THE LIGHT
WITHIN US

OTHER BOOKS BY CARL JAPIKSE:

The Hour Glass

BOOKS BY ROBERT R. LEICHTMAN, M.D. & CARL JAPIKSE:

Active Meditation: The Western Tradition

Forces of the Zodiac: Companions of the Soul

The Art of Living (five volumes)

The Life of Spirit (five volumes)

THE LIGHT WITHIN US

A Step-By-Step Guide

To Spiritual Growth

by Carl Japikse

ARIEL PRESS

Columbus, Ohio

Second Printing

This book is made possible by a gift
to the Publications Fund of Light
by James Edgar Shotts, Jr.

THE LIGHT WITHIN US

Copyright © 1987 by Light

All Rights Reserved. No part of this book may be used or reproduced in any
manner whatsoever without written permission, except in the case of brief
quotations embodied in articles and reviews. Printed in the United States of
America. Direct inquiries to: Ariel Press, 3854 Mason Road, Canal Winchester,
Ohio 43110.

ISBN 0-89804-042-6

TO

ROBERT R. LEICHTMAN, M.D.

THE LIGHT
WITHIN US

Preface

Humanity has been blessed by many great thinkers and spiritual leaders. Jesus. Paul. Socrates. Pythagoras. The Buddha. Krishna.

One of the least known of this small band of profound thinkers is the founder of Raja Yoga, Patanjali. According to Western scholars, Patanjali (pa TUN ja lee) lived sometime between 800 and 300 B.C., although Hindu sources state that he lived much further back in time—in the neighborhood of 10,000 B.C.

Patanjali left behind him a short treatise on the steps involved in the practice of Raja Yoga—a system of achieving union with the soul through the enlightenment and training of the mind. The text, as he wrote it, consists of 195 "sutras" or short instructions in Sanskrit. These sutras—a word which springs from the same roots as the English word "suture"—stood alone, with no commentary.

Over the years, of course, countless commentaries have been written on the "Yoga Sutras of Patanjali," as they have come to be called. Some of the commentaries have been illuminating; some have been utter rubbish. But the text has been preserved and is one of the most complete and profound statements on the steps involved in spiritual growth.

Naturally, there have been many translations of this text into English. Many of the early ones attempted to be direct translations, which has rendered them highly obscure and difficult to read. Almost all of them have been highly steeped in inbred traditions of the Eastern approach to meditation and spiritual growth. As a result, they are outdated and perhaps even a little dangerous to the average Westerner interested in personal and spiritual growth.

It should be stressed that Patanjali's basic ideas are not in any way out of date. Correctly applied, they are just as fresh and as challenging today as they were thousands of years ago. But the thought-forms and standard philosophy which accompany the instructions in the various commentaries frequently miss the mark. Indeed, the passive Oriental approach to just about everything in life has managed to render Raja Yoga, which is supposed to be the yoga of the mind, almost worthless to anyone who happens to have a well-trained mind! This unfortunate state of affairs is due to the fact that the *common* teaching of Raja Yoga consists of little more than exercises in focusing the attention and the passive observation of life. This degradation is completely contrary to the original teachings of Patanjali, of course, but this discrepancy seems of little interest to those who continue to champion the passive approach to life.

My own interest in these instructions began when I picked up *The Light of the Soul* by Alice A. Bailey, which is certainly one of the most outstanding renditions of this ancient writing. Reading *The Light of the Soul* is like attending a mental feast; the commentary is filled with wonderful mental nutrition. The insight it provides is neverending, for as many times as one might read it, it is not possible to exhaust its potential for inspiration.

In leading classes on *The Light of the Soul*, however, I found that many students had difficulty following all of Alice's complex ideas and esoteric references. Although she did a heroic job updating and Westernizing the text, there is still an abundance of Sanskrit words and hard-to-comprehend ideas. I found myself providing my own commentary on both the words of Patanjali and on the text written by Mrs. Bailey.

Over the years, I have examined a number of other translations and interpretations of these sutras, and have become convinced

4

that there is room for yet one more—a commentary which endeavors to present these instructions to the Western mind with the same clarity and precision as Patanjali originally presented them to the Eastern mind thousands of years ago.

To achieve this goal, I have taken a number of liberties. First and foremost, I make no claim to being a scholar of Sanskrit. The rendition of the sutras—I call them instructions—in this book are often free and liberal. Yet to my mind, they convey the original intent of Patanjali to the modern Western mind better than the standard translations. They are sometimes based entirely on my intuitive understanding of the original thought-form associated with the instruction—or, in some cases, on my intuitive examination of the archetypal forces associated with them.

Second, I have cast out all Sanskrit terms—and most of the standard esoteric terms. These terms have their place, but if the reader is interested in the original Sanskrit, he should seek it out, and if he is interested in the esoteric interpretation, he should read *The Light of the Soul.* It does a far better job of handling these terms than I would.

Instead, I have tried to focus my commentary so that it becomes a complete step-by-step guide to spiritual growth. It is written to challenge the thinking of people at every stage of spiritual growth and service, from the very first step to the most advanced stage. It is also written in a way which is designed to be immediately useful to the twentieth century, Western spiritual aspirant— perhaps even the twenty-first century aspirant!

In approaching this book, I am writing specifically for those who are interested in growing spiritually, not just personally. There are many books and courses available on how to be more selfish without feeling guilt, how to get what you want without antagonizing others, and how to feel better about yourself. This book does not cover these topics! It deals strictly with the steps involved in growing in spiritual consciousness—i.e., becoming aware of the nature of spirit, integrating its qualities into our character and work, and learning to work as a soul.

There are three major aspects to the human being: the monad, the soul, and the personality. These are also referred to as spirit, consciousness, and form. The personality consists of the mind, the emotions, and the physical form. We tend to be focused almost exclusively in this personality. The soul is something greater than the personality; it is the part of us which created the personality—the light within us.

The goal of any legitimate spiritual growth is to switch our polarity from being focused in the personality to being focused in the soul. Once this has happened, then true spiritual growth can begin. Yet this is often more than many people want. Lots of people would like to have a little help from spirit from time to time in their lives—but they would prefer to keep spirit at a safe, comfortable distance otherwise. This is neither possible nor desirable. In order to grow spiritually, we must be ready to serve spirit.

Patanjali assumes that those using his instructions are dedicated to serving spirit and focusing their consciousness in the light within them. But he takes each step one at a time, dividing his text into four books.

In Book One, we will examine the nature of consciousness and learn to distinguish it from sensation and form—our normal means for awareness and action.

In Book Two, we will examine the means for integrating the soul and the personality, so that they are able to act as one. Integration is one of the most important of all psychological techniques. Until the soul and the personality are integrated, the personality is estranged from its heritage and the soul is unable to fully express itself.

In Book Three, we will consider the creative skills and talents which arise as a result of this union, and outline the steps involved in reaching creative mastery.

In Book Four, we will deal with the theme of self-realization and the nature of the soul as light. We will examine the light within us individually and the light within the world—the Christ.

It may surprise some people that a book of instructions on yoga mentions the Christ—especially since Patanjali lived before the time of the Christ. Yet if Jesus could say, "Before Abraham was, I am," this should not be viewed as too much of a mystery. Reality is reality, after all, whether in the West or in the East. We refer to certain inner realities as the Christ life or the Christ consciousness. The Hindus refer to the same realities using slightly different terms. But the realities are one and the same. I have merely chosen to use those terms which the majority of Westerners are most accustomed to—and comfortable in using.

Some people will latch on such minor points, of course, and reject the book on that basis. These, obviously, are people who are more interested in sustaining their prejudices than in growing in spirit. To grow in spirit, we must be willing to entertain new ideas about the soul, the nature of consciousness, and God. Most of our ideas about divine life are based on a strange brew of assorted beliefs, concepts, and precepts. They are not very orderly or cohesive.

The great value of these instructions is that they do build a strong structure of thought in our awareness as we proceed through the text, one instruction after the other. They are not just random observations, but a well-disciplined group of ideas which lead us, step by step, out of the focus of our personality and into a fuller awareness of our soul.

They help us discover the light within us—and what we can do with it. I hope you will find them as practical and as helpful as I have.

I

THE NATURE OF CONSCIOUSNESS

1. OM. The focus of spiritual growth is consciousness.

Sensation is the innate mechanism of perception for the personality; consciousness is the means of awareness of the soul. The goal of spiritual growth described in this text is the integration of the personality with the soul. Book One will describe the nature of the soul and consciousness. Book Two will describe the means by which integration of the personality and the soul is pursued. Book Three will describe the creative applications of consciousness through the enlightened personality. Book Four will paint a portrait of the personality which has been fully illumined by integrating with the soul.

There are three aspects to the human system: the personality, the soul, and the monad. In terms of awareness, these three levels could be defined, respectively: sensation, consciousness, and oneness. It is not the purpose of this text to concern itself greatly with the monad or oneness, although methods of attaining this state of being are certainly implied. The goal for the vast majority of spiritual aspirants is learning more about consciousness and how to expand it, use it, and consecrate it. Therefore, the text is primarily a guideline to soul contact.

Hence, the first instruction begins with the word "OM." This is a mantra or sacred word from the Eastern tradition. In the Western tradition, the closest approximation to this word is the "Amen." Properly, it is used not just at the end of prayers or songs, but as a mantra sounding the Christ force. As a mantra, the OM is to be sounded mentally. It can be spoken verbally, but its real power comes through silent concentration on the force of consciousness it represents. The OM can be used for purification, attunement, and the charging of awareness.

Esoterically, the OM is the sound of the energies of the soul's patterns and qualities. Thus, this first instruction indicates that the whole idea of spiritual growth is to learn to sound the OM correctly—in the way we live our life. The way the word is sounded physically is much less important (although useful); even the way it is sounded mentally is still not as important as the way we express the qualities and forces of the soul in our daily activities. As we think, act, and express ourself in accord with the way the soul would have us think, act, and express ourself, we learn to sound the OM. We grow spiritually.

As a mantra, the OM should be sounded in the mind, using our creative imagination so that it is as though *the soul itself is* saying the OM. It can then be directed at the etheric, astral, or mental bodies to purify them. Or, it can be used to attune to other souls, a Master, an inner planes group, or the Hierarchy. It can also be directed at a force center in one of our subtle bodies to charge it with extra energy. Properly done, it summons the power of the soul for the purpose at hand.

At the same time, it must be emphasized that long sessions of sounding the OM do not constitute a perfect or complete spiritual exercise. It is unfortunate that there are so many aspirants who assume that learning to sound the OM and hear it mentally constitutes a tremendous step forward spiritually. Expressing the qualities and forces of spirit in our daily activities is the true work of spiritual growth.

It was to the OM that John referred when he wrote: "In the beginning was the Word, and the Word was with God, and the Word was God. He was in the beginning with God; all things were made through him, and without him was not anything made that was made. In him was life, and the life was the light of men. The light shines in the darkness, and the darkness has not overcome it." The OM, therefore, is sounded through focused acts of consciousness. While many people shy away from the example of the Christ, being unable to imagine themselves in any way touching His robe, it is not too difficult to imagine sounding the OM through our acts of love, courage, compassion, and tolerance and our expression of dignity, wisdom, hope, and beauty. Yet they are the same.

The OM is the word of consciousness. It should therefore be obvious that any "sound" of the OM in physical, astral, or mental substance is not the OM itself. It is a projection of its true reality, its true spiritual force. The OM is a perfect expression of pure consciousness. Sounding the OM is not unlike going to an echo canyon, shouting a word, and hearing the echo return. In this analogy, the speaker is the monad. The word which he speaks is the soul. The echo is the personality. Or, to put it in another triplicity, the speaker is oneness, the word is consciousness, and the echo is sensation. The purpose of this text is to learn about the nature of the word and how to speak it. To do this, however, we must learn to distinguish between the echo and the word.

The true sounding of the OM fills consciousness at every level. It causes each of our subtle bodies to be infused with an awareness of the next higher level. It *animates* the mind, the emotions, and the etheric bodies. The work of integration begins with this capacity for animation.

2. To achieve the full use of consciousness, the spiritual aspirant must first restrain the mechanisms of sensation he has been accustomed to using.

The principal mechanisms of sensation used by the human personality are the physical senses, the emotional body, and the concrete mind. The average person makes all his observations and draws all his conclusions through these three mechanisms—primarily, the first two.

Unfortunately, very few people have control of these mechanisms. Indeed, the mechanisms of sensation tend to hypnotically control the average person, not the other way around. The typical individual accepts what he sees as the truth, reacts without thinking to his emotions, and is easily led to believe in ideas which appeal to him, without considering their logic, relevance, or validity. The strength of the hypnotic effect of these mechanisms of sensation can be quite strong, since the substance of the etheric, astral, and mental bodies is composed of elemental life forms which automatically respond to impulses of their own, unless disciplined by the human "lord of the form." In addition, the average person is highly susceptible to the seductive force of mass consciousness.

The use of consciousness cannot be mastered until the spiritual aspirant learns to master these mechanisms of sensations—the physical body, the emotions, and the concrete mind. The need for this should be obvious. To employ an analogy, a person interested in becoming a composer of piano music must first learn to play the piano, read music, and understand the principles of harmony. In learning to play the piano, he must practice finger exercises and drills, to develop coordination and timing. In learning to read music, he must learn phrasing, rhythm, and the ability to make the notes on a sheet of music come alive when played. And in learning to understand the principles of harmony, he must do more than study them abstractly. He must practice applying them to his own compositions. Only when these basic skills are mastered, requiring many years of discipline and effort, will he be ready to compose.

Just so, the spiritual aspirant must spend a great deal of time learning to regulate and properly use the mechanisms of sensation, before he can truly work with consciousness. Above all, he must learn to "restrain" these mechanisms so that they do not automatically react to the impulses of the innate, elemental lives, or the influence of mass consciousness, but to his own control. In no way does "restraint" mean that the spiritual aspirant stops using or tries

14

to destroy these mechanisms, any more than a would-be pianist would cut off his fingers because he finds them clumsy and awkward.

This last point is important, because it is not well understood by spiritual aspirants. The emotions and the mind are not enemies of spiritual growth to be defeated and avoided; the mechanisms of sensation are themselves *extensions* of consciousness in the physical, astral, and mental worlds. To learn the nature of consciousness and how to use it, we must respect these extensions of consciousness and their proper focus. Most of all, we must learn to bring these mechanisms of sensation under the control of the soul, so that we are able to use the mind to express the wisdom of the soul, the emotions to express the love and goodwill of the soul, and the physical form to implement the constructive plans of the soul.

This instruction is actually a logical continuation of the first. It is not the goal of spiritual growth to learn to *hear* the OM, but rather to *sound* it ourself, through our acts and thoughts. If our emotions and mind are busy expressing something else, or being impressed by elementals or mass consciousness, then it is not possible to sound the OM through them. We cannot afford, in other words, to allow our emotions to dwell in fear, worry, or pettiness, because these forces contaminate the body of our emotions and spoil its capacity to sound the OM. We must exercise the level of control needed to keep our mechanism healthy and harmonious with the soul.

In an age when the average person willingly exposes himself or herself to "punk rock" and other aberrations of mass consciousness, the call for restraint is apt to go unheeded. It has become popular to indulge our mechanisms of sensation, not restrain them. But indulgence is never the road to genuine enlightenment. Through the ability to restrain the emotions and the concrete mind, we discover the true meaning of freedom.

3. The goal of the spiritual aspirant is to know himself as he is in reality.

It is popular in this day and age to talk about "making your own personal reality," but this is an illusion of the emotions. The emotions can fantasize an infinite number of "personal realities," but for this very reason, it is impossible for the spiritual aspirant to know himself through the emotions. If "reality" can be revised on a daily basis, such "reality" is not a suitable foundation for identity and self-knowledge.

Reality is that which is found in the mind of God—not in the mind of the spiritual aspirant. The mind of God is universal consciousness. Therefore, as the aspirant shifts his focus of attention from the level of sensation to the level of consciousness, he becomes aware 1) of the nature of reality, and 2) of his identity within reality. Moreover, as he becomes aware of the principle of consciousness alive and active within himself, at the level of the soul, he begins to understand that his share of consciousness links him with universal consciousness. He is a proper son or daughter of God.

Note that this instruction is worded "to know himself as he is in reality," not "to know that he exists in reality." We can arrive at the latter conclusion through intellectual deduction, and while it may be helpful to know that we exist in reality, it is certainly not the goal of spiritual aspiration. Knowing ourself as we are in reality requires us to make a direct realization at the level of the soul, then test the validity of our realization by applying it in daily life. More simply put, we discover the presence of God within us, then *realize* it by "practicing the presence of God."

Too many of us know ourselves only as we exist day by day. We know our problems, fears, anxieties, and poor self-images. But we do not know ourself as we exist in reality. We deny our true

16

identity, by believing our personal lies. For this reason, often the first step the aspirant should take is to define a healthier self-image and animate it with consciousness. If we think of ourself as sinful, or weak, or unworthy of God, it will be impossible to work toward such a noble goal as this instruction sets forth. Instead, we must begin to think of ourself as a proper son or daughter of God, able to act creatively, wisely, and lovingly in life. We know that God exists within us, as the light within us, and so we begin to behave accordingly.

To summarize, the aspirant is called on to learn about his divine nature; identify with this divine nature as the true source of his ideals, self-image, inspiration, purpose, and life; become aware of the life and qualities of consciousness; and begin identifying with the soul's perspective on the phenomena of life—karmic patterns, lessons to learn, the meaning of illness or failure, and so on.

Only when we take on this goal—to know ourself as we are in reality—do we gain the perspective which will eventually enable us to break the hypnotic bond of sensation.

4. The consciousness of the average individual is identified with the diverse needs and expression of his physical, astral, and mental bodies.

Instruction 3 defined the goal of spiritual growth; this one clearly states the major problem to be hurdled. Consciousness has become entrapped in its own extensions in the physical, astral, and mental worlds—its mechanisms of sensation. The inner person is unable to discriminate between our ever-changing thoughts, feelings, and sensations on the one hand and the archetypal realities of the soul on the other.

As Alice Bailey points out, these "modifications" of thought,

17

feeling, and sensation are virtually infinite in variety; urges, wants, desires, and fantasies tend to reproduce themselves very easily. Instead of being exhausted by repetition, they have the effect of exhausting the individual, until he determines to control them. As the inner person identifies with these modifications, he becomes increasingly confused and perplexed by their seeming complexity. This state of identification with the modifications of thought, feeling, and form is an entrapment of consciousness, yet at the same time a part of a necessary procedure. The inner man can only become creative and conscious in the world of form if he becomes familiar with the substance of that world. As a result, he allows himself to become entrapped, in order to gain a working familiarity. Once this has been gained, however, it is necessary to disengage from the entrapment.

Owing to the hypnotic pull of etheric, astral, and mental substance, this disengagement or detachment is not easy. We constantly fall back into believing in the power and reality of this substance, forgetting that the true power and reality of life exists at the archetypal levels of the soul. The failure to discriminate properly is often very subtle in nature, adding to the difficulty. Nonetheless, as we learn to distinguish between *what we do* and *what happens to us* on the one hand and *who we are* on the other, we gradually learn the difference between sensation and consciousness, between the diversity of form and the unity of consciousness.

As understanding is gained of how fully we have allowed the diversity of form to entrap us, it is right and proper to experience a certain amount of regret that opportunities have been missed, mistakes have been made. This regret should not be allowed to become an emotional reaction of self-condemnation or guilt, however, which would just be another instance of getting stuck in the traps of form. Rather, it should have the effect of gently and lovingly cleansing our awareness of the impurities of our errors, so that we will be better prepared to encounter the soul.

Reduced to plain English, this challenge to spiritual growth may seem deceptively straightforward. Yet it can be extremely subtle in the ways it thwarts our forward momentum. Many an aspirant has dedicated himself or herself to the work of the soul, only to begin to question, as complications arise, the wisdom and even the benevolence of the soul in arranging the circumstances of his or her life. The complaints always seem reasonable enough, but the fact remains that we are identifying with our circumstances and supposed needs—not with the capacity of the soul to provide for us whatever we need, whatever the circumstance. We become entrapped again in form.

It should be added here that this entrapment is a literal one, not just a figurative one. The substance of the etheric, astral, and mental bodies has a life of its own, which is referred to esoterically as the "innate life." This innate life has certain cravings and tendencies which can easily lead us astray, unless restraint is practiced.

The innate life of the etheric (subtle physical) body seeks comfort, sex, pleasure, and money.

The innate life of the astral body (the emotions) thrives on fear, anger, stimulation, excitement, and the control of others.

The innate life of the mental body aggravates tendencies toward arrogance and pride, separativeness, and the urge to condemn and criticize.

An emotionally-focused person, for instance, might easily be driven by his fears and need for security to try to control others and the events of his life. This obsession, however, would blind him to the higher realities of consciousness, creating a major hindrance to the light within him.

The three temptations Jesus faced (one physical, one emotional, and the third mental) poignantly illustrate the subtlety of all temptations the aspirant faces, and the steadfast detachment needed to conquer them. Each temptation illustrates the problem of dealing with the innate life of our three vehicles; each was resolved by reaffirming the strength and supremacy of the life of consciousness. This instruction indicates the *roots* of temptation and how to overcome it.

5. Consciousness is whole, but the expression of consciousness through form produces five states, which are either painful or nonpainful for the individual.

At the level of the mind of God, consciousness is whole. Duality is known, but not experienced. Each divine thought is complete in itself, even though it is still growing at its own level. But as these divine thoughts are projected into the world of form and manifested, they can be "known" in any of five states of mind. At the emotional level, they generate five basic reactions. And at the physical level, they produce the five physical senses. These are the mechanisms of sensation.

The projection of consciousness into form further produces a basic split or duality which must be understood and accounted for. The interaction of consciousness and form results in what is known esoterically as "the pairs of opposites." Mentally, the opposites would be thesis and antithesis. Emotionally, they would be like and dislike. Physically, they would be pleasure and pain. Philosophically, it is often said that the whole of human life is spent seeking pleasure and avoiding pain; many philosophers consider that an adequate meaning of life. Yet, neither one of the extremes is to be embraced by the spiritual aspirant, as this would only keep him or her focused in the world of sensations, with its myriad modifications. Rather, the aspirant must find the higher correspondence in consciousness which is the unmodified origin of the pairs of opposites.

Thus, neither intimidation nor subordination are part of right human relationships—but cooperation and harmony are. Neither fear nor possessiveness of money is correct—but generosity is. Neither jealousy of or contempt for the rank or position of another person is correct—but respect for his or her achievement and authority is.

The soul is detached from issues of both pleasure and pain. Instead, it is focused in its creative plans and projects. If pleasure or pain must be incurred in order to fulfill its plans, it will incur them, but its clear vision of what it is trying to accomplish is not affected or distorted by them. It is focused in consciousness, not sensation.

As long as the spiritual aspirant believes in the opposites of pain and pleasure, or any other set of opposites, he will be at least partially hindered in his understanding of and use of consciousness. Fully detaching himself from these opposites is a long process requiring great patience and dedication, but important gains are made with every triumph.

Until then, it is useful for every aspirant to reflect on the fact that most of the self-deception we must overcome can be traced to the desire for pleasure, whereas by far the most growth which occurs is motivated by our desire to avoid pain. When we realize that both of these states are mere sensations, we can free ourself from this rather bizarre inversion.

6. These five states are correct knowledge, incorrect knowledge, imagination, sleep, and memory.

Patanjali is describing a principle of consciousness, not an aberration of it. The intent of each of his instructions is to

21

demonstrate how consciousness behaves. Once we understand this, then we will be able to adjust our own thinking and behavior to conform with the ideal. Many commentators seem to forget this, however, and immediately assume that the modifications of mental activity are by definition distortions of consciousness and therefore something to avoid. This is an erroneous perspective, since the rich diversity of thought, feeling, and physical expression helps consciousness express itself through the world of form—which is definitely something the soul is interested in. If we remember that the modifications are indeed modifications, and keep ourself focused in the unmodified consciousness of the soul while employing the modifications creatively, there will be no problem. What must be understood is that each of these five mental states can be used both legitimately and foolishly. Each has its creative potential and its pitfalls.

As Edgar Cayce said, "The mind is the builder." To be a builder, the mind must be used very actively. But we must also take care that this activity be wisely focused. Our goal should be to learn the purposeful use of each of these five states and dedicate ourself to perfecting this usage, shunning all uninspired uses.

As each of these five states is examined in its own individual instruction, it will be interesting to note the range they cover, from quite sublime uses of the mind for reaching out and discovering reality as it is (correct knowledge) to very concrete uses of the mind for structuring subconscious and instinctual patterns of behavior (sleep and memory).

The underlying thought behind this instruction can be summed up: the word is made flesh through the mind. Those who try to sound the OM without using the mind and its modifications are doomed to failure. Through proper sounding of the OM, the modifications are brought under control and can be used creatively. The key is this: the OM is not sounded literally, but by expressing the highest qualities of the soul in daily life—its love, wisdom, goodwill, dignity, grace, strength, and joy.

The person who truly thinks actually sounds the OM constantly, through the quality of his thoughts.

7. Correct knowledge is the observation, evaluation, and application of divine archetypes.

Few people actually think. They jump to conclusions, they let their minds drift, they stew and brood, they exchange "ideas" like money-changers in the temple, and they energize prejudices and preconceived notions. But few *think*.

Correct thinking is a threefold process beginning with the observation of a specific ideal or archetype in the mind of God. This stage of observation is a bit more profound than the ordinary experience of observing an accident across the street, however; it is more like an intense saturation of our awareness with this quality. Once the ideal or force has been observed and registered, it is then evaluated and examined, for the purpose of drawing conclusions about how this current of divine life can best be expressed—and for the purpose of tapping the power to do so. The third stage of thinking, then, is the actual manifestation of this divine force through our own creativity, behavior, or self-expression.

The distortions of this modification occur when thinkers observe data other than divine archetypes and forces and make decisions based on this erroneous observation, or when they take a genuine observation and distort it through improper evaluation or misapplication.

Spiritual writers frequently refer to the hall of ignorance, the hall of knowledge, and the hall of wisdom. The first hall is filled with naive people who have not experienced much of life. The second is

23

filled with people who accept facts as truth. The third hall, much less crowded, is reserved for those who have learned to interact directly with divine ideals, principles, and archetypes. Correct knowledge is not based on facts, or even such intellectual skills as logic. Facts and logic are necessary to the correct implementation of knowledge, but they do not generate knowledge. Correct knowledge is that which is derived from the intuitive observation of divine reality.

This is a very simple principle, but it requires much work and hard practice to incorporate into our own thinking. We must get in the habit of working "top down," from the perspective of divine archetypes. In dealing with beauty, for example, do we believe it to be in the mind of the beholder—or defined by the divine force of beauty? In working with kinship, do we get caught up in silly notions of sisterhood and brotherhood—or do we comprehend our common heritage in the life of God?

The spiritual aspirant must become accustomed to the fact that the phenomena of the worlds of form consist of two kinds:

1. Those forms and activities which are a reflection (even if imperfect) of a divine blueprint.

2. Those forms and activities which are not. They are the "creations of the created"—they have no roots in divine archetypes.

Correct knowledge helps us separate the first type of phenomena from the second. It reveals to us the meaning, relevance, and creative purpose behind the phenomena—which is always absent in category number 2.

Simply put, it can be said that correct knowledge leads us to a practical realization of the old truism: "As above, so below." If we can trace what we find "below"—in the worlds of form—to roots in higher dimensions, then we are dealing with correct knowledge. Otherwise, we are not.

In general, the mind state of correct knowledge is used to focus

24

the mind on the abstract patterns which govern life, become aware of them, and use them creatively. The best way to train the emotions to cooperate with this mind state is to imbue them with a strong sense of *idealism*.

8. Incorrect knowledge is the observation of the imperfection of form.

This state of mind can be just as useful as the preceding one to the spiritual aspirant, when correctly used. The form world is inherently imperfect. The work of humanity is to assist in rendering this imperfection more perfect. Obviously, this work cannot proceed unless it is possible to perceive that which is imperfect—so it can be corrected. In this context, correct knowledge is the perception of the ideal; incorrect knowledge is the perception of that which is flawed or limited. It is, essentially, knowledge of any aspect of the world of form.

The problem with dealing with incorrect knowledge is misconstruing it to be correct, and applying it instead of archetypal inspiration. The proper way of dealing with it is to define the distortion or imperfection as clearly as possible, and then consider which ideal or archetype it distorts. From this point on, the mind state of correct knowledge should take over.

An example of this distinction between correct and incorrect knowledge can be drawn from the Bible. The statements of Jesus in the New Testament are as close to formulations of correct knowledge as is possible. Yet the correct knowledge lies not in the words Jesus said, but in the ideas and qualities being expressed through the words. When fundamentalist Christians then interpret His words literally, they fall into the trap of incorrect knowledge. They are worshipping their knowledge of His words, rather than using His words as they were intended—to lead the reader to an awareness of His correct knowledge.

Incorrect knowledge is *not* the opposite of correct knowledge; it is more like a companion. The knowledge gained is not incorrect (unless it is used out of context); it is simply knowledge of the limited, flawed conditions of life. The mind still functions as described in instruction 7, through observation, evaluation, and application, but as it does, it compares the incorrect with the correct. Indeed, this state of mind is indispensable for anyone living and working in the worlds of form, as long as we do not come to believe in the imperfection we behold. The tendency to become cynical or pessimistic is a sign that we give too much credence to incorrect knowledge. By the same token, the ability to sustain faith and optimism in the face of seemingly impossible odds is an indication that we process incorrect knowledge wisely.

An excellent example of the proper use of incorrect knowledge might be found in the work of a clinical psychologist. To be effective, the psychologist must be familiar with all the varieties of psychological illness; otherwise, he could not heal them. But knowing what is wrong is not enough; the psychologist must also have correct knowledge—an understanding of the spiritual design for the enlightened human personality. Together, these two types of knowledge give him the ability to help his patients.

The use of incorrect knowledge is one of the primary assets of the spiritual man in cooperating with evolution. It should lead to the growth of consciousness, never retard it. The best way to train the mind in using incorrect knowledge is *discrimination*, separating the wheat from the chaff. The best way to train the emotions to cooperate with this mind state is to fill them with a strong *aspiration* to correct that which is imperfect.

26

9. Imagination is the mind state used to shape expressions in the world of form.

Man was created in the image of the Creator. Therefore, he is also a creator—and it is not only acceptable to work with images, but something which should be encouraged. The process of working with images is the imagination, and through the properly controlled creative imagination, all patterns of form are created. But when the images man creates do not conform to the realities of the mind of God, they become mere fancy: glamours, illusions, and enchantments. Nonetheless, because the mind is the builder, these fancies acquire an aura of realness, serving to entrap the individual. Fears, doubts, anger, and lusts form one pole of this fancy; unreal spiritual expectations form the other.

The imagination is the mechanism used by the abstract mind to build patterns, by the concrete mind to build thought-forms. Obviously, this process can be used both constructively and destructively. The imagination can be used to build a healthy self-image—or a prejudice.

The legitimate use of the creative imagination is to recognize a need through incorrect knowledge, determine the archetype which would fill that need through correct knowledge, and project an appropriately constructed image into the world of form through the imagination, thereby shaping a new and better form, attitude, habit, or condition. Yet the mind state of the imagination is very easily distorted. Misleading images of ourself, of the groups we belong to, and of the nature of the spiritual life are readily formed and can seriously delude us. While the average person may believe that figments of the imagination have no power and are just empty thoughts, the spiritual student comes to appreciate how powerfully the images he holds in his mind and heart can influence the nature of his life.

A good example of this would be the images we create of other people. More often than not, our impressions of others are more fanciful than accurate—we relate to our projections of what we think a person is like, rather than the true person. As a consequence, we frequently treat others in inappropriate ways, thereby harming the relationship. To establish proper relationships with others, we must first unbuild the false images we have constructed of them, and replace them with images based on the ideal patterns being focused by their souls into their lives. We should create an image based more on their potential than on their flaws. This is not to imply that we should ignore their flaws, but awareness of their flaws is more the province of incorrect thinking than the imagination.

Our fanciful images are the "graven images" Moses warned us about, engraved in astral and mental substance. To use the mind state of imagination properly, we should follow the model of God, who scraped together mud and clay and spittle and then breathed into it life, producing the human form. If the forms of mud and clay and spittle we shape are based on archetypal patterns and filled with the life of spirit, we are using the mind state of imagination properly.

The purpose of the image is to generate a matrix for self-expression. Images of fear are powerful magnets that draw in the substance of fear and focus it. The use of fantasy in sex likewise creates a matrix which draws in forces and patterns the average person—or the typical therapist—does not comprehend, and would probably be revolted by if he did. By the same token, however, speculation about the way the soul would have us think tends to draw in the substance of insight and intelligence. In the hands of an intelligent aspirant, the creative imagination can be a powerful tool.

It is important to weigh the value of imagination carefully. Most people confuse this mental process for *wishing*, which is a function of the emotions. Wishing is the realm of fancy—mere whimsy. True imagination produces projections of reality, not wishes or fantasy.

The best way to train the mind in using the imagination is through *realization*, the direct apprehension of reality. The best way to train the emotions to cooperate is to fill them with a strong sense of *faith*.

10. Sleep allows unconscious forces to influence our mind state.

The word "sleep" is obviously being used symbolically. The mind state it refers to is one which operates at subconscious and unconscious levels—hence, the conscious mind is "asleep" while this mind state is operating. It has nothing to do with whether the physical body is sleeping or not.

All ideas require a time for incubation and maturation between the time of conception and the time when they are ready to appear in form—mentally, emotionally, or physically. Seeds are planted in the subconscious and unconscious levels of our thinking, so that they may develop even while we are consciously pursuing other ideas, other activities. We are asleep to them, but they are growing and becoming a part of ourself in spite of our lack of awareness.

A simpler example does involve the processes of sleep. We often spend some of our time asleep at night preparing for the events of the day to come, but most of our memory of this preparation is forgotten when we awaken. Nonetheless, valuable information has been "seeded" in our subconscious and unconscious, so that it can quickly arise to the surface when needed at the critical moment. It might be added here that normal sleep does allow the astral and mental bodies to "float" free and return temporarily to a

29

kind of reunion with the soul. This, in turn, enables the soul to cleanse, heal, and enrich the contents of our subconscious.

As valuable as this mind state is to the creative process, there are still many distortions of it. Many people try to render the conscious mind passive, in the hopes of becoming more attuned to inspiration or intuition. It has become quite common to believe that meditation is a process of stilling the mind and shutting out all mental images. This is a modification of the mind state of "sleep" that hinders the development of consciousness, not helps. It opens the individual to being manipulated psychically, and deadens the sharpness of the mental faculties.

In general, any trance state has the potential to deaden consciousness and our sense of identity. If used with great care and moderation by skilled mediums, the trance can produce results that cannot be duplicated in any other way. But the vast majority of trance work—psychically, hypnotically, or mediumistically—is unnecessary. It usually makes far more sense to learn to translate the unconscious into something which can be understood consciously. This is certainly a goal of genuine meditation.

The spiritual aspirant must learn to keep his conscious mind active and alert, yet at the same time become more aware of the way ideas incubate in the subconscious. To properly control and use this mind state, it is important to "map" the subconscious and become familiar with its associations, habits, and contents. Unless these are of high quality, the sleep of the mind will tend to traumatize and manipulate us. It will bias our thinking even while we believe ourself to be objective; it will leave us vulnerable to blind spots. It can likewise become a channel through which we are exposed to psychic attack.

Aa we gain control of the subconscious, however, and learn something about the scope of our interaction with the unconscious, we gain control of this mind state. This is not only a tremendous step forward in working with inspiration, but it also gives us a means of detecting unseen influences and becoming aware of the ways in which they are trying to manipulate us.

It should be noted here that the unconscious mind referred to in this instruction is *not* the Freudian unconscious of dark forces, urges, and repressed memories, which is really the sub-basement of the mind. Instead, it is the supraconscious mind—an aspect of our personality closely attuned to our divine wisdom and the storehouse of memories of our inner planes experiences and studies.

Paradoxically, the final result of the proper use of "sleep" is a conscious personality which is far more awake than it was before—awake to the qualities and talents of the soul, and alive and active in the physical plane. The best way to train the mind in using sleep is the intelligent practice of *invocation*, while the emotions can be taught to cooperate with the process of sleep by schooling them in the lessons of *patience*.

At all costs, however, avoid passiveness.

11. Memory preserves what we know.

The mind state of memory is vital to evolution. Without the capacity to remember what we have learned and the mistakes we do not wish to repeat, we could not add to the foundation of knowledge we have established. We would remain static. So, there is great creative potential in the mind state of memory, when correctly understood. In animals, for instance, memory is a vital aspect of instinct, which preserves the heritage of the species. In man, learning is achieved by repeating a lesson until it becomes automatic and "drops below the threshold"—becomes a natural talent or expression.

Our most central memory should be of the nature of the soul

and consciousness. When too immersed in emotional reactions and mental confusion, the remembrance of our true identity can help us break the spell of our reaction or confusion. The daily memory of the spiritual qualities we are trying to express can likewise help us learn to express them.

The common use of memory is actually a misuse of it, as it is tinged with heavy feelings of pain, regret, and remorse which can trap us in mundane experiences and associations, our painful reactions to past traumas, and the petty reactions of the personality.

Memory preserves the talents, strengths, and good qualities we have achieved, as long as we focus it properly and do not use it to recall a poor self-image, fears, or other distortions of form. In approaching this mind state, we should strive to remember as the soul remembers. The soul remembers those experiences of the personality which are imperfect only long enough to correct them (which may require several lifetimes). Once the lesson is learned, however, and the personality is able to express an appropriate ideal, it remembers this *ability*—not the many mistakes incurred in learning it. More precisely, the mistakes are put in the context of the final triumph. It is the maturity gained which becomes immortal, through memory—not the errors and difficulty.

The best way to train the mind in the correct use of memory is *comprehension*, in that we learn completeness of thought, even back to its origins. In simpler terms, this means striving always to understand the meaning of our experiences and to recognize that we have always been guided by an inner, benevolent wisdom— even at our times of greatest confusion. The best way to educate the emotions to cooperate is by *blessing* our memories, as described in the essay, "Finding Meaning in Life," in *The Art of Living I*.

12. Control of these mind states is achieved through tireless effort and detachment.

This instruction calls on the aspirant to answer an implied question: who controls the mind? Is it the physical person? The emotions? The subconscious robot? A master or guru? Or the mind itself? In the average person, it usually is the physical urges, the emotions, or the subconscious, or some combination of the three, that control the mind, to the detriment of growth. In highly intelligent people, the mind may try to control itself, but this effort implies a level of objectivity the mind does not possess. In the East, control is often given to a master or a guru, but this usually blunts the aspirant's sense of individuality. A true master or guru will stimulate the mind of his or her disciples, but never assume control of it.

The answer, of course, is that it is the soul which must control the various mind states. Nonetheless, there is a great measure of work to be done, by the personality, creating conditions which will enable the soul to seize this control. Primarily, this work is done by refining the skills of detachment.

Detachment requires us to discipline our habits, urges, desires, convictions, intentions, and attitudes, while putting the soul in charge. The phrase "tireless effort" implies that the whole process must be governed by a part of us greater than the personality—a part which does not tire. This is the soul.

Putting the soul in charge of the mind is *not* achieved by passive surrender to God, while blissfully ignoring our problems. It is achieved by maintaining a constant mindfulness that our soul has a vital and authoritative role to play in our life, and we must be attentive to its design and direction. In practical terms, this means that we must learn to use the light within us to examine our motives, plans, and self-expression, striving always to refine them to be more in harmony with the wisdom and love of our soul. We must make the effort to detach from our preconceived ideas and self-serving defenses and shine the light of our higher wisdom on every facet of our thinking, feeling, and activity, until we have aligned them with the authority of the soul.

The implied question of this instruction can also be answered by stating that it is the qualities of consciousness which must control.

It is joy which must control.

Love must dominate.

Wisdom must direct.

Peace must reign.

We must practice the presence of God.

13. Tireless effort requires a steady dedication to using these mind states for the purposes they were designed to fulfill.

Learning the proper use of the mind and human personality is not an easy task. The person who will be disappointed if he or she does not achieve enlightenment by the end of the year will indeed be disappointed. To paraphrase Thomas Paine, the lessons of spiritual growth are not for "summer soldiers and sunshine patriots who, in the face of crisis, shrink from the service of the soul." They require dedication, perseverance, and strength of resolution. They require tireless effort.

Still, it is not just practice which makes perfect: it is perfect practice which makes perfect. Dedication and tireless effort are not enough, if the techniques being used actually hinder spiritual growth, rather than advance it. In other words, we must not just develop the mind so that we can use it to read cheap novels.

We must train it in the skills of correct knowledge, so that we can understand the purpose, meaning, and eventual outcome of our activities.

We must train it in the skills of incorrect knowledge, so that we can perceive errors before we make them, and correct them.

We must train it in the skills of the creative imagination, so that we can create those thought-forms which will help us achieve our goals.

We must train it in the skills of right memory, so that we come to understand the meaning and value of our past experiences.

We must train it in the skills of interacting with the higher unconscious, so that we can become more creative—and draw closer to the light within us.

This is the real work—the tireless effort—of the spiritual aspirant. Time spent in meditation "emptying the mind," repeating a simple mantra endlessly, or trying to set the spine on fire is time wasted. These practices do absolutely nothing to bring the soul closer to the personality. They may actually deceive the personality into believing it is in touch with the soul (in all likelihood, it is in touch only with its own subconscious), but this kind of self-deception actually adds to the obstacles to be overcome.

The proper kind of training, practiced until mastered, restructures the personality so that the wisdom of the soul finds expression through the mind and the love of the soul finds expression through the heart. Spiritual training is therefore always active, always practical. It helps us transform our habits, values, priorities, thoughts, feelings, and skills, so that they express more and more of the light within us. In this way, we come to recognize the soul as our true guide and master who can work without exhausting itself.

We may feel that the reason the mind is hard to discipline is because we are bombarded constantly by pettiness and stress. Yet if there is pettiness in our life, it is a reflection of our own state of mind. If there is stress in our life, it is a reflection of our own state of

mind. It is not pettiness and stress which make it difficult to discipline the mind—it is our lack of attunement to divine archetypes
and ideals. We are not yet able to hold the mind steady in that
attunement.

This is what produces control of the various mind states—the
ability to hold the mind constantly in a creative mode. The tireless
effort to which we should aspire is the ability to use the mind as the
soul would use it. And it very much is a "tireless effort," not only in
the sense of never tiring or becoming a summer soldier, but also in
the sense that this effort produces no strain or friction. The soul
does not struggle or sink into inertia. It acts with perfect peace and
poise—not a state of resting or being inactive, but rather the
capacity to act in the face of great confusion, chaos, or stress and
remain in absolute control of the mind and personality, perfectly
attuned to the divine ideals of life.

This should be the goal of all spiritual aspirants, even if difficult
to attain.

**14. This steadiness of the mind will be reflected in our
values and convictions.**

Many people have a great admiration for specific spiritual
qualities and ideals, then turn about and behave in ways which
directly contradict their beliefs. The lawyer, for example, may have
a firm commitment to justice, yet act in ways which undermine the
practical application of true justice—without ever realizing it. The
spiritual worker may claim to be motivated by love, then employ
fear as a way of stirring up others—again without recognizing that
his use of fear obscures his attempts to express love.

This instruction confronts this all-too-common dilemma. It
states that it is not enough to have strong beliefs in spiritual ideals.

Part of the "tireless effort" of controlling the various mind states is translating the divine ideals and qualities of life into values and convictions that will govern our life and behavior in every possible situation. These values and convictions, then, are used in turn to generate priorities, habits, and commitments which are in harmony with the spiritual ideals we serve.

"Value" is perhaps the most underrated word in the English language. In a society which accepts "situational ethics" as standard operational procedure, it may be difficult to grasp how important values are to the process of stabilizing consciousness. Yet the aspirant needs to make the effort, reviewing what he values and then examining whether or not these values match spiritual realities. Where they do, they need to be strengthened; where they do not, they need to be replaced by something more enlightened. And we need to train both the emotions and our physical impulses to accept the leadership of these values and commitments.

Where there is a lack of ethics—or the presence of situational ethics—the aspirant will be vulnerable to instability and inconsistency of thought and action, as well as paradoxes and contradictions. In this instruction, Patanjali warns us to add discipline and consistency to our faith and good intentions in serving God. By implication, he also warns us to beware the instability and weakness which result from letting the emotions control our life, instead of the more stable spiritual principles. Therefore, the spiritual aspirant must strive to define his ethical principles and purposes in living based on the soul's direction and design, and work to achieve consistency in applying these principles in all that he does.

15. Detachment is the process of freeing our desires from their attachment to forms on every level of self-expression.

An attachment is a projection of psychic energy which binds the entity that projected it to the object grasped. In humans, attachments most commonly take the form of likes and dislikes, beliefs and disbeliefs, urges, lusts, longings, and addictions. The problem with attachments is that they represent a portion of awareness which is magnetically trapped by excessive interest in the object of attunement. Instead of being attuned to divine ideals and archetypes, the individual is attuned to his attachments. As a consequence, the light within us is ignored in preference to the glitter of the attachment. The activity of the mind is diverted from its proper state, focused in something else.

Many attachments are quite subtle, and even masquerade as spiritual values. The idea of needing to "get off the wheel of rebirth," for example, is just as much an attachment as materialism is. It tends to block out the light of the soul's creative purpose, which includes rebirth as a very important feature.

The practice of detachment must become an important feature of the daily activity of the spiritual aspirant. It is best achieved by realizing that the true spiritual man is not attached to any form (physical, astral, or mental), but is *attuned* to the divine ideals and archetypal forces of the soul. As attachments are discovered, therefore, the spiritual man turns his attention away from them and seeks out the higher correspondence to that attachment in consciousness. Due to the principle that "energy follows attention," the attachment thereby withers, and is replaced by a proper attunement. When focused in consciousness, there can be no attachments, for these are only possible in the finite realms of sensation.

It should be pointed out that there is an enormous difference between an attachment and a relationship. We are meant to be "in the world, but not of the world": we are meant to have friends, make lifelong commitments, hold responsible jobs, take our duties seriously, and generally enjoy life. If we do not, our self-expression will be sour and one-dimensional, something which is not conducive to soul contact. What the aspirant must learn to free himself from are those unnatural relationships which bind him to servitude—addictions, obsessions, and longings—no matter how subtle they may be. Any desire or wish which is strong enough to take priority over contact with the soul becomes an attachment and must be mastered.

Attachments which are not mastered during physical life can be not only a block to spiritual growth but a real problem to be solved after death. Since most attachments are centered in the emotions, they can become far stronger and more demanding after death, when the focus of our awareness shifts from the physical to the astral planes.

Further ideas on detachment can be found in the essay, "The Practice of Detachment," in *The Art of Living I.*

16. Mastery of detachment produces knowledge of the nature of consciousness, as well as knowledge of consciousness in manifestation.

For a long time, the spiritual aspirant tends to think of detachment as gaining freedom from his attachments. The true state of detachment, however, is not defined in terms of the absence of attachments, but rather in terms of being focused in the light of the soul—the light within us. The detached person is focused in consciousness, not sensation. Consequently, he is able to think with clarity and objectivity, because his mind states are not distorted by attachments.

Identity is a good example of this principle. The origin of our identity as a human being is in consciousness, yet we think of ourself as a physical being. We search for our "roots" through our ancestors. We identify with being a man or a woman, an American or a European, a Catholic, Protestant, or Jew, and so on. All of these associations represent the form nature of our identity, however, not our true identity. We discover our true identity when we realize that we are the soul, and can say with understanding: "I am that I am." As long as we identify with something finite, we have not gained mastery of detachment. We have not learned to think as the soul would have us think.

The detached capacity to think as the soul would have us think can be focused on two levels: that of the soul and that of the personality. When directed at the level of the soul, it produces insights into the true nature of consciousness, the life of spirit, and the nature of the heaven worlds. The ability to think in this way is of great importance, as it produces an enormous step forward in creative inspiration, the understanding of human nature, and the comprehension of life.

When directed at the level of the personality, this detached state of thinking produces other results; it reveals to us the meaning and true value of events. We begin to realize that there are purposes and reasons for what happens to us in life which *transcend our personal benefit or harm*.

The practice of detachment also includes the ongoing search for the way divine life is involved in our daily events and activities. This leads us to understand the nature of consciousness in manifestation. In specific, we become aware of three qualities to be found in any manifestation of consciousness. In the Hindu tradition, these three qualities are referred to as the three *gunas*: sattva, raja, and tamas. These three words can be translated into English as rhythm, activity, and inertia. Or, they can be restated as creative potential, animation, and resistance. The detached person does not shy away from the effects of these three qualities, but rather seeks to use them consciously, intelligently, and purposefully. It is this knowledge which helps the aspirant become a creative contributor to life—an important aspect of the purposes of the soul.

17. One way the spiritual aspirant can enrich his use of consciousness is to examine the nature of any object: its form, its quality, its purpose, and that which animates it.

The seat of consciousness is the soul, but it does project itself into manifestation in the form worlds for creative purposes. Therefore, it is only reasonable to conclude that much can be learned about the nature of consciousness by contemplating the manifestations of consciousness and, through the process of thinking, by tracing their appearance back to their roots. In practical terms, this means examining the form as it appears on the physical plane, appraising the quality expressed astrally, discerning the purpose to be found on the concrete mental plane, and ultimately identifying with the divine essence which animates the form. This is found on the abstract levels of the mental plane. It is the light within the form. As Paul put it, the whole of creation reveals the invisible nature of God.

A good example of this process at work would be the common act of reading a book. As we read, we should evaluate not just the style of the author, but far more importantly, the quality, the purpose, and the originating cause which animates this book. The quality would include such elements as the motive of the author for writing and the balance and fairness with which he writes. The purpose would be the intent of the author in presenting this book to the public. The cause would be the original inspiration. From this evaluation, we would be able to judge whether or not the author was responsive to archetypal inspiration while writing—or whether

41

he was guided merely by his own perspectives and reactiveness.

In making this kind of assessment of consciousness "from the bottom up," it is necessary to proceed with a great deal of detachment. It is all too easy to identify excessively with the object itself, its quality, or its purpose, forming a glamour or illusion about the object which interferes with the pure perception of consciousness. It is also possible to "invent" a divine archetype to suit the fancy of the moment and falsely believe it to be a legitimate ideal of the mind of God, when it is not.

Still, great understanding can be gained from this form of meditation, providing that it is always used to trace back to the roots of consciousness.

18. The aspirant can also develop his use of consciousness by focusing directly on divine archetypes, qualities, and forces, free of external impressions.

This instruction is almost the mirror image of the last one. Instead of starting with an object and tracing back to its roots in consciousness, we are now told that it is also possible to focus the mind directly on these roots—the light within the form. In other words, instead of considering the joy of a joyful person, we can attune our mind directly to the archetypal force of joy itself, at the level of abstract thought.

The capacity to use the mind in this way requires a good deal of practice, for the average person is not used to thinking at abstract levels—even the average aspirant. Almost everyone thinks in terms of images, words, memories, and theories. These are all forms and would represent external impressions. To focus directly on the light within, the mind must be free of these external impressions. This requires great care, for it is easy to fall short of the mark and tune into humanity's thought-forms about these divine forces—not the divine forces themselves.

The key is to speculate on how the soul would have us think, feel, and act in the expression of some particular divine force or quality. If this reflection is done in a light meditative state, we are bound to receive some good insights. We may even get specific ideas on how these forces and qualities can be applied to our conflicts, challenges, and so on. This does not in any way diminish the direct perception of these forces—it simply educates us about their application to our circumstances.

19. One does not acquire these skills of consciousness merely by shedding the limitations of the physical body.

Many people have learned something about the inner dimensions of life by speaking with disembodied humans through mediums or by reading books which detail such communications. There is certainly a lot of valid literature which has been derived through mediumship, the books of Eileen Garrett and Stewart Edward White, as well as the twenty-four books in *From Heaven to Earth*, being prime examples. But it must be understood that there is very little difference between the insight of a nonphysical and a physical human being. Nonphysical humans are able to operate astrally as freely as we now operate physically, but this does not in any way give them any clearer spiritual vision than we possess. The astral plane is not the home of spirit—in many ways, it is more polluted and corrupt than the physical plane. Even the concrete mental plane is not the home of spirit. One must be able to focus in the consciousness of the abstract mental plane in order to interact directly with spirit at its lowest level.

This level of spiritual maturity can only be reached by following the principles and practices outlined in this commentary. Shedding the physical body through death—or astral travel—does not in any way, shape, or form produce enlightenment. It is the activity of learning to express divine wisdom and love which leads to spiritual maturity—not the ability to step out of the physical form.

20. There are five methods to be used to explore the higher realms of consciousness: belief, the right use of energy, memory, meditation, and realization.

It is assumed that the spiritual aspirant has mastered the basic lessons of spiritual growth and learned to work at abstract levels with some facility. He has learned to control the modifications of the mind alluded to in earlier instructions, and can use the five mind states creatively. He is ready to explore the realms of divine life and the mind of God.

It is interesting to view these five methods as the higher correspondences of the five modifications of the mind. One of the great principles of life is "As above, so below." The nature of consciousness is not all that different from life in manifestation—just a great deal more subtle, pure, and powerful. In this instruction, Patanjali is presenting a key to scientific exploration of the archetypal realms of life. It is also a short course in the right examination of any facet of life.

Belief is, of course, something more powerful than the uninformed opinion the word is usually used to describe. The spiritual use of belief is that it defines the scope of the examination to be undertaken. Belief in the archetype of peace, for example, is a statement which implies that even though we have not yet examined it, we have strong reason to expect to find such a divine force when we look for it. This belief may be based on scripture, the

44

testimony of others, or our own intuitive glimpse, but it is a solid belief. A "belief" that cows can be taught to speak English is not based on any genuine evidence. It therefore does not qualify for this kind of belief. In the way the word is being used in this instruction, it it only possible to believe in things which do exist.

The second value of this spiritual level of belief is that it enables us to recognize that we have the right and capacity to make this exploration. A lot of aspirants believe in divine peace, yet do not believe that they could become a genuine agent of any divine force. They have been taught to believe that they are sinful, unworthy. Enlightened belief gives us the strength and courage to pursue intelligent examinations of the inner life. In specific, it focuses our emotions to accept and embrace the experience of contacting the soul.

The right use of energy is the second skill to be learned. As soon as we contact a quality such as peace, we are immediately struck by the force of its characteristic energy. It enters not only our awareness but also the whole of our life. To examine it, therefore, we must strive to understand the nature of its energy and what it means for a human to express it. Those who are intelligently studying astrology or the seven rays are learning some of the basic lessons of this skill—if they recognize that each type of energy they are studying is alive and active in life, not just some inert abstraction. The right use of energy implies that our motives and intentions are directed solely toward learning to use these energies to serve the soul—not for personal entertainment or frivolous pursuits.

Memory does not refer to the memories of personal experience stored in our subconscious. Rather, it is the capacity to tap into and use the accumulated wisdom of the soul. At an even higher level, it is the basic endowment of purpose and intent in everything ever created, including divine laws, archetypes, and principles. As we tap into this cosmic memory, we are able to "read the record" of this facet of divine life.

Meditation is not just a means for contacting the life of spirit; effective meditation builds the bridge in consciousness through which the soul can direct guidance to the personality, and the qualities of divine life can be directly known. The word "contemplation," which originally meant "laying out the design for a temple," perhaps conveys the nature of this type of meditation better than the connotations of meditation popular today.

Realization enables us to identify completely with the force of the archetype, so that we are one with it and it is one with us. We become an agent of this force—an incarnation of it.

These five methods are not separate techniques to be used independently; rather, they are the five elements of a single process of intelligent examination.

21. These five methods require a will that is intensely alive.

Mere curiosity is not enough to reveal to us the higher realms of spiritual consciousness. In order to activate the five methods listed in the last instruction, we will have to overcome a great deal of personal confusion and individual glamour, as well as the illusions and limiting prejudices of humanity and society. If this effort were sustained only by our personal interest—or even our personal will—we would give up after the first few struggles with our blind spots, deceptions, and veiled hypocrisy and follow the path of least resistance. Fortunately, our effort to grow toward the light within us is met ounce for ounce by help from the light itself. As our determination to grow increases, it is nurtured by the will of the soul.

The simplest and most effective way to mobilize and energize the will is to lead a life dedicated to knowing and expressing the life of the soul. We must repeatedly dedicate ourself to knowing the truth of our spiritual design and giving it expression. In this way, the will can become intensely alive in our own values, priorities, love, and dedication. This in turn leads to a state of determination which enables us to overcome all personal obstacles and grow through every experience.

At the level of the personality, the will must be focused through the mind. If allowed to be captured by the emotions, it may be distorted into stubbornness, rebelliousness, and other problems. Even when focused at the level of the mind, there is the danger it might feed vanity and egomania. But if properly controlled with detachment, it can be translated into such useful qualities as determination, steadfastness, and courage.

The intensely-alive will is exemplified by those individuals who are willing to take on a lifetime of great adversity in order to quickly overcome karma and learn new lessons in life. Nothing is allowed to stand in the way of such people.

Until the will is somewhat activated, the more sublime aspects of consciousness cannot be approached. We will tend to be satisfied with attuning to group thought-forms about divine life, instead of making direct contact with divine life ourself. The will gives us the ability to penetrate through the clouds of human opinion and even the outer appearances of divine life, so that we may interact with the inner, living reality.

22. As the will is expressed—intensely, moderately, or gently—it produces definite impacts on consciousness. It is therefore best to combine the use of the will with the activation of the love nature.

This instruction refers to the expression of will in the life of the soul and the daily life of the aspirant. The will is an expression of the Father, the first aspect of God. As the will nature is expressed, it has a definite impact on consciousness. This impact can be favorable or unfavorable, depending upon how well the expression of will is controlled. At times, it is quite appropriate to express the will intensely, as in facing difficult crises. But at other times, it might be quite inappropriate, leading to distorted conditions of stubbornness, insensitivity, egomania, or destructiveness. Then, a more moderate or gentle use of will may be better.

There is much the aspirant must learn about the use of the will. Many sincere religious people, for instance, have strong adverse reactions to anyone who is able to express the will intelligently and effectively; they believe that a person who is able to "get things done" is dangerous and needs to be curbed. This suggests that these people have overdosed on meekness somewhere along the line, and need to restore balance to their life.

It is important for all aspirants to learn to express the will skillfully, as conditions require, with intensity, moderation, and gentleness. We must also respect the impact the will can have on consciousness—not only ours, but the consciousness of others as well. In these three levels of intensity there is an important parallel to the three gunas or qualities of energy in manifestation.

Still, it is true that the pursuit of the will aspect alone would lead to terrible conditions of imbalance. In spiritual aspiration, there is frequently a great temptation to focus on one aspect of God and ignore the others. This is not wise, for all three aspects are expressed by God as one. Therefore, the wise aspirant will combine the use of the will with the activation of the love nature, the second aspect of God, and express both actively in his or her daily life, through service.

The love nature is activated as we learn to express compassion towards others, treat all of life benevolently, and approach God with reverent devotion. Many people equate the love nature with their emotions and feelings. While there is no question that the activation of spiritual love will *transform* the quality of our emotions, it is equally important to realize that the emotions are not the only mechanism for expressing divine love. Love can be expressed through the mind just as much as through the emotions—and, naturally, at even higher levels as well.

Much is made of the distinction between the occultist and the mystic. To be precise, the occultist strives to know and understand God, whereas the mystic strives to love God. It is thought that the occultist operates exclusively through the mind and the mystic operates exclusively through the emotions. But true spiritual growth cannot be limited to one facet of the personality, nor to one aspect of God. Ultimately, we are all aspirants, striving for enlightenment. This means that we know God, love God, and respond wisely to His will—at all levels of our being and in every facet of our life.

The model for the proper use of the will should always be that of the Christ, who said: "My Father is always working, and so am I."

In reading all of these instructions, it must be remembered that their purpose is to show us how to become aware of, respond to, and learn to express the light within us. This understanding and use of consciousness is not gained by accident or guesswork, or because God favors us personally. The consciousness of the soul is a logical and accessible science. It is a science requiring dedicated study and hard work, but tireless efforts made are rewarded. There is no whim involved; the universe functions by law, not whim. The aspirant must expect to study and understand those laws, and then adhere to them and use them creatively. When this advice is followed, significant growth can be made.

23. By intense devotion to the soul, knowledge of the love nature is gained.

This is a straightforward instruction. If we want to learn to play the piano, we must spend our time practicing—not reading books or watching television. Likewise, to know love we must express love. We must love the soul and the way it loves.

It must be understood, however, that devotion is not just a good feeling or a superficial profession of allegiance to the soul. It is a deep respect and affectionate commitment to the light within us. Properly expressed, it fills our whole being with love—the mind as well as the emotions, the subconscious as well as our conscious impressions. And, we cannot exclusively love the light within ourself alone. For this love to have any real meaning, it must be directed toward the light within all of creation. This principle was wonderfully stated by Jesus in the admonition: "As you do unto the least of these my brethren, so you do it unto me." The aspirant must learn that whatever he does to others, he is in effect doing to himself— to the Christ within him, the soul, the light which inhabits not only his consciousness but also that of the whole of creation.

As we touch others, and life itself, with goodwill, affection, harmony, charity, and compassion, therefore, we are both expressing and demonstrating our devotion to the soul.

24. Being a part of consciousness, the soul is unfettered by the limitations of form. It can work creatively with cause and effect and the principle of manifestation.

The soul is the master for the individual spiritual aspirant. From time to time, the aspirant will encounter teachers on the physical plane who can impart needed instructions in spiritual practices, the

50

transformation of character, and enlightened living. These teachers should be respected and heeded. But they should never be regarded as a master responsible for the aspirant's development and growth. Even the Christ does not assume this responsibility! Each of us is responsible for our own growth and development spiritually.

As we grow in consciousness, we begin to realize more and more profoundly that the soul, the light within us, is our true teacher and master. It is inspired by the divine plan and has developed a timetable and blueprint for our own growth, creative activity, and service, not just for this one lifetime but for a whole sequence of physical incarnations.

These comments are not meant in any way to detract from the work and stature of the Masters. There are humans of advanced standing who have mastered the art of living and therefore deserve the label "Master." These individuals are actively involved in guiding the development of the whole human race, and many spiritual aspirants are well aware of a special relationship with one or more of these Masters. Yet even where such a bond exists, these Masters do not displace the soul as having the primary responsibility for the individual's growth and development. Actually, the Masters are more interested in how the aspirant can help them with their projects and service.

At one time, a close relationship between aspirant and guru was desirable. At this stage in humanity's growth, however, the value of this type of bond is declining. Aspirants throughout the world are being encouraged to recognize their own soul as their true master.

And the soul is well equipped to play this role. For long eons, the soul has been guiding the process of creating one personality after another, each one a bit more responsive to the light within it than the previous ones. It has full knowledge of what must be faced in each life, both to satisfy antecedents already set in motion and to fulfill the current opportunities for growth and creativity. Indeed, through this experience of millions of years, the soul has developed great skill in working with both the law of cause and effect and the principle of manifestation.

The Law of Cause and Effect is one of the great principles of life. It is referred to in the Bible in the statement: "As you sow, so shall you reap." This is not a passive statement of "going with the flow" of effects; it is a very active statement of the value of working at the level of causes—the archetypal realms of divine life—to produce effects in the worlds of form. The average person deals only with effects. The challenge to each aspirant is to learn to contact causes and work with them, rather than be enslaved by the effects. The soul is able to comprehend life's events as *effects* of earlier impulses, mistakes, indiscretions, good works, or intentions. It is therefore able to predict effects and work creatively to balance behavior in such a way that the growth potential of any given life is maximized.

The Principle of Manifestation is the impulse of the soul to work in the worlds of form. There are certain schools of thought, especially in the East, which claim that the soul dislikes working in the worlds of form and wants to get off the wheel of rebirth as quickly as possible. This is a rather bizarre notion with little supporting evidence. Once the personality develops to the point where it can express the qualities of the soul with little if any distortion, why would the soul suddenly quit incarnating?

The soul does not incarnate on the earth plane because it decides it wants a sojourn into form. It responds to a divine impulse—in this case, the divine impulse to illuminate matter. The personality is an elaborate mechanism which has evolved over millions of years to allow the soul to fulfill its purpose. As the personality becomes an effective agent of the light within it, then the soul begins actively to use it to express its love, wisdom, joy,

52

beauty, harmony, and other qualities. In this way, the soul fulfills its role as master to the personality.

The principle of manifestation is one aspect of the divine will—the need to "express below what is above." The unenlightened personality, lacking will, tends to do whatever it wishes, whenever it pleases. Therefore, the effects it creates are ephemeral and of little consequence. The soul, however, seeks always to honor the divine will; whatever its choices and plans for the personality, it can be assumed it has a noble purpose.

25. In the Christ, the light of the world, consciousness expands to infinity. In the soul, the light within us, our awareness expands to infinity.

In form, the darkness of the world, consciousness contracts to a single point. By identifying with this "pointedness" to some degree, we begin to think of identity and individuality in terms of singleness and selfishness, both of which are distortions of Oneness. Our awareness contracts. Eventually, however, that which contracts begins to expand. We become aware of the Christ, macrocosmically, and of the soul, microcosmically, and slowly learn new ways of viewing life. First, we learn to act unselfishly. But mere altruism is not enough. We must expand our awareness and develop a true "group consciousness"—the ability to identify with the Christ and act as though we were One with God and all of life. Then the light within us is able to illuminate the darkness of our life, and becomes a light in our world. Indeed, it is the nature of light to be inclusive—to eventually permeate the livingness of all things.

This instruction is a powerful statement of the nature of growth. It is the function of the soul to evolve. The soul is perfect, yet evolving. This is a concept which often puzzles spiritual aspirants,

53

who think of perfection as some static state of completeness. It is hard for them to conceive of perfection becoming more perfect. But this is because they are thinking in terms of forms, not qualities. Love is perfect in itself, but we can become more perfect in our expression of it. And as we do, we add something significant to love, and it becomes more perfect as well.

The Christ consciousness is perfect and free from limitations, but a vital part of its perfection is its impulse to evolve. It is designed to expand to infinity. It is for this reason that Jesus told the parable comparing the kingdom of heaven (the consciousness of the soul) to leaven, "which a woman took and hid in three measures of meal, till it was all leavened."

Evolution occurs at the soul level, but requires the action of the personality (the woman), which serves the purpose of hiding the light of the world in form until the form is illumined. In this way, the form becomes transformed, but it is actually consciousness which has expanded.

Esoterically, the word "expansion" is preferred to the word "evolution" to describe the processes of growth in consciousness.

26. In the Christ, the light of the world, the first born are taught the nature of their birthright. This is not a function of time, but of consciousness.

The "first born" are the human souls involved in the vast work of bringing heaven to earth. They are "first born" because the soul must be created before the cycle of personality lives can proceed. In the creation of the soul, individuality is shaped as an active principle. This is our birthright.

The key to recovering our birthright is to use the Christ as a model for the lessons to be learned. Through the Christ, the light of the world, we can learn what it means to act as the soul, the light within us.

It is commonly accepted that evolution is a function of time, but it is not. It is a function of consciousness. This is alluded to in the statement by Jesus, "Before Abraham was, I am." Abraham represents the first born; Christ, the light of the world. Abraham is the symbol of individuality; Christ is the symbol of universal awareness. Evolution occurs within the context of time, but is caused by the basic design of consciousness. First the Christ, then Abraham. First the soul, then the evolution of individuality.

27. The word OM is the light of the world. This is consciousness.

There is no spiritual lesson more fundamental than understanding that consciousness is the word of God. Jesus used this idea to overcome temptation, saying, "Man does not live by bread alone, but by all of the words which issue forth from the mouth of God." In this way He put the form world in its proper perspective, as a projection of consciousness.

The greatest difficulty the aspirant has is learning to distinguish between consciousness and the forms of consciousness—between the light within us and the bodies which house this light. Properly sounded, the OM declares that the light of the world is present and expressing itself through form. To sound the OM, therefore, we must detach ourself from sensation and form, and identify with consciousness.

We do not become conscious of the OM—the OM *is* consciousness. We learn to recognize its sound in our life; we learn to recognize the presence of God within our thoughts, aspirations, and acts. As we do, we hear the OM more and more clearly. And the more we learn to express the presence of God in all that we do, the more we become a conscious part of the light of the world.

28. By sounding the OM so it resounds through all levels of awareness, consciousness finds expression in form and the mechanisms of sensation become attuned to consciousness.

It must be reemphasized that the OM is best sounded by acting as the soul would have us act, thinking as the soul would have us think, and expressing the emotions as the soul would have us express them. In other words, as we fill our mind, heart, and creative endeavors with love, joy, beauty, gracefulness, wisdom, dignity, peace, compassion, and goodwill, we sound the OM. But whenever we let ourself be filled with worry, anxiety, pessimism, confusion, anger, or hate, we sound only discord.

The link between the personality and the soul must be carefully constructed, both by the aspirant and the soul. The personality can chant "OM" for eons, but success in attuning to the soul will come only when it learns to express the archetypal qualities and forces of consciousness in daily life. The soul responds to this effort by gradually revealing more and more about the nature of these qualities to the prepared personality.

Once these basic principles are understood, it is possible to sound the OM to invoke the light of the soul, to purify the subtle bodies of the personality, to align the mind, emotions, and physical body with the soul, and to charge the vehicles of the personality with subtle force. Through practice and repetition, this establishes a strong link between the soul and the personality, so that the soul can act through the personality and so that the personality can attune itself quickly to the soul.

29. This produces self-realization and the removal of obstacles.

Many people fear that pursuit of the spiritual life will lead to a loss of identity or sense of selfhood. This fear is the by-product of a number of specific distortions in traditional religious thinking:

- The advocacy of "selflessness" instead of unselfishness. Selflessness implies the denial of our selfhood, yet individuality is one of the great characteristics of consciousness. It can be very harmful to aim for selflessness. The true goal is unselfish altruism.
- The idea of "getting the self out of the way," so that God (or the soul) can step in and direct the personality without interference. The only problem is that if we truly get the self out of the way, there will be nothing left for God or the soul to act through. The soul needs the personality for effective self-expression.
- The notion that nirvana is like becoming a drop in the ocean. This is the result of an unfortunate use of metaphor to describe atmic consciousness. The soul has a distinct identity as an individual as well as a full member in the body of humanity. Rumors that we will disappear into the cosmic allness or the cosmic void are total nonsense. The only thing that disappears is the vanity and foolish egotism of the personality.

As consciousness expands, so does our sense of individuality. The goal is self-realization, not self-denial. Self-realization is the full identification with the consciousness of the soul, our true Self. It has nothing to do with being in touch with our feelings or our bodies, which would more accurately be called self-indulgence. Gradually, we learn that the soul is the self. The personality, by contrast, tends to be a mass of attachments.

This instruction highlights an interesting point. Due to the nature of selfhood, the obstacles to be removed are all internal. All significant conflicts in the life of the aspirant are found within, not

57

without. They are sometimes mirrored by outer events, but the real conflict is an inner one. The outer events are simply our *projections* of inner distress. As such, they must be resolved within, by modifying attitudes, changing habits, establishing new values or talents, and so on. Any effort to blame problems and conditions on others distracts us from our opportunity to learn and move toward self-realization.

There is a strong measure of the quality of hope associated with this instruction. When meditated on, the instruction attunes the mind to what Paul referred to as "Christ in you, your hope of glory." Hope is an important aspect of evolution and must be contacted and known by the aspirant who wishes to discover the full nature of consciousness.

30. The obstacles to a true understanding of consciousness are the lack of physical purity, the lack of interest in attuning the mind, the lack of a genuine need to know, the lack of carefulness, the lack of dedication, the lack of detachment, the lack of objectivity, the inability to concentrate, and the inability to hold the mind steady in the light of consciousness.

The obstacles are all defined as a "lack" or "inability" for a very good reason. It is not what we have in excess which keeps us from contacting the soul; it is always what we lack. It is not our anger, worry, or fear which hinders us; it is our lack of compassion, poise, and love. Had we compassion, we would have no anger. Had we poise, we would have no worry. Had we love, we would have no fear. It is never wise to think of consciousness as the opposite of form. Consciousness is the realm of divine ideals, patterns, forces, and qualities. Not knowing how to express these ideals and qualities—or knowing but being too lazy to do so—is the true hindrance.

In working with this instruction, we should take care not to dwell on what we lack. The better response is to focus our tireless efforts on becoming more attuned to the qualities and forces we need.

The lack of physical purity. It is possible to have a "well-energized, symptom-free" physical body and yet lack physical purity. Such a body may be able to jog twenty miles, but be totally unable to register the impulses of the soul. Without purity, contact with the creativity of the soul will overstimulate sexual urges. Without purity, contact with the fires of consciousness will lead to nervous disorders. Physical purity is achieved primarily by cleansing and strengthening the etheric body, the subtle counterpart to the dense physical body. Some benefit may be gained by such physical practices as hygiene, cultivating an aspiration for good health, and moderation in diet, drinking, and smoking. A diet which keeps the consumption of meat to a minimum, for example, can help create an etheric body made of the most refined etheric matter, and therefore most able to respond to the soul. Nonetheless, the real focus of attention must be placed on consciousness, not the form. The etheric body must be attuned to the ideal patterns of energy distribution known to the soul. It is the etheric body which provides the real pattern of our health. And as we develop spiritually, eventually the etheric body becomes a "sounding board" for the soul's expression; impressions are registered not just in the brain, but throughout the entire system.

The lack of interest in attuning the mind. The mental body is still quite feeble in most aspirants; it has not been adequately trained. In moments of inspiration, they may use the mind, but in moments of crisis or decision, the mind tends to be abandoned and the emotions are used instead. This immediately shuts the door on the one link between the personality and the soul—the mind. Feeding the mental body and strengthening it should be of paramount interest to all spiritual aspirants. This is especially important since so much of our use of the mind is necessarily focused in mundane issues. It takes a concentrated effort to counteract this, by deliberately using the mind as much as possible to explore the realm of meaning and causes.

The lack of a genuine need to know. This obstacle has also been called "wrong questioning" or "doubt." Many aspirants are more interested in finding what is wrong with life or discovering questions which cannot be proven than they are in actually learning about the nature of consciousness. Wrong questioning tends to hold the mind in the finite ideas of form, making it impossible to approach consciousness, which is infinite. Therefore, it is necessary to learn what might be called "right questioning," which starts with the assumption that every legitimate question has an answer which is helpful and attainable. Rather than ask questions for the sake of idle curiosity or gossip, the aspirant asks questions because he has a genuine need to know the answer. Moreover, he knows that he must seek an enlightened answer, and that the soul and its friends are the best source for this guidance. A genuine need to know guarantees a response from the levels of consciousness, because it permits the soul to evoke evolutionary changes from the personality in return.

The lack of carefulness. Caring is one of the hallmarks of love. The soul cares—it cares about the divine plan, it cares about humanity as a whole, and it cares about the welfare of the personality. The aspirant who seeks to learn about consciousness is entering realms of potent energies which are to be used creatively and productively. If used carelessly, these energies can be misdirected and cause harm. The aspirant must therefore demonstrate his responsibility in using the archetypal and divine forces of consciousness; any irresponsibility will be an obstacle to be overcome. One of the best ways to demonstrate this responsibility

60

is to establish the habit of examining our motives and our behavior, weighing the consequences of what we do and what we leave undone. In particular, we should strive to eliminate selfishness as a hidden motive for our acts, and make sure that everything we do demonstrates the caring of the soul.

The lack of dedication. This obstacle is also called apathy or laziness. It is one of the most common problems among spiritual aspirants, who are so comfortable in their old ways of thinking and behaving that they do not respond to the calls issued by the soul. The lack of dedication is not only a problem in staying with a discipline of personal growth, but is even more an obstacle in the field of service. Promises are made but not fulfilled as completely as they might be.

The lack of detachment. The simple way of defining this obstacle is *lust*—lust for power, lust for sensual experience, lust for psychic experiences, lust for comfort, lust for spiritual growth, or whatever it might be. Any form of lust magnetically entraps the aspirant in form, blocking out the light of the soul. This obstacle is removed through the practice of detachment.

The lack of objectivity. We are accustomed to believing what our senses perceive, ideas that are presented to us, and even our emotional states. Even when our perceptions are not erroneous, however (and they often are), our interpretation of them is usually subjective. It is based on what we have believed in the past or what seems right. This opens the door for enormous confusion and multiple mistakes. To remedy this condition, we must discipline ourself to thoroughly consider all options and compare them to meaningful archetypal patterns in consciousness. These archetypes and principles, being the objective reality of the mind of God, are the true basis for human objectivity.

The inability to concentrate. This eighth obstacle is the condition of not being able to contact the light within us, the soul. It is corrected by becoming aware of the nature of consciousness and trying to express the qualities of divine life as completely as possible in daily life. The great block of concentration for the average aspirant is his intense responsiveness to mass consciousness, social conditioning, and peer pressure. It has even become popular in some circles to "mellow out" and "go with the flow." If ever there was advice designed to keep us from contacting the soul, that is it.

The inability to hold the mind steady in the light within us. Once a person is able to contact the light of the soul, the inability to remain focused in this light can still be an obstacle to be hurdled. Perhaps the simplest example of this problem is the aspirant who receives good insights, then fails to act on them or use them as a basis for intelligent change. The other classic example is the person who registers genuine growth, then backslides into the customary habits of the personality. This problem is resolved by taking steps to sustain our spiritual intent and goals. Insights must be grounded and the love of the soul expressed, or all real progress will be held up.

31. These obstacles not only interfere with a true rapport with consciousness, but also lead to conditions of regret, pain, nervousness, and chaos in the personality.

It is not necessary to dwell excessively on these conditions. They are the somewhat melodramatic reactions of the person who responds to life without the light of consciousness to guide him. They can also be found in society as a whole, because society, too, tends to block out the light of the soul. In the individual, these conditions lead to accidents, awkwardness, injury, fatigue, self-pity, confusion, despair, and illness. In society, they lead to war, crime, oppression, panic, and pessimism. Each of these reactions is characterized by the same problem: the person or group who is experiencing it *believes that the obstacle causing it is real!* As we have seen, this is not true. The obstacle would vanish if the divine archetype or quality which happens to be missing were cultivated.

Therefore, when confronted by regret, pain, nervousness, or chaos, we should keep our sense of humor and balance, and not overstate the problem. To take the problem too grimly would be tantamount to denying the reality of consciousness—the ability of the light within us to resolve this difficulty. The problem must be dealt with, of course—but not on its own terms! It must be met with the healing force of the light of the soul.

A certain amount of suffering does figure in any human life, of course. This is perfectly normal. The unexpected does happen, and even enlightened people will experience moments of loss. But suffering should be relatively short in duration. When it becomes prolonged, it is a sign that contact with the light within us is more imaginary than real.

The intelligent person learns to make his suffering work for him, by trying always to acquire some wisdom from the lessons inherent in his pain or misery. He recognizes that recurrent suffering may well be the natural action of divine law encouraging him to stop behaving in improper ways and begin cultivating a more enlightened approach.

Indeed, this instruction provides us with an excellent understanding of why it is so important to practice thankfulness and blessing as daily spiritual rituals. We should be just as thankful for the exposure of pain or chaos in our life as we are for success and pleasure, because these conditions remind us of the need to cultivate a better and stronger expression of the qualities of consciousness. We should likewise bless the problems life forces us to deal with, so that we may more quickly understand what the genuine solutions to them are.

32. The obstacles are removed by intense application of the appropriate divine archetype or quality. The result is perfect poise or peace in expressing this divine force.

Poised expression is a dramatic contrast to the chaos, pain, nervousness, and regret mentioned in the last instruction. Yet it is the hallmark of the individual who understands the nature of consciousness and acts accordingly. When he confronts an obstacle that blocks the light within, he strives to comprehend what he lacks and cultivate its expression. Knowing this, he may be confused from time to time, but never panics. He may suffer on occasion, but never dwells in emotional pain or anguish. He honors the true nature of peace by always acting with poise.

The key word in this passage is "application." We do not overcome obstacles merely by basking in harmony or some other divine quality. We must build harmonious conditions, heal those that are disharmonious, and serve the divine force of harmony. Just wishing on the star of harmony is never enough.

The next seven instructions describe seven archetypal qualities and indicate how each can be expressed with poise. There is good reason why so much attention is given to poise—it is one of the principal hallmarks of the detached person. The benediction of the enlightened individual truly is: "My peace I leave you."

33. Peace is achieved through the expression of the ideals of compassion and tenderness, devotion to purpose, and the transcendence of pleasure and pain, good and evil.

One of the great disturbers of peace is our sensitivity to our private hurts, the injuries suffered by others, and the distress of humanity as a whole. Peace is restored, however, when we learn that this sensitivity can be used creatively, to touch others with compassion and tenderness and help heal their wounds. Moreover, if we are devoted to purpose, we can deal with the crises of our own life, as well as the serious problems of the international scene, without personalizing them. We *serve* the purpose, and the purpose cannot be served by personal anguish. It is only served by intelligent action and loving help. Therefore, we transcend the opposites of pleasure and pain, good and evil, and enter into peace, even in the midst of imperfection and hurt.

It is important not to gloss over these suggestions as though they were occult platitudes. We can all be compassionate and tender at times, but this instruction is suggesting something more powerful—using the power of compassion and tenderness to *heal* wherever distress exists, within ourself, others, or society. By the same token, it is easy to regard ourself as devoted to purpose—and then forget all about this purpose and become absorbed in self-centeredness. This does not bring peace. To activate our devotion to purpose, we must demonstrate it through active service.

This instruction describes the work of love in action, or transforming love. It encourages us to leave our personal reactiveness behind—our sympathy and self-pity, our self-indulgence and self-centeredness—and cultivate an impersonal, nonreactive expression of the higher emotions. In this way we can stop being so devoted to our own welfare, and transfer this devotion to a higher purpose.

The keynote of this instruction is loving service. It outlines the path to inner peace through Ray 6, the ray of Idealism.

34. Peace is also achieved by breathing harmony and creativity into the unbalanced conditions of life.

This instruction is commonly interpreted in terms of the

physical practice of pranayama, the science of breathing. It should be noted, however, that pranayama literally means "the wise control of energy." It is therefore somewhat misleading to reduce this idea to the regulation of the physical breath. It is far more relevant to study this instruction in the context of the need to harmonize spiritual aspiration with creative inspiration, thereby creating balance—and peace. It is very easy for the aspirant to throw himself or herself out of balance, through intense zeal or fanaticism on the one hand, or through intense involvement in a world cause on the other. In such cases, there is great need for a healthy measure of harmony to restore balance and help the aspirant once more tread "The Noble Middle Path."

In practical terms, it should be noted that harmony is most often achieved by promoting cooperation and creative change in unbalanced conditions. Conflict is often a sign that the people involved have become polarized in their views—unwilling to look at the situation from any perspective than their own. In many cases, the resulting impasse can only be resolved when a mediator succeeds in finding a common ground on which all parties can cooperate.

The keynote of this instruction is integration. It outlines the path to inner peace through Ray 4, the ray of Harmony and Creativity.

35. Peace is achieved by training the mind to recognize higher correspondences and express the realities of heaven through the lower correspondences on earth.

The mind that is unable to rise above mundane levels is never at peace; it is constantly confused, in doubt, and limited. It is therefore important to train the mind to look for the higher correspondence of every fact, event, habit, attitude, idea, or belief it encounters. As the mind begins to see some of these correspondences, they lead it gradually into the realm of archetypes and divine qualities. As the reality of these inner patterns and forces is confirmed, confusion, doubt, and limitations are dispelled. The mind attains a new sense of stability, and with it, peace. In addition, it is now prepared to express these archetypes through the lower correspondences of the physical senses, the emotions, and the mind.

This approach to peacemaking encourages evolutionary change toward spiritual perfection. It is an important model for all efforts to establish peace, in our personal life or in the life of the nations of the world, for it leads to a higher perspective that dispels confusion. It stimulates an awareness that peace must be accompanied by inner growth, or it is shallow and perhaps even meaningless.

The keynote of this instruction is divine discovery and application. It reveals the path to inner peace of Ray 5, the ray of Practical Knowledge.

36. Peace is achieved by identifying with the light and radiance of the Father.

This instruction is often interpreted to advocate a withdrawal from the frustrations of life into a blissful contemplation of the light within us, but it is of course much more active than this idea suggests. If we truly identify with the light and radiance of the Father, we must perforce radiate this light into our life, just as the Father radiates His light throughout His entire creation. We must illumine all the dark spots and shadows of our activities, thoughts, habits, and relationships. It is this participation in illumination which produces peace, more than the mere contemplation of God's light.

In addition, the more we understand and deal with the *purpose* of any activity, project, or condition, the more we can act with peace. Guided by this purpose, we know we are contributing something worthwhile. But what does it mean to understand purpose in this way? We must identify with the purpose and intent of spirit—not the wants of the personality. We must truly act on the words, "My Father is always working, and so am I." We must identify with the will of the Father, seeing our individuality as an expression of it—not as a burden to bear, but as a wise and useful source of our self-expression. In other words, by seeing our individual radiance wholly within the context of the radiance of the Father, we achieve peace.

We draw our ability to think, feel, and act—our whole life—from the Father. As we discover what this really means to us, we will also understand that it is true for everyone else, as well as all of creation. As a result, our over-individualized state of self-interest and inadequate cooperation will be tempered, and we will find ourself more at peace with our surroundings and our brothers. We will begin to see our ties with others more clearly, knowing that while our contributions must be highly individualistic, the same divine purpose guides us all. The same divine purpose radiates through the noble work of every individual.

The keynote of this instruction is divine participation. It illumines the path to inner peace of Ray 1, the ray of Will.

37. Peace is achieved by spiritualizing the stupor and allurement of matter.

It is interesting to consider this instruction in juxtaposition to instruction 36, which suggests identifying with the light and radiance of spirit. By contrast, we are now encouraged to deal with the dull heat and tempting nature of matter. We do not identify with these aspects of matter, of course, for this would not produce peace. Rather, we spiritualize them, through purification, detachment, and the use of matter for constructive purposes. Once again, it is important to realize that we are not being encouraged to avoid form or physical manifestation, but to spiritualize it.

There are those who try to deal with the seductive nature of matter by rejecting it; there are those who try to deal with it by indulging and glorifying it, as in tantra yoga. Neither of these efforts leads to peace or union with the soul. Instead, they hold the aspirant trapped in matter. Peace is found by illuminating the stupor and allurement of matter—by transforming greed into generosity, laziness into diligence, lust into creativity, and contempt into respect.

It may seem odd to some to discuss the stupor and allurement of matter, but these are accurate characteristics. Too much association with materialism can actually dull our awareness, leading to conditions of inertia, nihilism, pessimism, apathy, laziness, and selfishness. We must also beware the seductive pull of matter, which can aggravate tendencies toward greed, possessiveness, envy, vanity, and competitiveness. Since the aspirant is continuously involved in redeeming these conditions, he must take care not to be infected by them.

A good example of how easily we can be infected by the stupor of materialism is the pervasive notion, especially in the East, that peace is a state of quiet rest—or, even worse, quiet nihilism. Nothing could be more of a perversion of the truth. Peace is a divine force which comes into our life as we cultivate its expression. Of all of the divine forces, it is quite possibly the most active, the most invigorating, and the one that stimulates our intelligence the most. It enables us to remain poised and in possession of a clear head in the midst of turmoil and chaos. This series of instructions is demonstrating seven different ways the aspirant can work with the force of peace to establish poise in his life and perfect his character. But the first step which must be taken is to lift humanity's concept of "peace" out of its ill-bred associations with passivity, rest, and inactivity and restore to it its proper meaning.

Esoterically, there is another meaning to this instruction as well. The etheric, astral, and mental bodies of the average person tend to be composed of matter from the lowest subplanes. Little peace can be found in these regions. As each one of us enters upon the spiritual path, we begin the long task of refining the quality of energy in our subtle bodies. This is not done by dwelling on the impurities and trying to purge them, but rather by calling on the light and radiance of spirit. As we work daily to cultivate our expression of these qualities, they inexorably cast out the impurities and improve the quality of our subtle energies.

This, in turn, is the great model for spiritualizing matter—the work of redemption. If we complain and gripe a lot about our work, we lower its potential quality and value. We have been seduced by the petty side of our nature. Conversely, if we learn to respect the value of our labor and our job, and perhaps even discover that we can express joy and excellence through our work, we spiritualize our activity. We create peace.

There are many practical opportunities to create this kind of peace. A mother who resents the time and energy required to care for her children is trapped in selfishness. Yet her neighbor, who cherishes her children and delights in nurturing them, is able to use the same opportunity to make an important contribution. She creates peace.

The keynote of this instruction is consecration, in that we make even the most mundane routines of life holy and meaningful through our dedication and cooperation with the divine plan. It outlines the path to inner peace of Ray 7, the ray of Constructive Activity.

38. Peace is achieved through the conscious control of dreams.

The word "dreams" is one which invites a number of interpretations. It can refer to actual dreams remembered from sleep, to daydreams, to visions or ideals of the future, and to creative projects. The capacity to dream is really the capacity to speculate, anticipate, and plan. If these dreams are based on fantasy, they will not produce peace. But if they are based on archetypal realities, they will indeed lead to peace. Our dreaming must therefore be controlled by the soul; they must be dreams of consciousness and the mind of God, not dreams of the lower worlds.

Worry would be a good example of "uncontrolled dreaming." It creates all manner of wild speculation, little of which is likely to come to pass. It excites us, but serves no useful purpose. In fact, intense worry about "worst case scenarios," the anticipation of failure, and the fear of embarrassment or rejection can actually do us a great deal of harm. These anxieties dissipate our energies, generate glamours, energize bad habits, and tend to invoke what we fear. To counteract these problems, we need to calmly examine the goals and purposes of the soul, and replace our worries with this certain knowledge. This creates peace.

The right use of dreams is in speculation, evaluation, and planning. Our dreams should prepare us to invoke and apply specific divine qualities and forces for our work, our relationships, our growth, and our responsibilities. In this way, we focus our creative energies constructively, generate an efficient and disciplined structure of thought, and invoke success for our efforts.

The great dreams are those on the scale of the American Dream. This is a vision of freedom and individuality which constantly reminds us, as citizens of this country, that we do have a divine mandate to perfect the expression of these ideals.

71

As much as possible, we need to define the "great dreams" which motivate us, and carefully define them in terms of serving the light within us.

The keynote of this instruction is intelligent discipline. It reveals the path to inner peace of Ray 3, the ray of Active Intelligence.

39. Peace is achieved by becoming responsive to that which is dearest to the heart.

The disciple John wanted to be the one closest to the heart of his master, the Christ. This was not a selfish desire, as it might appear, but rather an esoteric statement of the peace which comes from working at the heart of any divine energy. It is also a very practical guideline. To establish peace in any aspect of life, we should try to act from the heart of this facet of life. If, for example, we have a poor relationship with a friend, we should try to ascertain what the heart of the bond is—its purpose and meaning. Having understood this, we then consider what is "dearest" to the heart of this relationship—and become responsive to it in all that we do.

This instruction also highlights the need to avoid living our life at the level of petty and superficial appearances, as so many people do. Instead, we need to be centered in the heart of things—the real issues of intrinsic worth, quality, and purpose. As we learn to work from the heart of life in this way, we move closer to the soul. Peace is generated because we are moving away from the superficial elements of life and coming closer to our true spiritual center.

For the advanced aspirant, this instruction is a call to become responsive to the inner groups which claim the loyalty of the soul, thereby entering into a whole new level of activity.

The keynote of this instruction is goodwill. It portrays the path to inner peace of Ray 2, the ray of Love-Wisdom.

40. As peace is mastered, the capacity to work with divine laws, principles, and archetypes is perfected. The realization of the aspirant now extends from the infinitely small to the infinitely great.

It must be remembered that these instructions into the nature of consciousness are logical and progressive. The reason why the realization of the aspirant now extends from the infinitely small to the infinitely great is simplicity itself: all things large or small are manifestations of divine laws, principles, and archetypes, which have no size. The same divine blueprints used in constructing a galaxy can also be used in building a molecule. Therefore, by working with the archetypal patterns of consciousness, the aspirant has access to all manifestations of these archetypes—in other words, everything which has the breath of life.

Actually, the capacity to work with divine principles and archetypes breaks down most of the limitations we experience in our ordinary efforts to think. For example, it lets us understand the basic principles of fields of knowledge in which we are not thoroughly familiar with the facts and data so many people believe to be knowledge. Thus, a person who is thoroughly accustomed to working with the divine principles of electricity would find that he can apply the same principles to understanding human psychology. The facts and data of these two fields of study differ widely, but there are amazing correspondences at the level of principles.

Working with divine principles and archetypes also helps us transcend the barriers of space. Intelligence pervades the universe; as we develop our intelligence, we attune ourself to all expressions of intelligence, wherever they may be. Just so, love pervades the universe; as we develop our expression of love, we attune ourself to all expressions of love in the universe. Indeed, all divine archetypes—joy, goodwill, grace, and peace, among others—pervade the

73

universe; as we learn to express these qualities in our life, we attune ourself to their expression throughout the universe.

Mastery of the peace described in the preceding seven instructions occurs in graded steps. The first level of peace is the peace of controlling the emotions, producing the ability to properly express the qualities of love, harmony, and devotion. The attainment of this state of peace brings with it the conscious ability to think in four dimensions. This is still the level of form, but is a major step forward in the thinking capacity.

The second level of peace is the peace of the disciplined use of the mind, producing the ability to work directly with creative inspiration. The attainment of this state of peace brings with it the ability to think in five dimensions. It introduces the aspirant to direct cognition of archetypes, principles, and laws.

The third level of peace is the peace of the intuition, producing the ability to identify directly with the consciousness of any form. The attainment of this state brings with it the ability to think in six dimensions.

The fourth level of peace is the peace of the spiritual will or nirvana, producing the ability to be at one with the larger life in which the aspirant lives and moves and has its being. The attainment of this state brings with it the ability to think in perfect wholeness.

41. When peace has been achieved, then the consciousness of the spiritual person, like a pure crystal, takes on the perfect nature of any divine force being expressed. Simultaneously, it reveals the nature of the individual, the quality of his consciousness, and the divine essence being expressed.

This instruction describes the end stage of human evolution, the avatar. The avatar is a spiritual person of such perfection that he is able to become an incarnation of a divine quality. He is so identified with this divine force that he brings it to life in his life, for the whole of the lifetime.

He does not just contemplate joy; he *becomes* joy and expresses it in his life.

He does not just proclaim the value of love; he *becomes* love and uses it to help others with goodwill and benevolence.

He does not just extol the virtues of wisdom; he *becomes* wisdom incarnate and focuses new light into all that he does.

Identifying this completely with divine archetypes does not diminish the sense of individuality; it enriches it and lifts it up to a new level of realization. The aspirant no longer thinks of his soul as "God in man"; he now views the whole of his activities on the personality level as *man in God*.

Those who reach this level become the great creative geniuses of science, art, literature, government, finance, and religion. The nature of their individuality becomes wholly consumed in expressing the divine energy they represent in ways not seen before on the planet. Everything they think and do is colored by this work. No sacrifice is too great if it contributes to an expression of this aspect of divinity. Examples of this type of avatar would be Rembrandt in the field of art, Abraham Lincoln in the field of government, Nikola Tesla in the field of electricity, and Andrew Carnegie in the field of philanthropy.

Individuality is the heart of consciousness. The attached personality has no real sense of individuality. He is basically like all other members of the species, an expression of what has been called "herd consciousness." But the detached person understands his heritage. He knows that his individuality lies not in personal quirks and idiosyncrasies, but in *what he can do* and, even more importantly, *what he is doing*—with his opportunities, his resources, his talents, and the divine forces he has learned to contact and express in his work.

The spiritual person, therefore, does not try to assert his "uniqueness." Instead, he tries to refine his consciousness to the point where it can act like a pure crystal, focusing one or more of the divine qualities or archetypes of life into his self-expression. The measure of his individuality is twofold:

1. His ability to express this divine force without distortion or aberration.

2. His capacity to apply it in new and meaningful ways which revolutionize human awareness, at least in a small way.

42. Such a person is able to work dynamically with divine forces, because he has learned to translate their power, quality, and structure into ideas, a vision, and a useful application.

The divine qualities and archetypes, by their very nature, are interested in expressing themselves in the worlds of form. As we become skilled in meditating and contacting the light within us, and dedicate ourself to acting as an agent of divine life, we will find our access to these divine qualities expanding rapidly.

It is important to appreciate, however, that serving as an agent of the divine forces requires great skill—not to contact them necessarily, but to express them intelligently. Any number of people have been prematurely overshadowed by divine inspiration, only to misapply it. They did not know what they were doing. It is not enough just to believe in the benevolence of life. There are specific skills to be mastered in translating divine forces into ideas, shaping those ideas into a vision, and then working out a useful application which still expresses the essence of the divine force that originally inspired us.

The process described in this instruction is the meditative state of contemplation leading to creative work. The seed of a creative idea is taken into the light within us and slowly nurtured into an application which can be expressed through our character, our work, or our growth.

43. When the mind is not conditioned by the past, or by the need for a creative application, the spiritual person is able to discern the pure origins of thought.

This is not an easy instruction to comprehend, as it deals with a pure state of abstract thinking—what Alice Bailey refers to as "perception without judicial reasoning." As we have seen earlier, this abstract perception of the divine mind is unconditioned by words, images, symbols, feelings, or concrete ideas. It is also unconditioned by the memory of experiences and events in the worlds of form. This is not to say that the function of memory is suspended—for it is a legitimate state of mind—but it is focused out of the realm of personal experience and into the realm of consciousness. The mind is trained not on what has been known, but on what is knowable.

This is true discernment—the perception of archetypal reality without any preconditioned expectation of what these archetypes are. As long as our expectations are preconditioned by our personal assumptions, we will not perceive the archetypes as they are, but rather as we want them to be. This latter kind of perception, of course, is one of the greatest problems for spiritual aspirants, who want to make contact with the soul—but on their own terms. They want the soul to fulfill *their* expectations of what it is like. As a result, they set themselves up for enormous disappointment and frustration.

True discernment must occur at the level of consciousness itself. It cannot be achieved by tracing from form to consciousness.

77

This kind of thinking is a useful way to prepare the mind to discern, but is not discernment itself.

This instruction also provides us with a clue to working with memories. Consciousness utilizes memory, but not for the purpose of preserving the past, like photographs in an album. It remembers in order to learn, by focusing on the living essence of the past, not the events themselves. Unfortunately, many people are enslaved to the past. They carefully preserve the feelings of regret, humiliation, anger, or despair they have associated with specific memories. Instead of learning, they remain stuck in a repetition of the past, like a scratched record. Their negativity clogs up the memory and confuses their thinking capacity. Such people need to cleanse the memory of this kind of negative reaction and put it in a new context—the context of hope and optimism. Thereafter, whenever they recall the memory, instead of being buried in anger, they are heartened by the recollection of how this episode in their life strengthened them, taught them to value decent behavior, and so on.

The light of consciousness is not mired in the past. It is moving, growing, and busy animating life. We should be, too.

44. Through active work in exploring the divine mind and using its qualities and forces creatively, the spiritual person is able to become aware of even more subtle things.

The soul is not the highest aspect of our being; consciousness is not the end all and be all of universal experience. The ability to work at the level of consciousness described in the last few instructions may seem phenomenal to the ordinary reader, but it is actually quite elementary. It is the crowning achievement of human growth, but just the introductory achievement of true soul consciousness.

78

The more we work with divine forces and qualities, the more we come to realize how vast our opportunities to grow have become. We begin to sense the incredible organization of intelligence and benevolence which pervades all of life. These occasional glimpses help us put our individual efforts and trials into perspective.

45. Form, consciousness, and spirit are seen as a continuum of Oneness in manifestation.

The aspirant becomes aware of the three in One and is able to work creatively with the fires of all three aspects: fire by friction (form), solar fire (consciousness), and cosmic fire (spirit). He can act as an individual, a son of Man, and a son of God without the need of shifting his focus of consciousness or sense of identity.

We are still dealing with consciousness, but realize that consciousness can have three expressions: knowing about forms, knowing about knowing, and knowing about spirit. The process of learning becomes something more important than just acquiring a new recipe for fudge. Fudge may have its place in our life, but we do not overrate it; we put it and everything else in the context of what the soul, and spirit at its higher level, is trying to accomplish.

This instruction also suggests that there is an eventual synthesis of spirit, soul, and form, leading to a new continuum of cooperation from one level to the next in the work of redemption and the fulfillment of the divine plan. In this light, we can once again clearly see that spirit, the soul, and matter are not antagonistic toward one another; they are all part of the life of God. It is therefore just as foolish for the spiritual aspirant to reject "the material world" as it is for the dense materialist to reject spirit!

46. The aspirant now realizes that consciousness itself is a radiation of spirit.

Form has become fully integrated with consciousness, and is now seen only as the manifestation of divine archetypes. When he thinks of forms, the aspirant actually thinks of them first in terms of their archetypal essence and only secondarily in terms of their manifestation. And yet he is still confronted with a duality: not the duality of form and consciousness, but the duality of consciousness and spirit. Through his use of consciousness, he becomes aware of the monad. But he knows very little about the monad.

At this stage, the aspirant begins working more consciously with divine energies, as opposed to ideas or patterns. His efforts to heal, serve, and be creative become much more powerful. He begins to experiment with the processes of radiation.

47. Focused in the highest level of consciousness, the aspirant holds himself steady in a realization of spirit.

The ability to hold himself steady in the realization of spirit may be brief in terms of time, but it lifts the aspirant to the highest potential of consciousness: awareness of the Father. The Two in One becomes the One.

This gives the aspirant more than just a glimpse into a high state of enlightenment—it reveals a basic characteristic of consciousness at work. Consciousness dominates matter by sounding a keynote which embodies the power of its purpose. As this keynote is sounded from the level of the soul, over years or even eons, the personality—and matter itself—inevitably responds.

To grow, therefore, we must learn to act as consciousness acts. By magnetically holding our attention in the purpose of our work, for instance, we can gradually infuse our attitudes, talents, and even the work itself with the essence of this purpose. The key, as always, is the steadiness with which we hold this realization.

Esoterically, this instruction represents a shift from the personality meditating to its higher correspondence. The soul is meditating on its "soul"—the monad. The ability to glimpse this indicates that the work of building the "bridge of consciousness" (what the Hindus call the antakarana) is well under way. This is the bridge which links the mind of the enlightened personality with the soul. As a result, the aspirant also begins to glimpse the reality of the spiritual triad, the reflection of the monad in atmic, buddhic, and abstract mental substance. It should be noted, however, that it is always *intelligent service* which first draws the attention of the triad and leads to the need to build the bridge of consciousness.

48. The aspirant therefore has a perfect understanding of divine ideas and their origins.

He has acquired "all knowledge," because he is conscious of the purpose of divine ideas and qualities and the sublime impulses of which they are projections. To put this symbolically, he not only hears the Word perfectly as it is uttered, but is aware of the One Who is uttering the Word. And he has learned to identify so completely with the Word that he is the Word itself.

Nonetheless, he is not yet identified with the One Who utters the Word, even though he can hold himself steady in a realization of that Life.

At this stage, the aspirant is able to work at the atmic level, by identification with the spiritual triad. The atmic plane can be thought of as the epitome of knowledge, the apex of consciousness. A tremendous amount of stability attends this instruction. There is

81

no residue of doubt, confusion, or misunderstanding. Only perfect understanding remains. There is a clear perception of divine law and a pure identification with divine qualities and forces.

Realization, as a mental process, reaches its highest state—the immediate and full grasping of reality.

49. This comprehension is ineffable to the mind which has not been trained in the nature of consciousness.

It is the "peace which passes understanding." This comprehension is based entirely on the principles of the infinite potentials of consciousness and spirit, and is therefore incomprehensible and even foreign to the mind which is used to thinking exclusively in finite terms—the mind that has trouble even with fourth-dimensional concepts.

This level of comprehension cannot be acquired by reading scriptures, being blessed by a guru, or any artificial means. It unfolds step by step as we follow the instructions given us by Patanjali.

50. As it is gained, all lesser modes of comprehension must pass away.

At this point, to return to more finite methods of thinking for the purpose of comprehending life would not only be foolish, it would be evil. They may have been appropriate at one time, for one stage of growth, but they are not appropriate now. If used, they would interfere with a divinely-tuned mechanism of consciousness. They would interfere with the unfoldment of evolution.

And yet, even though these modes of thinking must be left behind for the purposes of comprehension, a reasonable facsimile of them may have to be used for creative expression. Traditional forms of logic may be unnecessary, for example, for the individual focused on the atmic plane—and represent a hindrance to comprehension, because they would grossly slow down the processes of consciousness—yet when this individual presents some new truth for others to digest, it will be best if he expresses it in logical terms. Otherwise, he is inviting distortion of the truth he presents.

This is one of the problems of spiritual leaders who do achieve the higher levels of consciousness: they frequently fail to express the new realizations they gain as clearly and as precisely as they might. As a result, the unenlightened aspirants who follow them develop the idea that the higher levels of consciousness are something akin to mush. Nothing could be further from reality.

51. When this state of consciousness is itself transcended, the aspirant is One with Life.

The *awareness* of Oneness is not the same as full *identification* with Oneness. The next step in development is therefore the transcendence of consciousness and entrance into the pure life of spirit. However, the purpose of this book is to deal with the nature of consciousness. Therefore, once this step is made, the commentary ends. The reader should not conclude, however, that no growth is possible after this point. From one point of view, only now does the growth of the true man begin.

In this final instruction of Book One, Patanjali sets forth an interesting idea: that the whole of growth is like climbing a ladder, one rung after another. At each rung or plateau, it is transcendence which helps us grow—catapults us to the next rung, so to speak. What is transcendence? It is the ability to rise to a higher perspective and thereby neutralize the lower one. We may not be ready to enter fully into the life of spirit, as described here, but each of us is at some rung on the ladder of growth. We have the opportunity to take the next step forward, but are not quite sure how to do it. Yet if we summon the impulse to grow within us—the divine impulse of evolution—it will give us the stimulus we need to make the next step.

THE PROCESS OF INTEGRATION

1. Integration between the soul and the personality becomes possible as the aspirant learns to act with divine will, compassion, and skill.

Integration is a psychological procedure for transforming something which is fragmented or divided into something which is *whole*. The divers pieces are made integral, or one. We saw in the study of Book One that the ultimate spiritual goal is the achievement of Oneness, through which we reveal the fullness of both divine will and human competence. Therefore, integration of consciousness at any level is desirable.

There are two basic steps in the integration of human consciousness. The first is the integration of the mind, emotions, and the physical body into a single, cohesive, dynamic personality. The second is the integration of the personality with the soul. The second step of integration cannot proceed until the first phase is well under way, for the soul is virtually unable to express itself through a disorganized, ineffectual personality.

Both of these processes of integration occur very slowly and gradually, and require many lifetimes to complete. In spite of many claims to the contrary, integration is *not* a magical procedure produced by wishing for it, fantasizing it, or bribing a guru to do it for you. It is a piece of work that only the aspirant can do for himself, in cooperation with the soul. There are many simple ways it can be described: as the blending of diverse elements of consciousness, or the harmonization of the different functions of consciousness, or attunement to the ideals (or rays) for the personality or the soul. Each of these conveys an important element of integration, but it should be kept in mind that the most important feature of integration is the result: wholeness. Integration is a multidimensional activity which has to be thought of in multidimensional terms to make complete sense.

We are dealing, in other words, with something more profound than pouring chicken broth, beans, and meat into a pot, heating them, and producing soup. Mixing ingredients together is *not* integration. Integration involves transformation; it leads to the development of something whole. It therefore goes beyond just learning to use the mind, emotions, and physical body actively in life. A different analogy may help.

If a European leaves his mother country and migrates to the United States, he has the opportunity to integrate himself into the culture of his new country. But simply working, eating, and sleeping in America is not enough; the foreigner who does not learn English, become a citizen, or modify old habits and customs is not really participating in the wholeness of the American life experience. Of course, becoming an integral part of a new country is a long, slow process. It takes years of practice, for example, just to learn to think in English, let alone master the idioms and grammar. It also takes a long time to adjust to new modes of political thinking, to different lifestyles and customs, and to an appreciation of the indigenous literature, arts, and sciences. But it can be done, and it does not require a repudiation of the older ways of approaching life—just a new definition and focus for them.

The integration of consciousness is much the same. The personality is not integrated by eliminating the emotions in favor of the mind. Nor is it integrated by stubbornly staying emotional and childish, refusing to learn to think. Rather, integration is achieved as each of the three bodies is brought to its fullest, most enlightened expression, coordinated to work smoothly together, and directed to be constructive, active, and efficient in life. Correspondingly, the integration of personality with soul does not require that the personality abandon everything it cherishes; after all, the soul wants to act *through* the personality, not around it. On the other hand, integration cannot occur as long as the personality tries to interpret the life of the soul in terms of its own selfish wants and fantasies. Integration enriches both the personality and the soul; ideally, they become partners in a mutual effort. The single goal, purpose, or ideal that they serve in common is eventually the most powerful integrating force.

The integration of the personality occurs at the level of character, in the essence of our mind, emotions, and physical energy, not the substance of the bodies themselves. Changes do occur in the substance of the bodies as integration proceeds, but the true changes occur in consciousness, not form. It is therefore important for the aspirant to break the habit of thinking of the three bodies as *forms*, and begin thinking of them as intangible principles or expressions of consciousness. This is not easy, because most of us still have the tendency to think of the physical body as real, the soul as something less real. It requires a major reversal to realize that the body is but a temporary focus for our real individuality, the light within us.

One of the principal ways we make this reversal, and initiate the work of integration, is to adopt a specific theme for each of the three bodies of the personality—a theme which will link that body with the soul as it is perfected and added to our self-expression. The three themes set forth by Patanjali are:

Acting with divine will, the theme which should guide and become the integrating force of the mind. This is not just the worship of divine will, but the active translation of the *qualities* of the will into defined purposes, plans, and goals, and the *force* of the will into the courage to initiate work on these plans, discipline ourself, and persevere in our projects.

Acting with compassion, the theme which should guide and become the integrating force of the emotions. This produces a major reversal in the use of the emotions. Instead of being mired in selfishness and defensiveness, we learn to use the emotions to enrich the quality of life—our own, that of our friends, our work, and nationally.

Acting with skill, the theme which should guide and become the integrating force of the physical body. The key to any incarnation is how successful the person is in contributing to the ongoing growth of humanity. This requires a wide variety of skills, differing with each person.

It should be added that the theme of the soul, as it seeks to act through the personality, would be to express the glory of God in thought, emotion, speech, and behavior.

2. As integration occurs, the personality expresses more and more of the light of the soul. Its flaws and deficiencies are gradually eliminated.

The goal of integration is not to *combine* the personality with the soul; after all, the personality lives a relatively short span of years, then dies. What purpose would it serve to combine an immortal soul with such a temporary vehicle? None at all. But it is useful to make the personality fully *compatible* with the soul, so they can act as partners.

An analogy which helps clarify this point is that of the sculptor. When he is just beginning to learn his craft, his sculptures are quite ordinary, unrefined, perhaps even distorted. But as he becomes a master of his craft, his work becomes embodied with the stamp of his genius and individuality. They inspire the people who contemplate them. They are a legitimate contribution to civilization.

The soul seeks the same result with its creation, the personality. It does not want a personality which is mired in mass consciousness; it wants one that can express the full range of individuality. It does not seek a dull personality; it seeks one which radiates the light of spirit, the genius of mind, and the compassion of love. The difference between the work of the soul and the work of the sculptor is significant, however. Because the soul is dealing in such a pliable medium as consciousness, the work of art it has created (the personality) is *able to grow!* A block of marble is unable to help the sculptor do his work, but the personality is able to make a significant contribution to the process of integration—and is expected to do so. Indeed, it has been created to do so.

When the personality first realizes it has the potential to contribute to the work of the soul, it is still motivated primarily by personal, selfish drives. It continually seeks reassurance that it is getting more out of the endeavor than it is putting in—or "sacrificing," as it is likely to view it. Eventually this ceases to be a relevant issue, however. It learns more about the true significance of growth and cooperates willingly with it.

The spirit of growth is the most important element in integration. The very substance of the bodies of the personality changes and becomes of higher quality. The organization of these bodies also changes, becoming more disciplined and efficient. These changes are enormous, but they occur gradually, so that the impact is not destructive. And they are all designed to bring about one result: the personality becomes more "light-bearing." It is not just attuned to the soul, but actually embodies the very qualities of the soul, to one degree or another. It radiates the light of the soul. This radiation is something more than charisma, which is usually just a function of the emotions. It is more an ongoing presence of intensity of purpose, genius, and inspiration. It is a presence which heals, builds, and serves.

But more happens in the process of integration than just the gradual enlightenment of character and creativity. The flaws and deficiencies of the personality are also eliminated. This is a point

91

which is all too frequently glossed over, as though the soul would be more than willing to accept the personality as it is, warts and all. The soul does care for its creation, even when it is grossly imperfect, but can only integrate with it when these imperfections have been removed.

The soul can only integrate with the physical body when its tendencies toward inertia, materialism, and dependency have been eliminated, by cultivating the virtues of productivity and self-sufficiency.

The soul can only integrate with the emotions when their tendencies to be selfish, reactive, negative, possessive, and antagonistic have been removed, by cultivating the virtues of generosity, helpfulness, optimism, goodwill, and benevolence.

The soul can only integrate with the mind when its tendencies to be separative, arrogant, and stupid have been eradicated, by cultivating the virtues of cooperation, humility, and wisdom.

The soul can only integrate with the personality when its tendencies to be irresponsible, absorbed in trivialities, ungenerous, and uncommitted have been overcome, by cultivating the virtues of responsibility, purposefulness, altruism, and dedication.

These flaws and deficiencies are all internal, in that they involve our attitudes and patterns of behavior. Some will be familiar to us, but some will not, because the roots of these flaws or hindrances may be much deeper than our personal conscious awareness. They may be patterns which originated in earlier lives—or in mass consciousness. Still, they must be dealt with, because we have accepted them and formed traits and habits of our own based on them.

These patterns do not evaporate by covering them up with positive thinking—or by praying to some deity to magically remove them from our lives. They are eliminated as we work with the proper techniques of mental housecleaning to remove them. By studying the archetypal patterns of consciousness, we determine the ideal way of acting or thinking in some aspect of life. The ideal is always that pattern which permits the maximum amount of the light of the soul to shine through. Then, we hold the ideal consistently in mind and strive, day by day, to eliminate or reform any attitudes and traits of behavior which obscure the ideal.

Mental housecleaning is sometimes discouraging work, because the magnetic patterns of the personality are often quite strong and stubborn. Ancient patterns which have influenced us for thousands of years do not submit in a week's time. Nonetheless, the light of the soul is stronger than any of these patterns—or, indeed, all of them. If we remain steady in our determination to invoke the light within us to remove these flaws and deficiencies, in time we will triumph. We will learn to act with the divine will, compassion, and skill.

It should be added, by way of emphasis, that the work of mental housecleaning is the primary way the personality demonstrates its dedication and devotion to the soul. It is *not* enough, as some believe, to flood ourself with white light in a quasi-meditative state and expect this automatically to clean up our character! Nor is it enough just to "unblock" ourself, as others advocate. We must actively cultivate the virtues and qualities of the soul—joy, wisdom, goodwill, courage, steadfastness, and harmony.

The reason for cleansing and purifying the personality, after all, is to train it to radiate the light of the soul. A personality which "expresses more of the light of the soul" is not just a personality with a large and glowing aura; it is a personality which demonstrates ever more of the skills, virtues, and qualities of the soul in its daily activities.

3. These flaws and deficiencies can be grouped in five categories: ignorance, the tendency to personalize, passion, hate, and attachment.

Each of these five categories is a distortion of one of the basic attributes of consciousness. Ignorance is the distortion of wisdom. The tendency to personalize is the distortion of the principle of individuality—we assume that we are our feelings, desires, and cravings, forgetting that we are actually a noble child of God, a proper citizen of the universe. Passion (which is used here in the sense of any intensely focused feeling—not romantic passion) is the corruption of the impersonal attitude of divine love. Hate is the perversion of the spiritual process of redemption—instead of transforming that which is imperfect, hate seeks to destroy it. Attachment is the result of mistaken identification—we identify with the limits of form, rather than the treasures of heaven.

Because these flaws are distortions of basic attributes of consciousness, the key to eliminating them lies in shifting our primary focus of attention away from the flaws and toward the ideals they fail to express—or, in so many cases, actually sabotage. We should not be *threatened* by the fact that we have these flaws, but realize that, in the process of eliminating them, we are able to learn valuable lessons about consciousness.

It is also important to realize that, if we are serious about our determination to integrate our consciousness, we must not indulge any of these flaws. It is right and proper to be patient as we pursue the work of mental housecleaning, and not demand perfection overnight. Obsessive perfectionism is self-defeating. But so is the rationalization that these flaws really are not that serious, after all. They are.

In this context, it is interesting to consider *why* these five kinds of hindrance produce difficulty. The reason is that they lead to the pursuit of the ephemeral and the unreal, thereby producing frustration, failure, and disappointment. Indeed, the only value of these hindrances is that they lead us time and again into suffering. The suffering, in turn, eventually inspires us to seek out and discover the spiritual laws and ways of living which will relieve our agony. It is sad but true: until we deliberately choose to walk the lighted path, suffering is probably the only force which will motivate us to grow and improve as a human being.

4. Ignorance is the cause of all deficiencies and flaws, whether they be conscious, subconscious, unconscious, individual or collective. Thus, until ignorance is overcome, the other hindrances cannot be fully eradicated.

Ignorance is not so much the lack of knowledge (which is finite and limited itself) as it is the opposite of consciousness. Consciousness is the state of knowing and the activity of applying what is known. It is the condition of the soul. And so, it is only logical that any obstruction to the light of the soul must be rooted, above all, in ignorance—not knowing. Anything which impedes the radiance of the light within us through the world of form is, by definition, an obstruction.

Just as it is helpful to think of consciousness in terms of movement, rather than in terms of stasis, it is equally illuminating to view ignorance in this way. The real problem of ignorance is not that we do not know some fact that we ought to know; facts are easily attained. Rather, it is that our attention is focused in something other than consciousness. We are *ignoring* our true source of wisdom! It may be because we are too absorbed in the pettiness and trivialities of life, or too interested in pursuing our desires, or too busy being angry and hostile toward others, or too absorbed in the seeming importance of materialism. But the fact is that we are ignoring the soul; we are ignoring what we have been commissioned to do. And this is a flaw, a deficiency. Until it is removed, we are hostage to it.

There are many aspirants who deliberately shun the cultivation of the mind as somehow hostile to the life of spirit. They claim that God is love and that therefore loving God is the only requirement of the spiritual life. Patanjali makes it abundantly clear that this is not so. Love without wisdom creates a very unbalanced condition. Indeed, there are many dangers to ignorance:

• Ignorance of the real causes of our suffering traps us in the conditions of our life, trying to solve problems through threats, intimidation, fear, and avoidance, instead of cultivating the spiritual qualities of tolerance, patience, and understanding.

• Ignorance of divine law deludes us into trying to evade the consequences of our acts, both of commission and omission.

• Ignorance of the skills, wisdom, and virtues of our own divine nature traps us in the pettiness and limitations of the unenlightened personality.

• Ignorance of the right use of the emotions traps us in possessiveness, jealousy, fear, hate, grief, worry, and frustration.

• Ignorance of the right use of the mind binds us in our own convictions, stereotypes, prejudices, and rules.

• Ignorance of the right use of the will traps us in arrogance, stubbornness, and isolation.

To put this idea as plainly as possible, the real threat to integration with the soul is stupidity and dullness—not the stupidity and dullness of others, or mass consciousness, but our own. This is true for each of us, at our respective levels of development and growth. The aspirant should never be too proud to admit it, or he or she will slow down the growth process tremendously. If we are sincere in our aspiration, we will carefully examine our areas of stupidity and dullness and correct them.

Consciously, this includes the lack of wisdom, undeveloped skills, gaps in our knowledge, and a lack of experience in expressing such qualities as compassion, joy, peace, and beauty.

Subconsciously, the problems of stupidity and dullness can be found in an innate resistance to growth, traits of laziness, habits of defensiveness, feelings of inferiority, guilt, fears, petty jealousies, and patterns of hypocrisy and self-deception.

Unconsciously, these problems can be found in repressed and suppressed patterns of behavior, susceptibility to the influences of mass consciousness, and perhaps even a sense of loyalty to unenlightened forces. The accumulation of the earthbound patterns and materialistic habits for all of our past lives—esoterically referred to as "The Dweller on the Threshold"—is also a major element of our unconscious dullness and stupidity.

Collectively, the problems of stupidity and dullness can be found in such universal conditions as our fear of death and the expectation that the proper response to the death of a loved one is a prolonged bout of grief. They can also be observed in the universal acceptance of anger as a legitimate response to opposition and frustrated desires.

Collective ignorance subverts the individual aspirant far more readily than is commonly understood. One of the strongest themes in modern mass consciousness, for example, is permissiveness—that we need total freedom (no rules) in order to achieve our full potential. This idea first gained popularity in the teaching of grammar and mathematics, but has since become the favorite theme of many unscrupulous but highly popular "spiritual teachers." They tell us that God makes no rules; therefore, if we are unhappy, it is because we have imposed unnecessary rules on ourself! There are many mottos to the permissive movement:

"Go with the flow."

"Do your own thing."

"Pursue happiness first, and all else will come to you."

"Just let it be."

"Get in touch with your feelings."

"We create our own reality."

The tendency to go along with whatever everyone else is doing—whatever is in fashion—is one of the strongest signs of vulnerability to collective stupidity.

"Stupidity" may seem too harsh of a word, but it is actually very precise. It means "lacking in intelligence." The stupid person is still buried in form. He has not yet discovered the power of consciousness to illumine form—at least in the areas of his stupidity.

This is a massive problem. Very few people, even spiritual aspirants, exercise the full range of mental faculties. Some people think well logically, but not by association. Others have high intelligence quotients, but lack common sense. Some are quite skilled in processing data, but are unable to speculate on its meaning. The saddest part of the problem is that so many people are willing to dwell in their stupidity! They fill their time with trivial activities, rather than applying themselves to training their minds.

A simple rule for dealing with ignorance is this: wherever darkness exists, there lies ignorance. Darkness is removed by applying illumination—by focusing the light within us upon the source of the darkness. We can never expect to be entirely free of ignorance, because the nature of light is to seek out the dark and illumine it. We can, however, strive to become an agent of light, so that we are never trapped or hindered by the darkness we encounter, either within ourself, within others, or within society.

5. The man who ignores the realities of consciousness, which are immortal, pure, infinite, and universal, becomes imprisoned by the seeming significance of sensation, which is mortal, polluted, finite, and personalized.

This instruction has tremendous implications, because we are, after all, designed to operate in the realm of sensation, with its mortality, pollution, finiteness, and overweening selfishness. This assignment was not a fluke of cosmic coincidence; we are meant to spiritualize this realm of sensation, by uplifting it and perfecting it, thereby making it more enlightened. Only by voluntarily submitting to partial ignorance and confusion could we achieve our goals. But the pull and temptation of ignorance is strong; it needs to be countered by a firm understanding of the nature of consciousness.

We do not overcome ignorance by retreating from the imperfect world of sensation into the spiritual realm, as some Easterners attempt to do. Rather, we do it by expanding our consciousness so it can work simultaneously in the form world and the soul world. We integrate these two spheres of activity in our own consciousness, knowing that "when the higher meets the lower, it remains the higher"—it purifies that which is impure and adds elements of immortality and infiniteness to that which is mortal and finite.

Immortality is gained by learning to create works that are "worthy of immortality." This is not as hard as it may seem; it merely implies that we strive to embody the immortal qualities of the soul—compassion, wisdom, joy, nobility, and intelligence—in all that we do. These elements cannot die, even though the forms we create do pass away.

Purity is gained by learning to contact and use the pure essence of energies, rather than the lower octaves. In other words, we use the essence of love, rather than its common expressions as sentimentality, possessiveness, or sensual attraction. We use the essence of courage, rather than its common expressions as boldness, bravado, and intimidation.

The infinite is gained not by spacing out, as common parlance puts it, but by learning to draw the energies we need to heal and sustain the forms of life from sources beyond our limited scope. We learn to contact and put to work the unlimited energy available to us—within the atom, within mankind as a whole, and within God's life. This is done by making sure that our works and acts are inspired and sustained by the infinite wisdom, power, and law of God. When we are inspired by our own wishes, we are unlikely to create something heaven would want to support or sustain. But when inspired by the soul—even in the way we treat others, face challenges, and solve problems—we will find that we can draw on the unlimited strength of the infinite.

Universality is gained not by giving up our sense of individuality, but by learning that the individual is a perfect microcosm within the macrocosm. The individual is able to "self" or "individualize" that which is universal, thereby putting the principles of the universe to work in his own daily life, moment to moment. In addition, we must recognize the collective burden we share with all other people and play our role in spiritualizing our culture and civilization through the expression of responsibility, goodwill, fairness, kindness, and creativity.

The more we begin to think in terms of immortality, purity, infinity, and universality, first, and in terms of mortality, pollution, finiteness, and selfishness, second, the more we overcome the bonds of ignorance. In no way does this mean that we pretend that we will never die, that our lives are flawless, that we have no limitations, or that we can spend all day contemplating cosmic verities. Rather, it means that instead of fearing the death of the personality—which would be ignorant—we view death in the context of the immortality of the soul. Instead of polluting our personalities with worry, negativity, and discouragement—which would be ignorant—we strive to cultivate the expression of tolerance, tranquillity, and gracefulness. Instead of limiting ourself by thinking only in terms of the circumstances of life and our reactions to them—which would be ignorant—we strive to see how these circumstances help fulfill the plans of the soul. Instead of continually thinking only of our personal needs, activities, and frustrations—which would be ignorant—we put our personal priorities in the larger context of what the universe is trying to accomplish and how we can contribute to it.

There are many practical ways these ideas can be applied. One of the simplest is the general realization that the events we encounter, even the negative ones, have no actual impact on the reality of the soul. The death of a loved one, the loss of one's job, the break-up of a marriage, or the disloyalty of a friend can cause the ignorant personality enormous stress. But to the person who has conquered ignorance and become an agent of light, these are just events, nothing more. They must be dealt with responsibly and intelligently, but they do not endanger his immortality, purity, infiniteness, or universal connections. They do not diminish his light.

It must also be understood, however, that not all issues of mortality, pollution, finiteness, and personalization are quite so obvious. In many cases, they are quite subtle, and color the thoughts and acts of even advanced aspirants. It is helpful to understand the fuller dimensions of these problems.

The problem of *mortality* also involves recognizing those fads and facets of life which lack divine inspiration, and therefore have no real substance. Most rock music, for example, is highly mortal—in fact, much of it dishonors the spirit of music—whereas the music of Bach has endured for centuries and will continue to do so.

We all know the threat of air and water *pollution*, but do we also recognize the true impact of polluted emotions, thoughts, and

101

philosophy? When we mix affection with possessiveness, we pollute it with envy. When we mix the urge to reform with resentment, we corrupt it with vengeance. When we mix our intent to help others with guilt or fear, we pollute it with shame and intimidation. When we mix Christianity with Marxism, we pollute the forces of goodwill and brotherhood with exploitation and bigotry of the worst sort.

It is easy to see the *finiteness* of fixed ideas and prejudices, but many open-minded people nonetheless make terribly incomplete assumptions about major issues—the common assumption, for instance, that criminals would never choose their lifestyle on their own. They must have been driven to criminality by poverty, weak genes, or some other factor. The possibility that people with weak values, a poor self-image, and underdeveloped character restraints might consciously choose a life of crime is something they somehow never grasp.

The subtle coloring of ideas through *personalization* is not much different. Groups which advocate financial assistance to the poor often talk about the need for everyone to pay his or her "fair share" of taxes, yet they never talk about the need for everyone— even the poor—to contribute his or her "fair share" to the prosperity of the country, nor the corollary right of everyone to keep a "fair share" of his or her own productivity.

Ultimately, it is the integration of the mind with the divine will or intent of the soul which eliminates the obstacle of ignorance. This also implies that the emotions and the physical energy have been brought under the supervision and control of the mind, and are therefore responsive to the guidance of the soul.

6. The tendency to personalize life is an error of identification.

There are many ways the tendency to personalize life manifests. The most obvious is the person who thinks only in terms of self-centered interests—the person who subscribes to the philosophy of "looking out for number one." But the person who becomes completely absorbed in his problems and suffering is also personalizing life, and so is the individual who becomes caught up in the most trivial and petty elements of existence.

Other examples of personalizing life would include:

• The person who takes any suggestion, whether critical or not, as a personal insult or an attempt to embarrass him.

• The person who becomes obsessed with grief after the death of a loved one or close friend.

• The person who is competitive to the point of proving himself superior by defeating others.

• The person who is so absorbed in his own activities and achievements that he is unaware of what others around him are doing.

• The person whose wish life and fantasies become more real to him than his actual responsibilities, relationships, and accomplishments.

The tendency to personalize life is the single most important factor determining our self-image. When we have eliminated this flaw, we view ourself as a proper child of God, a creature of intelligence, love, and talent cut from cosmic fabric. This is a healthy self-image. But as long as the flaw exists, either consciously or subconsciously, our self-image suffers. At the one extreme, it causes us to dislike ourself intensely, or at least feel inadequate; at the other extreme, it engenders enormous pride and egotism, which block out the light within us.

The tendency to personalize magnifies the limitations and flaws of the personality and emphasizes our smallness as an individual, by reducing every issue down to the most microcosmic level. It causes us to look for spiritual growth in the personality, for instance—even though the true drama of evolution occurs far more at the level of the soul than the personality. Nonetheless, we still expect concrete evidence—and we want it now! And so, our growth seems slow and torturous. Because we are so intensely identified with the personality, we forget that a span of sixty or seventy years is just a blink of the eyes as far as the soul is concerned. The soul has been at work for millions of years. It is our tendency to personalize which leads to the sense of suffering—not the slowness of growth itself.

In terms of humanity as a whole, the tendency to personalize is the root of superstition, which is still one of the great problems of the "world disciple." Superstition is the magnification of our fears and concerns and the assignment of magical powers to people, groups, or forces which do not have them. The greatest superstition of all is the so-called "dweller on the threshold," which is the sum of all our personal limitations, accumulated over the long eons of our spiritual evolution. The final showdown on the issue of personalizing life inevitably involves the confrontation between the soul and this "dweller."

To work effectively at the soul level, the aspirant must be able to set aside his or her tendency to personalize and leave it be. Eventually, this becomes complete mastery of this deficiency, but in the beginning, it is enough just to be able to do it when most necessary. A healer, for example, cannot afford to personalize his work—if he genuinely expects to contact universal forces of healing. Similarly, the tendency to personalize the use of intuition is probably the single greatest interference with the development of objectivity in the unfoldment of the intuition.

This flaw is best eliminated by making the effort to shift our attention away from the trivial and petty details of life and orient it to the universal qualities and forces of consciousness. If we identify with the essence of such qualities as love, wisdom, gracefulness, courage, dignity, and goodwill, we will gradually find less attraction in identifying with a sense of personality.

Working with esoteric symbols, presented in meditation by the soul, can also be very helpful in breaking the tendency to personalize.

7. Passion is the root of reactiveness.

This particular flaw is often referred to as "desire," but not all desire is by any means a flaw or deficiency. To term it such would be the equivalent of saying that the emotions and mind are flaws. These are more properly seen as tools or instruments of consciousness. Desire, for example, can be very useful in motivating the personality to fulfill the creative plans of the soul.

The real difficulty arises when the personality becomes more attuned to his desires or passions than to the direction of the soul. As a result, he becomes *reactive*—he is more interested in what life can do for him, than in what he can contribute to life. He becomes more interested in experiencing and tasting life than in *growing*. He becomes one-pointedly focused in some reaction or attitude—fear, hate, lust, affection, wishing, grief, bitterness, indignation, embarrassment, and so on.

Passion blinds us to higher motivations. It rejects the soul as the primary source of power and impetus in our life. Instead, it draws power from physical and emotional resources. It seeks pleasure. It covets comforts and riches. It longs for satisfaction and fulfillment. The passionate person expects life to provide all these things, and if it does not, he believes himself to be a hapless victim.

A good example of this is the common expectation of so many people that their occupation be "fulfilling." When we approach our work expecting it to fulfill us, however, we cast our expectations into a reactive mode. Given this definition, very few jobs, if any, will ever fulfill us. Something will happen to displease us—because, after all, we are not really interested in the quality of our work, but in our personal pleasure. By contrast, if we approach a job with the attitude of enriching it in every way we possibly can, then every day will be fulfilling. It is automatically fulfilling because we are filling it with a full measure of the light within us.

Another classic example of the perils of passion is the confusion which usually arises when people become crusaders. These people employ passion in the name of a noble cause, be it consumer protection, the feeding of the needy, or the rights of a particular minority. Apparently, they believe the nobility of their cause somehow rubs off on their tactics and behavior, and makes their passion right and proper. But it does no such thing. What these people, and many others, fail to recognize is that they are not being passionate in favor of consumer protection nearly as much as they are being passionate in despising big business; they are not helping the needy nearly as much as they are assailing society for allowing this to happen; and they are not supporting the affronted minority nearly as much as they are attacking authority.

We need motivation in order to accomplish worthwhile things, but our choice of motivation is very important. In time, the person motivated by passion becomes a slave to his emotions and lusts—a slave to his anger, his petulance, his willingness to compromise himself in order to obtain the object of his passion, and his reactiveness. His passion becomes just another form of addiction—an insidious and destructive addiction that can consume our life as much as alcohol or drugs. He ends up being driven instead of motivated.

Dispassion, by contrast, is not a state of being unmotivated; esoterically, it implies that the individual is motivated by something greater than his passions. Whereas the passionate person often wastes a great deal of time being annoyed and frustrated by what he dislikes, the spiritual person conserves his energies for the constructive work of reform and building, while remaining calm, dispassionate, and centered in his inner focus of enlightened plans and intentions. He is motivated by the light of the soul—by the impulse to grow.

The impulse to grow is a vital element of consciousness and is therefore present within every human being. But the person who is driven only by passion has not yet learned to cooperate with this impulse to grow; it can influence his life only indirectly, by forcing him into situations where he is caught between the proverbial "rock and a hard place," so that the only choice left will lead to growth. If the impulse to grow is recognized and activated, however, such coercion is not necessary, and the hold of passion gradually dies out. Projects are undertaken, commitments made, and alliances formed because they accelerate growth, not because the personality has a passion to pursue them.

The more we become involved in the true spirit of growth—seizing every opportunity to grow ourself, encouraging others to grow, and supporting the principle of growth in society—the more we neutralize the flaw of passion. We should therefore seek to nurture the seeds of growth.

8. Hate is a blight on consciousness.

Hate is more than just aversion. At times, love can involve the controlled elements of aversion; the love of truth, for example, might produce an aversion to falsehood. This does not mean that there is a hatred of falsehood, but simply a determination to avoid it, expose it, or reject it. Indeed, the magnetic nature of love includes the automatic repulsion of anything that is alien to the quality of that love.

The difference between love and hate is more fundamental. Love is constructive; it cares for life, wants to see it grow, and shares in the gains made. Hate is destructive. It is separative and antihuman. It is a blight on consciousness. Hate is the perversion of the redemptive essence of love. Where there is hatred, for whatever reason, integration is not possible, because hate actually *attacks* consciousness and seeks to destroy or sabotage it.

The moment a person starts to hate, he betrays the life of spirit. This is true even if he hates in the "name" of a religion or special cause. There is no justification for hatred in any circumstance—and the spiritual aspirant must learn this lesson thoroughly. He must demonstrate that he harbors no hate or potential for hate in his heart before he can be fully entrusted with the expression of the light within him.

This is not an easy lesson for some people to learn, since hate is so widely enshrined as a way of life in large segments of society. Many people do not believe it is possible to oppose a person, a threat, or a cause without hating it. They feel they must actively condemn, lest they be accused of being fainthearted. This is an illusion of the highest order. It is quite possible to avoid a person who is a bad influence without hating him. Instead, we can pity him with compassion and goodwill.

The worst level to fall to is the belief that hate can only be defeated with hate—or that we must hate evil. These are both lies. Destruction only adds to destruction—it does not diminish it. The only effective way to deal with hate is by cultivating love. Hating hate is still hate—and vicious by nature.

Some people, of course, will claim that they do oppose hate, but

108

add that it is all right to be angry in the name of righteousness! Anger is simply an expression of hate, and is as much devoid of the light of spirit as hate. Righteousness, it must be added, is only served by that which is itself right—not by anything destructive or harmful to life.

The Christ admonished His disciples (and therefore all aspirants) not to resist evil. This does not mean that we should accept it, but rather that we should avoid the trap of hating evil, thereby pouring large amounts of our time, energy, and creativity into opposing it. We best halt the progress of evil by doing good works and bringing heaven to earth—not by eternally fighting everything that is wrong. Esoterically, both loving and hating evil produce the result of feeding it, so the wise aspirant learns to focus his or her attention always on what is right and good and use this power to transform that which is imperfect or evil.

The most common forms of hatred are petty gossip, complaining, blaming, and fault-finding. These activities often seem innocuous, or at least justified, but they serve no constructive purpose or produce no helpful result. This does not mean that a boss should never criticize the poor performance of an employee or a parent should never punish an errant child. The difference lies in motive. Petty gossip and fault-finding are pastimes motivated by a desire to see others humiliated; they seek to destroy. Enlightened supervision of employees or children is motivated by a desire to help the other person grow and improve himself.

The skillful ability to express love is one of the central requirements of integration. Indeed, it is a given, because "God is love." How can we integrate with the God within us—the soul—if we cannot express love? The aspirant is therefore enjoined to become proficient in all expressions of spiritual love—compassion, goodwill, caring, benevolence, devotion, affection, kindness, harmony, and tolerance.

The best way to eliminate hate is through healing. This turns our attention away from harsh criticism and destructive activity and focuses us in a creative, restorative mode.

9. Attachment is the clinging to the forms of life. It is an aberration of the impulse to manifest.

There is nothing wrong with being incarnate in the form world and interacting with forms. The soul has freely chosen to work in this way, and therefore using forms for the purpose of building and creating new expressions for light on earth is neither a flaw nor a deficiency. But clinging to the life forms we have created, and not wanting to give them up, is. So is the acceptance of the forms of life as more significant than consciousness.

This flaw could also be called the "belief in materiality"; it blocks off the light of spirituality. The origin of this belief is the urge to reproduce—to preserve the species. But it becomes much more pervasive in time; it shows forth in the heavy emphasis put on family ties and obligations; in the importance given to sex; in greed and the desire for comfort and material accomplishment; and even in materialistic philosophies and positivistic science. This belief in materiality is a deficiency because it impedes creativity and distorts the process of building. These processes become seen only in terms of physical activity. The inner components are left out.

At its simplest level, an attachment builds up a habit pattern in the subconscious which drives us to crave for and possess the object of our longing. It can even distort our perspective to the point where we feel we must actually *prevent* others from attaining the object of our attachment for themselves.

Physical addictions are a good example of this flaw. The individual becomes dependent on alcohol, drugs, money, or some other gratification in order to exist. To someone who understands that the alpha and the omega of life is the soul, the illusion of addiction is obvious. But to the one who is addicted, the power of the illusion seems much stronger than anything else in his life.

To some degree, most people have addictions of one sort or another: forms they believe they must possess. It may be ties to the school they attended, or the trappings of prestige (such as an expensive car), or a certain routine at work. It could also be the tendency to become obsessed by specific events, memories, fears, or traditions. The hindrance of these addictions is that they inhibit us from wanting to change them—even when they are negative or harmful. The reason for this is that we have invested a certain amount of our own identity into these attachments. If the objects of our attachments were suddenly taken away from us, we would feel diminished as a human being.

It must be emphasized that there is nothing wrong either with forms or with the manifestation of consciousness in form; the former is part of the glory of God, while the latter is a dynamic facet of the divine plan. The problem arises only when we mistake the cake tin for the cake—in other words, when we give more importance to the outer form than we do to the inner consciousness which guides and directs the form. We lose sight of the fullness of reality and become absorbed in illusion.

In terms of energy, whenever we cling to the forms of life, we get bogged down in the resistance, inertia, and numbness of materialism. Attachments deaden our responsiveness to the inner life; we become dependent on the small measure of innate life we find within them.

It should also be clearly understood that we are often more strongly attached to things we dislike and hate than we are to objects and forms we like and love. Many Jews, for example, remain attached to the Holocaust by dint of the strength of their loathing and hatred for what happened; they desperately need to discover the strength to forgive. Many fundamentalist Christians become attached to evil by their intense condemnation of it. Most Marxists are attached to capitalism through their envy and resentment.

Whether the attachment is based in craving or loathing, however, we end up wedded to the object of our attachment—which makes it impossible to establish a true relationship with spirit. The attachment usurps the rightful place of the soul.

We do not correct this flaw by rejecting the importance of forms, but rather by seeing that their true value to us is as resource material for our creative and building work. As we deal with forms, we should take great care not to be hypnotized by their attractiveness; we should always strive to maintain control of our creative work. This is accomplished through the process of *sublimation*, not in the sense the word is usually employed, but in the esoteric sense of working with the subtle or sublime essence of energy within a form—not just becoming aware of it, but actually harnessing it as an animating force.

When everything we do, and every form we use, is seen as being animated by the light within us (or within the form), then detachment or withdrawal from the form is no longer difficult. It is just a question of withdrawing the animating life.

10. When correctly seen, the flaws and deficiencies can be eliminated by adopting and maintaining the proper mental posture toward life.

Many people believe that the obstacles they face are outside forces opposing their progress, happiness, and achievement. As a result, they wage battle with mythical beast after mythical beast, slaying only themselves. When correctly seen, however, it becomes clear that our flaws and deficiencies are all internal. They are the attitudes and behavioral traits—conscious, subconscious, and unconscious—which block out the light of the soul.

Some people, of course, have trouble understanding this basic principle. They believe themselves to be the innocent victims of the teaching of their parents and the immaturity of society, not to mention the accidents, natural calamities, and betrayals we all experience in life. It is true that we cannot *control* the behavior of others or the events of life—although we do *influence* these factors more than we suspect. But if we are centered in our spiritual self, it is possible to take these external threats or tragedies in stride. A friendship may have been shaken, but we know our capacity to make friends remains. A loved one may die, but we know our capacity to love and be loved remains. If we lack these inner strengths, however, then we will be vulnerable to all manner of fear, doubt, false assumptions, and distortions. It is for this reason that Patanjali tells us that all of these flaws and deficiencies are internal.

The key to removing these deficiencies is simple enough to explain, although more difficult to apply. We contact the appropriate archetypal ideal of the soul and hold it steady in our mind, until the strength of its light has dislodged and washed away the flaw. This process often requires years to complete, because it is necessary not only to remove conscious patterns of deficiency, but subconscious and unconscious ones as well. Yet it is not especially difficult work, if we are willing to work patiently and without relenting.

Nevertheless, many spiritual aspirants encounter great trouble in eliminating these flaws. Usually, the problem lies in not adopting the proper mental posture. They do not actually contact the power and authority of the soul. Instead, they try to get by with a rearrangement of the subconscious. This is the failing of most forms of analysis, hypnosis, and therapy. They put new labels on old problems, but do not really shift our attention from the personality to the soul. They do not provide us with a true spiritual perspective, or center us in our deepest, most humane values and ideals. The value of a proper mental posture is that it puts us in rapport with the courage, wisdom, joy, and love of spirit which let us face any and all problems as a mature adult, not as a frightened child.

It is also possible to grasp the work which must be done, but then do it with such heaviness of heart and grimness that the benefit is virtually negated. The person who knows he must give up bad habits, for example, but does not really want to do it, will probably make very little progress in eliminating these flaws. He has part of the proper mental attitude—he knows the ideal he ought to be honoring—but still lacks the key. He resents growth.

Just so, it is possible to know what needs to be done, but lack the courage to proceed. This, too, is a common failing among spiritual aspirants.

The "proper mental postures" which will negate the five hindrances have all been mentioned in the commentary on the last five instructions. Nonetheless, it may be helpful to restate them here, for easy reference.

1. The posture which negates ignorance is responsiveness to the wisdom of the soul.

2. The posture which negates the tendency to personalize life is identification with the universal qualities of life.

3. The posture which negates passion is cooperation with the impulse to grow.

4. The posture which negates hate is the expression of redemptive love.

5. The posture which negates attachment is sublimation.

11. The best way of establishing and maintaining these correct mental postures is through meditation.

A mental posture is a good deal more than a casual attitude; it is a carefully structured pattern for living, energized by the light of the soul. To be useful in eliminating flaws and deficiencies, it must be based on an archetypal pattern. As a result, it will always be affirmative, never passive. It is not enough, in other words, to adopt the ethic of "harmlessness," where we make it a point not to cause harm to any other living being. The true spiritual ethic is "helpfulness," where we make it a point to help others whenever possible, in addition to doing no harm. It is possible to be "harmless" and still express no archetypal reality. Yet it is not possible to be "helpful" without expressing some measure of love or goodwill.

A correct mental posture is more than just a good self-image or an occasional commitment. It is more than mere positive thinking and self-hypnosis—and more than just a good feeling about God and life. It is a vibrant, living mental state, in which we are *poised* in the strength and purpose of our values, convictions, and ideas, all of which are based on the solid rock of an appropriate archetypal pattern. And it is strong enough to influence every strata of our character, so that we will act consistently in all circumstances. We will act, not react!

Obviously, this type of posture does not just arise accidentally. It must be carefully built and nurtured. The fastest, most reliable, and most effective way of building these mental postures is through meditation. But just what is meditation, and how is it used in this way?

The simplest meaning of the word "meditation" is "thinking." When we are thinking—truly thinking—we are meditating. It is important to understand this, because it clearly indicates that meditation has nothing to do with physical exercises, incessant chanting,

115

hyperventilating, and other dubious practices. Nor does it have anything to do with feeling good, fantasizing, or acting out repressed emotions. It engages the mind.

But the esoteric use of meditation involves more than just thinking and reflecting on life. It always begins by making contact with the light of the soul, the light within us. If the meditator has already established direct contact with the soul, he begins by renewing this contact. If he has not, then he begins by renewing the highest level of contact he has previously made, by invoking the guidance of the soul, the ideal for his life, or the healing and creative power of consciousness.

In the light of this contact, and the recognition of the full authority of the soul in his life, the meditator then carefully formulates the correct mental postures, based on the guidelines presented in the previous instructions. He then applies them to specific aspects of his life, by reviewing how he intends to behave in any given situation or condition. He honestly examines where his flaws and deficiencies lie, and rehearses the optimum way he wants to behave in the future, so as to eliminate these flaws and deficiencies. This work must be done slowly and thoroughly to be effective—and the correct mental posture must be envisioned in great detail and vividness. It cannot just be some vague, ill-defined hope to be a better person. It should be a sharply focused, clear image of treating people with love and wisdom, of confronting problems with a greater sense of universality and creativity, and so on.

Once these mental postures are established, the meditator then focuses the light within him into this posture, so it becomes animated. He reanimates this pattern on a daily basis, in order to maintain it. Naturally, as he goes through the activities of his life, he tries as best he can to act in accord with the ideal mental posture—not his old flaws and deficiencies.

Meditative practices are not just limited to establishing and maintaining correct mental postures, of course. They are directly involved in every stage of the work of integration. The goal of meditation is always to link the personality with the light of the soul, and to focus this light into the work of the personality in some useful way—to heal, to create, to serve, or to inspire.

12. The aspirant who has learned to establish and maintain correct mental postures is able to act in harmony with the law of right action.

In the East, the law of right action is referred to as the law of karma. Few terms, however, have been encased in more nonsense and misinformation than the word "karma." The phrase "right action" more completely carries the full meaning of this concept.

Briefly put, the law of right action states that we are accountable for every act, every failure to act when we had the duty to do so, and every thought and feeling that we generate. Being universally intelligent, the fabric of life registers the impact of what we do and then makes whatever adjustments are necessary to continue serving the divine plan. These "adjustments" become the basis of our individual karma. Sometimes, they manifest very rapidly; at other times, there may be an interlude of many lifetimes before the adjustments occur.

In every instance, the law of right action operates impersonally, without any trace of favoritism. The law's only allegiance is to the divine plan. As we develop proper mental postures, based on serving the plan rather than our personal wishes and hopes, we begin to understand the law of right action. At first, our efforts to conform with this law may seem to be a constraint, but as we become more in harmony with its purpose, we discover that the law of right action is actually one of those "truths that will set you free."

117

While the word "karma" has been imported to the West from the East, most of the truth associated with it has been left behind. Even comedians joke about it, although they do not understand it. People refer to it casually, "Well, that must have been my karma." They are alluding to certain events which they assume are the consequences of earlier acts or indiscretions. They also assume that the slate is now wiped clean. This is not exactly true.

There are two principal components in karma or right action. Divine intelligence makes whatever adjustments are necessary to restore order and balance to the activity of manifesting the divine plan in the worlds of form. We, in turn, incur an obligation to serve as an agent for making these adjustments. Early in our development, we are usually a very unwilling agent. Later on, we accept our obligation with humility.

The more quickly we can accept our obligation to be an agent of right action, the more quickly we can harness this law for our own creative work and success. Conversely, the more we delay in accepting these obligations, or try to deny them, the more we will suffer.

When the word "karma" is used, the first thing we are usually taught is that there are two types of karma: good and bad. Good karma stems from the contributions we have made and the service we have performed; it leads to new opportunity. Bad karma derives from errors we have made and actions, thoughts, or feelings which have interfered with growth; it restricts opportunity and leads to repeated problems. In truth, however, the distinction between good and bad karma is artificial. It is the creation of the aspirant, who views certain kinds of circumstances as pleasant and others as painful. The universe itself views all karma as good, in that it maintains the order of the universe and leads always to growth. Properly viewed, no karma is punitive. It is all ultimately constructive and therefore "good." But this is a difficult perspective for the average aspirant to acquire.

Every action occurs within the context of the law of right action. Knowing this, the aspirant should seek to discipline his actions, so they all contribute to the work of the soul and in some way enrich the quality of life on earth. He does this not because he seeks the good reactions which will come to him as a result (although they surely will come), but because he understands that these good results will create a gridwork or matrix for subsequent growth and enrichment. Thus, he serves the soul not only with a single activity, but also by creating a seed which will continue to reproduce itself and bear fruit for a long time to come.

This does not mean that the aspirant becomes a rude, abrasive fanatic who tries to convert everyone else to his vision of the divine plan. Rudeness, abrasion, fanaticism, and the highly personal vision are all out of step with right action. They will produce restrictive adjustments even though undertaken in the name of the soul. To work in harmony with the law of right action, we must make sure that we honor the essence of all divine forces in whatever we do. We must be just in our expression of justice; we must be wise in our use of intelligence.

Establishing and maintaining the correct mental postures toward life serves the purpose of making the aspirant active, rather than reactive, which is the usual human condition.

13. As long as the seeds of his flaws and deficiencies remain in his character, the aspirant will be reactive to life and subject to the law of right action.

If creative action, inspired by archetypal patterns of consciousness, can generate a gridwork or matrix of subsequent growth and enrichment, then in the same way, unintelligent and selfish reactions to life tend to generate a pattern of subsequent difficulty and impoverishment. The threads of destiny in such a reactive pattern can become quite intertwined, as the individual tries to balance out one reaction with yet another reaction, never understanding that his elaborate and ingenious "solutions" are only serving to aggravate the actual problem. The simple example of this condition is the case of the individual who tells a lie to cover up the inconsistency of an original lie, then must continue inventing new lies to explain the ever-increasing number of inconsistencies. There is no end to such a pattern, except to start telling the truth. Just so, there is no end to the difficulties attending reactive behavior, good or bad, except to cease being reactive and to start acting as the soul would have us act.

A more subtle example of this same principle is the mother who loves her children possessively. The children react by withdrawing from her and by trying to gain freedom from her possessiveness. The mother will typically respond to the actions of her children by becoming even more attentive and affectionate—which in her mind, means more possessive—and she thereby compounds the problem. She is convinced she is doing the right thing, and cannot understand why her children create such a fuss.

The seeds from which these patterns of destiny arise are to be found in our flaws and deficiencies. They do not exist in the circumstances of life—these are just inevitable projections of the seeds. Rather, they exist at subconscious and sometimes unconscious levels of our character. To master the reactive principle, therefore, we must eliminate these seeds, and the visible flaws and deficiencies associated with them.

This often seems like a difficult undertaking to the aspirant, who wonders how he can become aware of the nature of karmic patterns set in motion in earlier lives but seemingly latent at this time. Of course, it is not really as difficult as it might seem. The latent patterns from earlier lives that need to be dealt with in the current lifetime always become visible in one way or another. No pattern is ever fully buried in the unconscious—there are always telltale signs and clues visible on the surface. It may take some outside assistance—from friends, therapists, or teachers—before the individual is able to interpret these outside clues properly, but they are there.

It is also possible for the aspirant to invoke from his soul guidance to help him better understand which patterns he ought to work to eliminate—and how to proceed. This would represent a very healthy attitude toward the work of integration. But a word of warning should be added: the aspirant who invokes this guidance will indeed receive it. He had better be prepared to cooperate with it.

It is not necessary to know details of previous lives in order to work on eliminating negative patterns of karma. Indeed, knowledge of such details more commonly distracts the individual than it helps. Always, our goal should be to contact the light within us—not the memory of earlier personalities and what they have done. As the instruction tells us, the seeds of our flaws and deficiencies reside in our *character*, not in our experiences, either in this life or another one. So it is in our character that we must grow.

Actually, until the problem has been corrected at the level of character, nothing of substance has been accomplished. Many people make the mistake of confusing character and behavior, for example, and then work diligently at changing their behavior, ignoring any growth in character. This is self-deception at its most refined level. A good example would be the person who is very passive, based on patterns of insecurity at the level of character. This person attends a therapy workshop, discovers that he is passive, takes a class in assertiveness, and becomes a born again boor. He feels quite proud of the "growth" he has made, but all he has done is exchange one reactive pattern for another. His basic character remains unaffected. In fact, all he is actually asserting is his sense of insecurity!

Further insight into dealing with karmic patterns can be found in "Finding Meaning in Life" in *The Art of Living Volume I.*

14. These seeds bear fruit according to their nature.

If the seeds of our behavior are inspired by helpfulness and productivity, they will bear the fruit of cooperation, achievement, and growth. If the seeds of our behavior have been shaped by selfishness, greed, and pushiness, they will bear the fruit of opposition, isolation, and deprived circumstances. The inner intent determines the quality of the outer results.

It is for this reason that it is wise to realize that the power of life is drawn not from our circumstances, but from consciousness. We should therefore focus our attention on the guidance of the soul, and cease being so morbidly obsessed with the superficial implications of events or how others will interpret them. If an aspirant breaks his leg, it is relatively pointless for him to try to ascertain whether it was the result of good karma or bad karma. The more germane question is: what is the growth potential of this event? What can I learn from this about becoming more sensitive to the needs and feelings of accident victims?

From the perspective of the soul, all elements of destiny are benevolent. They may be unpleasant to the personality, but if the personality learns something of value from them, they are, in the final analysis, beneficial.

15. As integration is achieved, the attitude of the aspirant toward his life in the three worlds of form changes. It becomes a mature attitude of joyful service. As a result, he is no longer hostage to adverse physical consequences, to emotional anxieties, or to mental errors. Instead, he is able to use physical circumstances as opportunities for productivity, the emotions to create a proper climate for his work, and the mind to supervise the work to be done.

This instruction is traditionally interpreted in terms of the pain and limitations that the spiritual man perceives while in incarnation, due to the imperfections of form—even the most subtle forms. One interpretation states: "All personal life is misery." This is a trifle melodramatic, and indicates one of the great weaknesses of the Eastern tradition: the persistent notion that physical life is unpleasant, something to escape at the first possible opportunity. As a result of this distortion in thought, an entire generation of aspirants in the West has come to believe that the whole goal of spiritual growth is to "get off the wheel of rebirth." Nothing could be more in error—or more destructive to the cultivation of genuine spiritual attitudes. The purpose of spiritual growth is to achieve integration between the soul and the personality. If the soul viewed all personal life as pain and misery, it would never agree to integrate with it. The simple truth is that the soul seeks to use the personality as its vehicle for enlightened self-expression. It cannot do so until all flaws, weaknesses, and deficiencies have been removed from the personality. Yet as this work progresses, the soul is able, step by step, to assume control of its creation. It does so willingly—and with great joy.

While it is certainly true that we all encounter pain in physical incarnation—in fact, can create a hell on earth if we are so minded—it is important not to dwell on this facet of life excessively. We are trying to integrate with consciousness. If we belabor the potential of pain too much, we will succeed only in integrating with pain. It will trap us in sensation and obscure our true heritage.

The true mode of the soul is joy. It is therefore incumbent upon the aspirant to express as much joy and cheerfulness as he can in his attitudes, purging from his self-expression any traces of grimness, pessimism, and sourness. This is not to suggest that we should become naively gleeful, pretending that there are no problems in this "best of all possible worlds." There are problems, but the solution to them lies in focusing the light within us upon them, thereby transforming them, instead of reacting to them superstitiously, thereby magnifying them.

The ideal attitude of the aspirant is *joyful service*. This, of course, is service to the soul and to God's plan. It is rendered on the physical plane but inspired by the soul.

As the individual becomes absorbed in this work, his preoccupation with self and with the difficulties of life tend to fade away, as being less important. He sees physical events as opportunities to serve. He views his emotions as an important instrument for conveying the joy, love, and peace of the soul to those he serves. And he regards the mind as the field of energy in which true service occurs, as he works to establish seeds of creativity and healing which will endure, inspire, and radiate.

16. Painful consequences, anxieties, and errors which have already been set in motion can be neutralized by establishing the correct mental posture.

This instruction must be read with care, lest the aspirant conclude that the principle of right action can be suspended or superseded for the benefit of a loyal follower. This is not the case: universal law is universal law. The aspirant does not seek to relax it or circumvent it, but rather tries to understand it and cooperate with it.

Once an action has been set in motion, it cannot be averted. But if the aspirant, in the interval between the time when the mistake was made and the time the reaction bears fruit, modifies his attitude and integrates himself more completely with the soul, he will be equipped to deal with the consequences with greater maturity. He will not see it as painful, but as a learning opportunity.

As he integrates with the will of the soul, he will see the value of taking immediate steps to correct errors which have been made, rather than hiding them or making excuses for them. By adjusting the error, or compensating any loss which has occurred, he learns that he can become his own agent of karma.

As he integrates with the compassion of the soul, he comes to understand that the soul knows no such thing as remorse, shame, embarrassment, or loss. Therefore, he gradually stops viewing the circumstances of life as punishment or threats, and begins to activate greater benevolence in dealing with others.

As he integrates with the creative talents of the soul, he begins to serve mankind more altruistically. This in turns builds within him a reservoir of skills, patience, and character strength which enables him to face crises much more easily than in the past. They are not so painful because they are more readily resolved.

The great hurdle in learning this lesson is the tendency of so many people to respond to adversity *defensively*, denying that they are responsible or trying to shift blame to someone else. Defensiveness does not in any way neutralize error or lessen distress; at best, it produces only temporary relief. We cannot avoid paying bills by moving out of town, after all; the bills remain due and must eventually be settled.

The correct mental posture for dealing with the vicissitudes of life is one of forthrightness, goodwill, and integrity. It does not try to assess blame; instead, it tries to solve the problem, by calling on the wisdom, tolerance, compassion, and guidance of the soul. As a rule of thumb, whenever we find ourself assessing blame or making excuses for activities gone sour, we have gotten off the right track. We are covering up instead of acting with wisdom.

The keynote of this instruction is a strong measure of *responsibility*. As we see that it is our duty to be responsible for our own acts—and responsive to the laws and patterns of the mind of God—

we generate the "correct mental posture." We neutralize the force or impact of negative reactions yet to come. We do not prevent them, but we certainly do diminish their impact on us. Fear and anxiety diminish as we integrate with the courage and strength of the soul; resentment and intolerance diminish as we integrate with the love of the soul; and the sense of being a victim diminishes as we integrate with the wisdom of the soul.

17. Because the negative seeds of character have been created in reactiveness, they are neutralized by cultivating a genuine sense of active involvement in the life of the soul. This is the state of detachment.

We are dealing here with a sequence of very fundamental ideas about human nature. The reactive person believes that the external circumstances of his life, the people he knows, and the way he is treated are the source of his psychological energies. He depends on them, and is thereby reactive to them. The enlightened person, by contrast, knows that these are more properly considered the field of his creativity, not the source of his energy. He draws his energy from the wisdom, compassion, and will of the soul. He is therefore detached from external conditions and able to interact with them creatively.

It is always startling to discover how much our character has been influenced by the life around us—how our passivity and reactiveness have led us to cultivate this feeling, take on that idea, and so on. It is part of our human nature to be sensitive to forces and influences around us. All too often, however, we fail to monitor this process and end up being responsive to moods, ideas, and feelings which we would normally find alien. We are not exercising sufficient control; we are being too reactive. We need to realize the full meaning of the idea that the personality must cease to be reactive to the forms of life and instead become responsive to the life of the soul.

One of the great dualities we must face and resolve is that of passive versus active. It is perhaps easiest to examine this on a global level, in terms of society. At this level, the passive pole is represented by the consumer, the welfare ethic; the active pole is represented by the contributor, the work ethic. We have become consumers of society, when we are meant to be contributors. We have adopted the idea that society ought to pamper us and give us everything we need. We even believe it is our "right" to have these things. It is hard to imagine a more passive, attached condition.

It is far healthier to think of ourself as a contributor or producer, actively involved in making life better. Instead of clamoring for our rights, we put the emphasis on fulfilling our responsibilities. Instead of seeking out personal satisfaction, we derive enjoyment from the successful achievement of a portion of the divine plan.

If we take our role as contributor too seriously, to the point of becoming absorbed in it, we will create new seeds of reactiveness. But if we pursue it with detachment, we can cultivate an ideal mental posture well suited for the modern aspirant, a person actively involved in the world but not of the world.

As long as we react to life, we will compound our problems. But as soon as we begin to act in life, by recognizing our creative potential and seeking to fulfill it, we learn the key to changing the seeds of negativity in our character.

It may be helpful, at this juncture, to remember that the process of integration is not just a blending of two elements—in this case, the soul and the personality. More properly, it takes two or more elements and creates a new *whole* which is greater than and different from the sum of the parts. Spiritual integration is not a piecemeal effort, where we overcome one flaw here, another deficiency there. From the very beginning, we have been designed to act as a complete system of consciousness. We are meant to be whole. And in order to be whole, we must be involved in daily life. Passivity is a destructive, counterproductive mode. In its place, we must cultivate genuine involvement.

This is a point which ought to be pondered by psychologists and psychiatrists, who tend, as a group, to ascribe most of humanity's problems to childhood conditioning and environmental pressures. These may often be contributory factors, of course, but what the vast majority of these professionals fail to appreciate is that it is the reactive mechanism of our human nature which perpetuates and magnifies these problems for us. We may have had a parent who was mean to us when we were a child, but now that we are an adult, it is our own reactiveness which continues to treat this as a problem! We may have grown up in a family where yelling and screaming was a normal means of communication, but now that we know better, why do we continue to behave in that way? As long as the professionals continue to treat the child we were thirty years ago, instead of the reactive adult we are today, no real cure can be possible.

Real detachment is not achieved until we are primarily identified with the spiritual work ahead—the plan of the soul and the work we have left undone—rather than the things of the past, be they triumphs or hardships. We become whole by integrating with our spiritual purpose and the life of the soul, not by perpetuating immaturity and irresponsibility.

Our wholeness may not yet be fully realized. But it is not a goal to achieve; it is a living reality now. And the sooner we recognize this reality and incorporate it into our daily thinking, the sooner we will recover our divine birthright.

18. The active and reactive mechanisms of consciousness are one and the same; they are composed of the same elements and governed by the same principles. What the aspirant experiences in life is therefore determined not by the constitution of his bodies, but what he does with them—and how he uses their innate potentials.

Both enlightened and unenlightened individuals appear on earth through the same kind of forms. The substance of their bodies may differ in quality, but it is drawn from the same basic reservoir of universal energy. Yet in the one, the bodies are used creatively; in the other, reactively. What constitutes the difference?

The difference is this: in an unenlightened individual, the bodies are used without purpose or plan, reflexively. In an enlightened person, they are instruments of the light of consciousness. In the former, the bodies are subject to any impulse that comes along; in the latter, they are responsive only to the integrative impulse of the soul. It is therefore the principles, goals, and qualities of the soul that integrate consciousness—not any aspect of the form world.

We must refine the vehicles of our personality in order to integrate with the soul. But it is not these vehicles which produce integration. It is not the nature of the form which produces enlightenment. It is always the presence of the soul. If a saint had the bad luck to be transferred into the body of a criminal, through some cosmic fluke, he certainly would not use it for criminal purposes. He would cleanse and redeem it. But if a criminal possessed the body of a saint, there shortly would not be much saint left. It is not the body that counts, but the consciousness using it.

Evidence that the personality is being used to serve, to heal, and to build suggests that integration is underway and the soul is taking possession of its creation. The success of the personality in pursuing these activities is a measure of how much integration has occurred.

19. In every expression of consciousness, there are four basic elements: the form, its quality or force, its purpose or direction, and that which animates it.

Hindu commentary on this instruction tends to complicate it immensely, bringing in all kinds of associations drawn from their philosophy. Yet it is just as powerful, if not more so, as a very straightforward statement. In dealing with any expression in form life, we must recognize that there is much more to it than just the outer appearance. There are also the intangible elements of quality or force, purpose or direction, and that which animates it. To be successful in any kind of integrative work, therefore, we must coordinate function, force, and direction into an effective unit, while making sure it is true to its animating life.

An analogy from the business world might help clarify this point. When a piece of office equipment breaks down, a repairman is sent to fix it. He arrives smiling, dressed in a three-piece suit, and with a briefcase of tools. This is the *form*. He has been trained to present the impression of complete competence. Whether he has competence or not, however, has little to do with his appearance. It is more an issue of *quality*—how well he does his work, and with what attitude. If he fixes the machine, for example, yet disrupts the whole office with his constant complaints, immature remarks, and self-serving demands, we might well rate his performance quality as quite low. *Purpose* or direction, by contrast, is an issue of what motivates this individual. Is he just trying to skim by in life doing the least amount of work possible and still get paid? Or is he loyal to his employer and devoted to being as helpful as possible to his clients? Finally, *that which animates the form* would be the company the repairman worked for.

It is popular in this day to believe that we can "dress for success" and it will come. This instruction makes it clear that nothing could be further from the truth. We must coordinate a proper appearance with genuine competence and dedication, a right sense of purpose, and an understanding of the larger forces we serve.

This is also an interesting principle to apply to the creative process. The creative genius is one who can touch an archetypal pattern of consciousness—the animating principle behind his intended work. Inspired by this, he then generates specific ideas for manifesting it, uses the emotions to set a tone or quality for his work, and gathers the physical resources needed. These he pulls together so that they work as one, and then integrates them with his inspiration. Everything he does is thereby infused with the light of his original abstract idea.

For those who want to explore the more complex thought-forms associated with this instruction in Hindu philosophy, it might be interesting to take the three attributes of consciousness—serving, healing, and building—and apply these four divisions to each one. The even more traditional might want to use the three attributes of matter—rhythm, activity, and inertia. In determining these divisions, however, it is always important to keep in mind the basic purpose of Book Two: integration. We do not integrate forms. We integrate consciousness.

20. The soul is pure consciousness. Being pure, it pursues its work in the worlds of form by reflecting itself in the mind.

It is useful to keep in mind that integration is the process of yoking together diverse elements and making them whole.

Why does the soul, which is pure consciousness, seek to express itself in form, which is impure? To fulfill its purpose and destiny by participating in the plan of God to spiritualize this planet.

131

How does the soul accomplish this? By embodying its light in form. This results in a certain degree of pollution of the light, producing flaws and deficiencies in human character. This, in turn, sets the stage for cleansing the polluted expression of consciousness.

Pure consciousness, however, cannot have a direct impact on impure expressions of consciousness, until the first stage of integration is completed. Therefore, it must reflect itself in the mind. The mind is limited in many ways, but is by nature much more responsive to the true light of consciousness than either the emotions or the physical body. As a result, the mind must serve as a reflection of the soul during the long stage of integrating the personality.

Due to this fact, this stage will proceed much more quickly if the mind is able to hold itself steady in the light of the purpose of the soul, and recognize it is as the primary focal point of integration. There are a number of reasons why this is not only sensible but necessary:

1. The mind can be aware of possibilities, while the emotions can only be aware of moods and the physical body can only be aware of physical sensations. The capacity to envision possibilities is crucial to the work of integration.

2. The mind can discern and discriminate among subtle differences, while the emotions can only like or dislike different qualities or forms. The ability to understand these differences is necessary for coordinating them.

3. The mind can be creative. The emotions can only imitate.

4. The mind can build up new things out of collections of old parts or ideas. The emotions can only possess.

5. The mind can direct and focus energies creatively or discharge them. The emotions can only react.

6. The mind can explore, discover, experiment, test, analyze, and verify. The emotions can only like or dislike.

It is for these reasons that the soul pursues its work in the worlds of form by reflecting itself in the mind. The mind, in turn, harnesses the emotions and the physical form to carry out the intentions of the soul. To grow spiritually, we must comprehend and appreciate the reasons for this "chain of command."

Various conclusions can be drawn from these statements. First, the work of integration can only proceed in its fullest sense if the mind is well developed and trained. It must be trained in all the usual intellectual skills, but most of all, it should be trained in skills which contribute to the work of integration. These would include abstract thinking, intuition, discernment, discrimination, realization, symbolic thought, and synthesis.

Second, the archetypal qualities of consciousness should be explored as thoroughly as possible, with the purpose of learning as much about them as is known. This work of discovery should primarily involve the aspirant's own meditative exploration, but should be stimulated by extensive reading of the writings of those individuals who are already familiar with the nature of these archetypes.

Third, the mind is not pure consciousness itself, but a reflection of it. Therefore, the mind can err, by establishing false ideals and values. The aspirant should remain flexible enough to leave these false ideals behind once they are discovered and constantly evaluate how well his ideals and values actually do reflect the pure archetypes and patterns of consciousness.

Fourth, the soul must be seen as the focal point of integration. As the skills of the personality grow, it becomes all too easy to rest on what we know—and stop growing. After all, we have made some real accomplishments to get this far, and it may be tempting to think there are few habits or attitudes left to improve. Without even realizing it, we can build up an attitude of smug superiority which blocks out more of the light of the soul than ever. Without putting ourself down in any way, therefore, we must daily reaffirm

133

our intent to integrate with the soul. And in difficult moments, when the personality falters in spite of its strengths, we need to confess to the soul:

"I am not able to do this alone. All of the talents of the personality are nothing without the light of the soul. I therefore ask you to help me respond to your chosen destiny, as I strive to do my best today. Let the light within me radiate through all that I do."

21. All of creation serves the soul.

This statement is fact, not speculation. The soul is a co-creator with God. It is so intimately integrated with the rest of God's life that all divine forces, laws, and beings will willingly and automatically serve the plan of the soul. And, as it seeks experience in the worlds of form, the same principle remains true. That which the soul needs to shape its personality and pursue its lessons in growth is made available. The whole world serves the soul, even as the soul serves the plan of God. Certainly, it is in our best interest as a personality to learn to serve the soul as well.

It is true that not all of creation is consciously aware of serving the soul, yet this does not diminish the significance of this statement. There is nothing which has been created which was not created either by the soul or by a creation of the soul. Moreover, the soul does not create on whim, but because it has a definite purpose. In some ways, the human personality does get out of control of the soul, but not as completely as some people apparently believe. In a very fundamental way, the creation still serves the Creator; because the soul chooses the basic nature of the personality and the circumstances it will deal with, it is able to guide even a highly reactive and rebellious personality in such a way that its purpose is at least partly served.

The power of this instruction must be understood before the work of integration will be successful. Much the same idea was set forth by Alexander Pope in his poem, *An Essay on Man*, at the end of the first epistle:

All Nature is but Art, unknown to thee;
All Chance, Direction, which thou canst not see;
All Discord, Harmony not understood;
All partial Evil, Universal Good:
And, spite of Pride, in erring Reason's spite,
One truth is clear, *WHATEVER IS, IS RIGHT.*

This is *not* an endorsement of the silly idea that we can believe whatever we want to believe, and it will be right for us; it is a declaration of the basic truth that what the soul creates in pure consciousness is, by definition, right. It may, for a period of time, go through a growing process characterized by imperfection, seeming chance, discord, pride, and even evil, but eventually the purpose of the soul is served.

We must stop thinking of God as "up there," somewhere in the abstract regions of life, and begin to realize that He is "down here," too, alive and well in the midst of our daily activities. Indeed, what every aspirant must learn is that it is "down here" that we discover the real power of the soul and the real presence of God—the power to spiritualize matter. The light within us really is within us—close by, at hand.

The problem is that we all too frequently forget that all creation serves the soul. We fall ill, and assume we are being punished by the soul. We feel guilty about something we have done—or failed to do—and feel unworthy of the soul. We pass through a difficult time in life, and decide that the soul is no longer interested in helping us. In these simple ways, we estrange ourself from the light within us.

But this is an unnecessary act in narcissism. Instead of feeling punished or guilty, we should ask ourself: "How can this episode of my life serve the soul?" We should also remember the words of Paul: "The knowledge that I have now is imperfect; but then I shall know as fully as I am known."

Because all of creation serves the soul, we should learn to look for the light of the soul within every circumstance, every challenge, every person, and everything with the breath of life.

22. As integration is achieved, the form world no longer seems to be a "separate reality." It is seen completely in the context of consciousness.

The average person has no understanding at all about consciousness; to him, what he can see, touch, and hear is the whole of reality. He is naturally aware of his emotions and some thoughts, but he believes these to be just the product of the physical system and brain. This is a state of near-total ignorance.

The aspirant understands the two principles of consciousness and sensation, but holds them separately in his mind. He regards God as being "up there" and has very little understanding of the relevance between "up there" and "down here," as he views the circumstances, pressures, and relationships of daily life.

Integration brings "up there" and "down here" together, until they merge. At this point, the aspirant realizes that they have always been integrated *in consciousness*—just not from the perspective of form. And so, while others are still immersed in the illusion of separateness, the enlightened aspirant knows the illusion to be false. Life is one.

By bringing up the idea of a "separate reality," this instruction raises the issue of illusion. This is a subject of some difficulty for many aspirants. In the East, it is very common to talk about the worlds of form as illusions. Yet common sense tells us that there is nothing illusory about the physical world. It is solid.

Esoterically, "illusion" is that which has the appearance of reality, but lacks the permanence of reality. To the degree that our identification with the physical form leads us to reject the reality of inner dimensions, we create an illusion. We mislead ourself. But the illusion does not exist in objective reality—only in our perception of it.

Illusion is not an issue of something being here or not being here. It is merely a sign that our limited perception fails to recognize the eternal, immortal, and pure essence of life, because our attention is entranced by sensations, feelings, and assumptions.

The physical world is quite clearly a part of reality, just as the emotional (astral) plane, the mental plane, and all of the spiritual dimensions of life are. Those who believe that only the spiritual dimensions are real are creating as harmful an illusion as those who believe that only the physical dimension is real. The truth is that each of these levels is a different octave or dimension in the whole scheme of reality.

As long as we approach life multidimensionally, acting with a sense of its wholeness, we will avoid the traps of illusion. But the moment we focus on one dimension and forget all the others, we begin to generate illusion.

Esoterically, there are three types of illusion the average person creates:

Maya, the illusion of the physical form. The physical limits of time and space are maya, as is the idea that consciousness is a product of form.

Glamour, the illusion of the astral form. Fears, hopes, beliefs, and passions are all glamours. The belief that our feelings define who we are is also a glamour. The term "glamour" is derived from

137

its ancient Scottish use, meaning "that which enchants or be-witches." In modern usage, the word "fascination" might be more correct. The great fascination of many psychics with dramatic changes and upheavals on earth is a classic example of this. These people have created such a strong thought-form of upheaval that it has acquired a limited reality on the astral plane. But there is no force of divine reality behind it.

Illusion, the illusion of the mental form. The common problem of mistaking a fragment of an idea for the complete idea is an example of mental illusion.

As integration is achieved, these illusions fall away; the spiritual person begins to see clearly. But others are still blinded by the same kind of self-enchantment.

The use of the phrase "a separate reality" in this instruction also deserves comment. It has become quite popular in some eso-teric circles to talk about "alternate realities," "separate realities," and even "simultaneous realities." All such discussion should be immediately suspect. There is one reality; within it there are many dimensions. Any perception of multiple realities is just that: a per-ception. It is in the best interest of the aspirant to strive to under-stand the wholeness and completeness of reality, rather than dissect the appearance of separateness or alternativeness.

The whole idea of "separate realities" is a product of low level astral perception. Untrained astral psychics will commonly see fragments of astral landscapes and events and make the wild assumption that these are scenes from a parallel reality. Actually, they are just images and impressions from one of the subplanes of the earth's astral plane—which is no more a separate reality than Detroit is a separate reality from New York.

There is another thought expressed in this instruction as well. Once completion is achieved on any one level, attention shifts to the next higher level and focuses there. The lower level is left behind; it may still be the scene of great activity, but it is not the center of growth and achievement. This is a very simple principle: when we enter college, we leave high school behind. We still deal with much of the knowledge and lessons learned in high school, but we are now operating at a higher level. Just so, when an entity passes from the animal kingdom into the human kingdom, the lessons of the animal kingdom are left behind—the focus is on being human. And when the human leaves the human level and enters into the kingdom of the Gods, the lower level drops "below the threshold." This is the underlying principle of initiation.

23. Integration produces a new kind of discrimination, based on the perception of wholeness.

Discrimination is the ability to separate the wheat from the chaff. The average person, however, views this process entirely in terms of form. He has memorized what is wheat and what is chaff and separates them in this way. But this is not true thinking. Why is the wheat considered wheat and the chaff, chaff? Because we value the nutritional value of wheat, and know that the chaff lacks it. None of this would matter, however, if we did not understand the purpose of wheat.

As used by the average person, discrimination is more a weapon that separates and divides than it is a tool which illumines and reveals. But as integration proceeds, we become more aware of the consciousness of the soul—and, as a result, more oriented toward thinking in terms of wholeness. The discriminative capacity of the mind assumes new usefulness. We start making decisions based on what serves the purposes of the soul: if a project does, we pursue it; if it does not, we avoid it.

We begin to think, in other words, in terms of spiritual purpose,

139

motive, intent, and goals. We evaluate the challenges and threats of life in terms of a growing spiritual perspective, not conventional wisdom.

Eventually, the spiritual person learns to use this mental faculty to distinguish between reality and illusion. This is of great importance, because there are many "voices" claiming to be authorities in spiritual matters. Some are, many are not. We cannot accept someone's authority merely because he asserts it and uses the proper buzzwords. We must evaluate the measure and quality of light he is actually bringing into life.

A good example of authority gone wrong is the popular notion today that it is important—even healthy—to "be honest" with our emotions. Yet whenever anyone talks about being honest emotionally, it is always to excuse being angry, rude, or judgmental. No one ever invokes honesty and then expresses forgiveness, compassion, or tenderness. So how honest are they being? In fact, they are being dishonest, because if they were asked, "In all honesty, do you enjoy it when someone expresses anger or rudeness to you," honesty would compel them to answer "no."

Discrimination allows the aspirant to pierce through such self-deception and honor true reality—that which is immortal and pure, spiritual in origin.

24. Integration also produces a new motive—the need to know.

For many eons, the Hindus have thought that the goal of integration with the soul was to get off the "wheel of rebirth." This is not so. The goal of integration is to create a finely tuned mechanism which allows the spiritual man to work wisely and effectively in the world of form. Such a person is not going to withdraw from life

140

right when he is on the verge of being able to do something useful. He is going to become more involved.

But doing what? The answer to this question lies in consciousness itself. This is the principle of knowingness. It will therefore motivate the individual who is fully integrated with it to focus the light of the soul in occult areas, discovering that which has previously been ineffable. He will break down limitations, hurdle obstacles, and contribute what he can to civilization. He will be motivated by the need to know.

At this level, of course, this is not especially a personal need to know. In some ways it is, but even more profoundly, it is humanity's need to know, so that it can learn to function more and more fully as an integrated unit of consciousness. It is our personality's need to know more about divine life, so that we can enrich human life according to plan.

There are many people who function without an awareness of the inner design. They grab hold of a problem of concern for others, locally, nationally, or internationally, and then identify themselves with this cause. Occasionally, they produce results, but often the problem is still just as serious at the end of their careers as it was at the beginning. They have managed to create a livelihood out of a human problem, but have not solved it.

The spiritual person does not behave in this way at all. He may dedicate himself to a serious problem, but he defines the problem in terms of what is lacking archetypally—not in terms of public prejudices. He works to supply this need, and once he has done so, he moves on to other projects.

It is for this reason that the esoteric teacher does not just teach what he knows. He intuitively determines what his students *need to know*, then examines the inner dimensions to discover the best way to supply these needs. This should be a role model for us all, whether we are in business, a scientist, a parent, or an artist. Our motive should always be to add to life that which the soul is interested in adding to life—as opposed to what we (or others) believe is needed.

25. When the aspirant can hold his personality steady in the service of the soul, integration is complete.

The meaning of this instruction is clear. It refers to the twofold process of integration already described—the integration of the three bodies into a cohesive personality, and the integration of the personality with the soul.

The end result of this work is the ability to hold the personality steady in the service of the soul. It is important to understand that this represents a significant challenge to humanity. For thousands of years, the aspirants of the world have been told that the task before them was to conquer the pain of the earth; their reward would be bliss and peace. This is an especially common doctrine in the East. Unfortunately, it represents an incomplete portrait of the spiritual man. Integration must join the personality with each of the three facets of the soul: its skill, its love, and the will. Those who believe that escape from earth into heavenly bliss and peace is the goal of spiritual growth have tapped only the love of the soul. As we also integrate with the skill and the will aspects, we come to realize that the ultimate result of spiritual integration is consistent involvement in the active service of the plans of the soul.

Once the basic work of integrating the personality with the soul is completed, there are other steps of integration to take:

• The integration of the individual with his ashram—the inner group through which he serves.

• The integration of the soul/personality with the Monad.

• The integration of the individual with the Christ.

As each level of integration is achieved, a new capacity for creative work is acquired. In fact, there is a steady stream of inspiration from the level of the soul into the personality. In this way, the ignorance of the personality is vanquished—not by reaching a state where "it knows it all," but by reaching a state where it has full access to the whole scope of consciousness, through the soul.

Ignorance yields to wisdom.

26. The aspirant is now identified with the archetypal realities of consciousness.

In the original text, this instruction reads: "Through discrimination, the aspirant is able to maintain this steadiness." This is certainly true, but it also reveals one of the weaknesses of the Eastern approach to integration. The way spiritual growth is described in many Eastern texts, it is almost as though we are expected to back in through the gates of heaven! By removing all obstacles to spirituality, we become spiritual. Unfortunately, it is not quite so simple. The soul cannot be known simply by removing all of the impurities of the personality! If we are going to build a house, it is true that we must begin by clearing the lot of the trees, shrubs, and debris that would interfere with digging the foundation. But just clearing the lot is not the same as actually building the house! Just so, spiritual growth involves much more than eliminating obstacles. We must also cultivate the virtues, knowledge, and abilities of our higher consciousness. We must explore the soul and its realms, *and learn to use what we find there to enrich our service.* We must learn to act and think as the soul acts and thinks, and to interact with the divine plan as it guides us.

This means that we must learn to think abstractly and interact with divine qualities and archetypes at their own level, as the soul would do. This is obviously beyond the reach of the beginning aspirant, who must be content with beginning lessons. But it is not only within reach but required for the advanced aspirant, who must begin acting under the inspiration of these forces.

We must not just honor love and seek to express it—we must become an incarnation of love.

We must not just honor joy and seek to be joyful—we must become a center of divine joy.

We must not just honor justness and seek to live by it—we must become a living example of divine rightness.

27. These archetypes are seven in number.

Words merely hint at these seven archetypal realities; many different words can be assigned to each. One way of listing them would be:

1. Authority.
2. Benevolence.
3. Economy.
4. Beauty.
5. Knowingness.
6. Service.
7. Glory.

Obviously, there are more than just seven archetypes or divine qualities; these are chosen because of their inclusiveness. Under each, there could be many subcategories, each representing a specific archetypal force. And there is nothing sacred about the choice of these seven labels. The reader may find it interesting to compare this list with other esoteric septenates—the seven rays, the seven messages to the seven churches in Revelation, and so on.

The important thing to remember about these archetypal forces is that each is a multidimensional energy which is living, growing, and seeking to project itself into form. To be integrated with these archetypal qualities is to lift the meaning of life into a context far beyond the imagining of the ordinary human being. But it is not enough just to become aware of each of these seven divine forces. The aspirant must demonstrate his ability to translate the power, quality, and intelligence of these forces into his creative work and spiritual service. In this context, each of these seven forces could be regarded as an "archetypal lesson" of spiritual growth. It is in this context that Patanjali presents them.

28. To be successful, the work of integration must be practiced consistently.

One cannot be a "lord of beauty" one moment and an alibi-making, defensive, and angry human being the next. For the work of integration to succeed, we must clearly understand the implications of the goal we strive for, and then work toward it in ways that are compatible with this goal. For one thing, this means striving to be as "whole" and as thorough in our efforts as possible—looking first for the purpose of our activities, then for the meaning, and finally for the right application. Second, it means acting with integrity—the active expression of integration—in every facet of life. Third, it means acting with a full sense of responsibility, not just by getting by with the minimum expected of us, but seeking instead to extend our responsibility and increase the contributions we make—in personal relationships, in our work, and in our role as a citizen.

In this regard, it is useful to keep in mind that we are dealing with universal intelligence, not personal intelligence. Our own enlightenment and illumination is incidental compared to the enlightenment and illumination of all manifested life. And so, it is healthy to realize that the practice of integration is really designed to integrate all life forms with the Oversoul. Our role as individuals is to serve as "midwives" for this birthing of consciousness.

While it may be disappointing to some, there is nothing "explosive" about spiritual growth. The real power of spirit is tapped by applying it consistently to life, achieving both a rhythm and a harmony which is in step with the rhythm of the archetype itself. Impatience with the human condition, and the desire to see reforms initiated without delay, often tends to alienate the aspirant from divine guidance, instead of drawing him closer.

There are many ways the typical aspirant, as well as the average person, slips off the track of consistency:

- In assessing his capacity to love, he focuses primarily on the affection and goodwill he has expressed to his friends, conveniently overlooking the way he traditionally treats strangers and opponents.

- He honors truth whenever it does not expose something he would prefer to hide.

- He cries out against injustice which touches close to home or is popular, but tends to overlook it when the injustice is in his favor, is remote, or is not a popular cause.

- He is eager to advocate charitable assistance to others as long as he is recognized for it—or as long as his role is mainly to call attention to the problem, while someone else provides the money and manpower.

- He is willing to serve God as long as God is willing to serve his personal agenda of wants and wishes. In other words, he gets to tell God what to do and interpret divine will to fit his convenience.

Obviously, achieving consistency in expressing the virtues of the soul is one of the most difficult challenges to the aspirant. Our capacity for self-deception is enormous. We must thoroughly understand that the work of integration is not designed just to bring us more comfort, tranquillity, and good feelings. It is meant to bring growth—a genuine transformation of our lifestyle. We learn to harmonize multiple forces, in thought, action, and words. To some degree, we may start to attract chaotic forces or conditions, especially unresolved conflicts from our own life, but only so that we can harmonize them and leave them whole.

29. There are eight spiritual practices leading to integration: obedience, detachment, attunement, transformation, transcendence, initiation, meditation, and enlightenment.

The word "leading" is used in this instruction with definite purpose; none of these practices is an "end in itself." Their purpose is to lead the aspirant closer to a true state of integration. As such, each practice is designed to produce a specific result. The first three serve the function of raising the quality of the three vehicles of the personality—the body, the emotions, and the mind—so that they are more receptive to light. The middle two integrate the personality as a whole and instill in it a greater awareness of consciousness. The final three, then, are practices which bring the soul closer to the personality, and harmonize the two, so that light embraces form and form receives light.

Each of these practices, moreover, develops competence and skill in the art of living. It is this competence that integrates consciousness and form, not just wishful thinking. But even competence must be developed with balance and proper intent. If a person has a high level of intelligence, but uses it only to set world records in solving crossword puzzles, he is not well integrated. The mind is simply overpowering the rest of the personality, and is not being grounded through constructive activity or loving service. The extent of integration is always measured by two factors: first, how well the ideals which motivate the individual embody the light of consciousness, and second, how well these ideals are manifested in the physical plane, through creative work or personal behavior.

It also ought to be kept in mind that a *spiritual* practice is by nature one that trains the aspirant to share in the life of spirit. It is therefore a practice which takes our attention off our self-centered concerns and focuses it more universally. It universalizes our consciousness, attunes us to the life and needs of humanity, and helps us to think in terms of the whole. It is in this context that these eight practices ought to be approached.

The first five practices will be discussed in detail during the remainder of Book II. The final three practices will be left for the beginning of Book III. A brief synopsis of these eight practices can, however, be given here.

1. Obedience. This is not obedience to a specific person, such as a teacher, or even to a set of rules or commandments. It is obedience to the light within us. At first, this might constitute obedience to a specific noble ideal; later, it becomes obedience to the soul. The practice of obedience prepares the personality to recognize a purpose and order higher than its own wishes, whims, and comfort.

2. Detachment. This is the process of training the personality to respond impersonally to the events of life, freeing it from its environment and attachments to this environment. This prepares the personality to become self-directed and self-sustaining, instead of remaining a slave to its emotions and to external forces.

3. Attunement. This is the practice of training the personality to respond to ideas and qualities higher than its own, thereby laying the groundwork for spiritual enrichment.

4. Transformation. As the personality learns to contact the forces and qualities of the soul, it is expected to use them to enrich its thinking, emotions, intentions, and activities. The nature of the personality is gradually remodeled to represent more and more of the higher nature of the soul.

5. Transcendence. This could simply be called the practice of "outgrowing." The personality has been conditioned in many subtle ways which must be outgrown and replaced by higher perspectives, as integration proceeds. Transcendence is the deliberate act to move to a higher orientation toward the phenomena of life, our self-concept as a spiritual being, and the meaning of what we do. It often involves the need to rise above cultural limitations and earlier teachings.

6. Initiation. This involves the esoteric application of directed force to both the soul and the personality, so that the processes of growth are accelerated. It is not something the personality can invoke, except by preparing itself to be ready, but it is a process the personality can learn to cooperate with, by *initiating* new projects, new service, and even new areas of growth.

7. Meditation. Obviously, the lower octaves of meditation have been involved in each of the earlier six practices of integration as well. At this level, it refers to the increased interest of the soul in working and acting through the personality; the science of meditation establishes the link between the soul and its wise, compassionate, and skilled personality, producing a state of communion.

8. Enlightenment. This is the final result of integration—the flooding of the personality with the light of the soul. It is a long and continuous process, beginning with an occasional glimpse of the light within us and building, gradually, until a steady illumination of thought, feeling, and action is achieved.

This synopsis of the eight practices of integration has been presented from the perspective of the personality, since this is where the consciousness of the aspirant is focused. But it is also useful to understand that these same eight practices are used by the soul in its activities, only in reverse order and with somewhat different labels.

1. Enlightenment. The soul's creative work always begins with an act of radiation—with the intent of sending light into the world of form.

2. Meditation. The soul focuses the light of consciousness into specific plans and ideals, which it then seeks to reflect into the mind of its enlightened personality.

3. Initiation. It stimulates the life of the personality so that it will be responsive to the new creative direction.

4. Inspiration. The idea is precipitated into the personality and begins to take shape as a creative idea.

5. The gathering of forces. As the idea emerges into the mind of the individual, it draws to it the resources, energies, and opportunities it will need in order to manifest. This happens as a result of the earlier stimulation of the personality by the soul.

6. The focusing of forces. The mind shapes the inspiration and its power into concrete plans for action. This includes recognizing the resources and opportunities available.

7. The magnetization of the spiritual impulse. The emotions are used to set a tone for the work to be done.

8. Grounding. The physical form is activated to perform the actual physical work required.

It is important to appreciate that these practices can be used in both directions, leading either to integration or to divine creativity. This is only reasonable, because the final goal of this work is to bring the soul and the personality to such a point of compatibility that they do work as one.

30. The five precepts of obedience are helpfulness, integrity, lawfulness, self-control, and generosity.

For obedience to be a genuine practice of integration, there must be a thorough and complete devotion to these ideals or precepts on the part of the aspirant. It is not enough just to pay them lip service, or to hold them up as lofty ideals which are solid in theory but bendable in practice. Each ideal must be brought alive in the life of the aspirant, or else it will not help the work of integration. Moreover, each must be fully expressed in the aspirant's life, physically, emotionally, and mentally. A good way to begin this practice is by making a thorough study of the nature of these five precepts—which goes far beyond just reading the short descriptions of each in this text. Suitable references are therefore given.

Helpfulness is deliberately chosen instead of the traditional ideal, harmlessness, because the concept of harmlessness is easily distorted to the point where some people refuse to take any action so that no harm can be done. Frequently the greatest harm is done by the moral coward who fails to do anything because he fears the consequences. What he does not take into account is the fact that karma is incurred just as readily by not taking action when it is necessary as it is by acting in ways that upset the balance of order. True obedience to helpfulness includes the idea of doing no harm, but extends it to embrace being helpful whenever possible and feasible. It orients the aspirant to a life of service, which is the dominant theme of genuine aspiration. Physically, helpfulness means refraining from doing anything, directly or indirectly, to harm someone else, but it also includes doing the things necessary to help those people who will suffer harm if no one offers aid. People who pass by the scene of an accident where no one is helping, in other words, are disobeying the injunction to be helpful, even though they are not responsible for the accident. Emotionally,

151

obedience to this ideal means refraining from any temptation to hurt other people with feelings of anger, resentment, hatred, or envy, either through visible demonstrations of emotions, spoken words, or just quiet perpetuation of the feelings. But it goes further than this alone, enjoining us to use the emotions to create healthy and enriched emotional climates at work, in the home, and wherever we have the opportunity. Contributing to a healthy morale at the office would be an excellent example of obedience to helpfulness. Mentally, obedience to helpfulness means establishing values and ethics which promote goodwill, while taking care not to endorse any idea or philosophy which promotes selfishness, the manipulation of people, or materialism. Helpfulness puts the spiritual growth of others—and the aspirant himself—first and foremost. As with the emotions, we must also realize that the quality of our unspoken thoughts is just as important as those that we express. The attitudes and values we radiate silently can be used both to harm and to heal. We must take care that they always heal. Above all, our effort to be helpful must be the genuine article, not just a clever public relations campaign to *appear* helpful, or it becomes harmfulness in disguise. More about helpfulness can be found in the essays "Cultivating Tolerance and Forgiveness" and "The Noblest Masterpiece" in *The Art of Living* series.

Integrity involves the practice of truthfulness and honesty, but includes more than this alone. The person who is obedient to this precept is not just truthful to facts and details, but more importantly is truthful to his ethics, values, and ideals. It likewise involves honesty to self—the light within us. Many people habitually delude themselves through clever rationalizations and elaborate excuses—in particular, by maintaining double standards which make allowances for their own errors and those of friends, while harshly condemning the errors of others. This is a lack of personal integrity. The aspirant seeking to obey this precept strives

152

for complete objectivity in thought and works diligently to purify the emotions and desires, so that they do not affect the mind's perspicacity. Indeed, at its highest level, integrity is the ability to work perfectly with the energies and qualities of consciousness, without distorting them. But this means the aspirant has learned not to surrender to fear, despair, resentment, or apathy in times of threat or crisis; he is able to maintain the integrity of his orientation toward the soul. More about integrity can be learned by reading the essay "The Pursuit of Integrity" in *The Art of Living Volume V.*

Lawfulness includes the obvious physical observances of law, such as not committing crimes. But the precept of lawfulness has its requirements on other levels as well. Emotionally, the attempt to steal the attention or devotion of someone else, by manipulating them, dominating them, or possessing them, is a violation of lawfulness. So is jealousy, which is an attempt emotionally to steal what someone else has. Vampirism is one of the most insidious of emotional crimes—the attempt to steal the energy of another person. Although this is quite common, it is to be scrupulously avoided. Mentally, the "rape of the mind" would certainly be an example of lawlessness—the forceful imposition of one's values and ethics on another person, through brainwashing, intimidation, or some other means. Yet the practice of lawfulness involves far more than just listing "crimes" and taking care not to commit them. At the level of consciousness, all of these precepts are affirmative. None is punitive. In its broadest sense, therefore, lawfulness is obedience to divine laws—especially the laws of right relationships. While the aspirant cannot be expected to have a comprehensive grasp of divine law, it is nonetheless feasible to apply the following tests: Are we treating others the way we want to be treated? Are we overcoming evil with good—or do we just try to kill it with malice, complaining, or bitterness? Do we place growth of character, knowledge, and ability ahead of our comfort and good feelings? Do we place the quality of life ahead of worries about appearances? Are we more concerned about doing our duty than avoiding it? To the degree that we can answer these questions affirmatively, we are lawful. More insight into lawfulness can be gained by reading the essay "Living Responsibly" in *The Art of Living Volume III* and the book *Stewart White Returns*.

Self-control is a precept with many applications. It is primarily self-discipline and purity in the use of any energy or opportunity. It involves avoiding the indulgence of excess, but also involves avoiding unnecessary self-deprivation—the so-called "poverty consciousness" which seems to affect so many "spiritual groups." The person who is sexually incontinent and promiscuous lacks self-control—but so does the person who arbitrarily maintains a forced state of chasteness or coldness. To give other examples, the person who spends money foolishly lacks self-control, but so does the person who relies on welfare to support him. The individual who craves approval from others lacks self-control, but so does the cynic. Obedience to the ideal of self-control leads the aspirant to accept the soul as the only authority in his life. He also learns that purity in the use of the energies and qualities of consciousness counts for far more than the appearance of conventional purity in the use of the energies of form. More insight into this ideal can be found in reading the essay "Enlightened Self-Discipline" in *The Art of Living Volume IV*.

Generosity is also a precept with applications on every level. The usual translation of this commandment is "abstinence from avarice." It is enough for the average person to set this as a goal, but the aspirant must cast all his goals in terms of consciousness, not the avoidance of the distortions of consciousness. There are plenty of people who have overcome greed and avarice, but it is exceptional to encounter someone who has learned to be generous. Life is structured to give, and by giving, grow. This is reflected in the

154

statement of the Christ that as we seek the kingdom of heaven, all of its treasures will be ours. This is generosity of the first degree! But we can only begin receiving these blessings of life as we master the precept of generosity ourself, and become obedient to it. We cannot interact selfishly with forces and energies which are inherently generous—our selfishness throws us out of harmony with them. Nor can we expect to interact with the soul, which is dedicated to meeting the needs of humanity and the divine plan, unless we learn to act generously, as a steward in God's vineyard. Physically, therefore, we must learn to be generous with money, time, and interest, where the need is appropriate. Emotionally, we must learn to be generous with our support, hope, compassion, and tolerance in dealing with others. Mentally, we must learn to be generous with good counsel, guidance, and the advocacy and defense of noble ideas. The precept of generosity is based on the principle that we have a duty to contribute as fully as we can to life and enrich its quality. As we learn to act in these ways, however, we come to realize that there is another side to generosity as well. It is the key to unlocking the abundance of divine life. In order to be able to receive in full, we must be able to give. We must understand that God does support life on earth. There are times when we are called on to be the agent of this support; there are also times when we must open our heart and receive. More on generosity can be gleaned in the essay "The Spirit of Generosity" in *The Art of Living Volume I.*

It should be clear from this description that the obedience required of the aspirant is not obedience to a teacher or guru—or even to a particular religion or spiritual school. Instead, the aspirant is expected to demonstrate to his own soul his readiness to act in harmony with the five major precepts of human living. Patanjali is not just setting forth five commandments that must be followed or else. He is listing five ideals or precepts which must become governing influences in the life of the aspirant, before the next stage of spiritual growth can proceed.

31. Obedience to these precepts, and to the life of the soul, is a universal duty which has no exception, regardless of time, circumstance, or crisis.

These five precepts are part of the fundamental design for ideal human behavior. All humans are expected to respond properly to them. It does not matter what race or nationality we are, or the circumstances we must deal with. Even crisis is insufficient reason for failing to fulfill these commandments.

Integration is not a process of personal convenience, to be pursued by the summer soldier or the sunshine patriot. Spiritual growth is not terribly difficult or unpleasant, but our obedience must be strong enough that it will not be shaken by the Valley Forge experiences of our life. If our obedience can be undermined, then it is not strong enough.

Above all, we must not fear crises. A crisis is a time of great intensity—a time when the soul is prodding us to rise above our limitations and learn to work at a higher level. There is always great creative opportunity at a time of crisis, if we can remain poised enough to recognize it and seize it. If, on the other hand, we become hysterical and believe that our life is falling apart, we will probably be too distracted to act properly.

Indeed, it is those very crises which tempt us to lower our standards that are the true challenges of growth. It is usually not much trouble to be patient and kind when all is going well; it is a lot different when we are tired, grumpy, and beset with troubles. It is a common habit of human nature to expect the rules to be suspended during difficult times. When people are sick, for example, they often expect to be indulged to excess. But the aspirant must realize that obedience means nothing unless it can be sustained during the worst of all times, as well as the best of all times.

In short, we need to reverse our perspective. Instead of racial or national ties, circumstances, or crises governing our life (and our reactions), we must install the soul as the true authority in our life. The first step toward doing this is to learn to obey these five precepts in all that we do.

32. The five ruling forces of detachment are purity, joy, the will, skill, and compassion.

Detachment, leading to identification with these ruling forces, represents a step up to a higher level of activity from mere obedience. We begin with obedience, or right observance, but as a spiritual practice, it is still rather passive. It is the least expected of any decent human being. Through detachment, however, we aim to create a specific tone or quality in our life. We try to inject something of the soul into our attitudes, behavior, and the way we approach our work and relationships.

The practice of detachment has already been thoroughly defined in Book One, in earlier instructions in this book, and in the essay "The Practice of Detachment" from *The Art of Living Volume I.* The commentary here, therefore, will be limited to examining how detachment helps the aspirant identify with these ruling forces—and how this promotes integration. Obviously, as long as the aspirant is attached to the forms of life—physically, emotionally, or mentally—it is not possible to identify with any aspect of consciousness. And so, he must detach from his lusts, unhappiness, dullness, resistance, and separativeness, in order to identify with purity, joy, the will, skill, and compassion. This is a long, slow process, requiring continual

157

attention, but it is only as difficult as the aspirant makes it.

The five ruling forces can be briefly described as follows:

Purity, at its simplest level, is the cleanliness and full potency of vitality, emotion, thought, and motive. Its value to the practice of detachment is indispensable; cleansing our thoughts, feelings, and habits is the first step toward realizing that we can control and guide them from a higher perspective. Purity also helps us deal with ambivalent feelings, so that we do not sabotage our personal resolve and intent in cleverly disguised ways. The best way to cultivate purity is to be mindful of our noble intentions.

Joy is more than happiness; it is the basic mood of the soul toward life—a constant delighting in every event, opportunity, and achievement. It is always present within us, no matter what the state of external conditions. Its value to detachment is that it creates a positive climate for the focus of our activity and shields us against the negative aspects of life. As we cultivate joy, we discover an inner source of strength which can help us sustain an enlightened mood even in the midst of tragic or threatening circumstances. The best way to generate joy is to be mindful of the abundance and goodness of our accumulated experiences. More insight on joy can be found in "Joy" in *The Art of Living Volume I.*

The will provides the power and courage to develop and sustain detachment. The intent to rise above hurt feelings plus the determination to be the right person and do the right thing are outstanding examples of the enlightened personal will in action. The best way to activate the will to become and stay detached is through sincere dedication to spiritual purpose.

Skill might also be called "the ability to do." It refers to the special mix of talents, skills, potentials, and attributes that the personality brings—or is able to develop—to the successful management of any problem or challenge of living. Its value to detachment is simple. The more we can rely on basic skills and strengths to help

158

us make our way in life, the easier it is to cultivate a detached perspective. Lacking in skill, we may be tempted to get what we want through manipulation or intimidation. But succumbing to that temptation would only bind us to outer circumstances. Skill, by contrast, gives us the chance to shape circumstances through our competence. It involves us actively in life. The best way to cultivate skill is to take charge of our life, seeking to learn something from everything we do.

Compassion is the expression of benevolence and kindness toward all people and all levels of creation. It cares for and nurtures the impulse to grow. The real test of compassion is our ability to relate to people we do not care for especially, and wholeheartedly recognize that their virtues and strengths far outweigh their flaws. As we learn to be ruled by compassion, we simultaneously learn to think and act impersonally, which is the heart of detachment. Compassion is best cultivated by expressing thankfulness for the potential in people and events and for the underlying benevolent spiritual life inherent in all things.

These ruling forces, of course, are all qualities that the average aspirant frequently touches, especially at peak moments. Before they become the ruling forces of detachment, however, we must learn to express them not just when everything is going well, but in particular when everything seems to be falling apart—when we are most inclined to behave reactively, immaturely.

The best time to express purity is when we are tempted to distort a divine energy to fit our personal needs.

The best time to express joy is when we are stuck in self-pity.

The best time to express the will is when we are on the verge of rebelling against the purpose of our work.

The best time to express skill is when we feel stupid and confused, incapable of fulfilling our responsibilities.

The best time to express compassion is when we think we are

159

justified in reacting to life with anger or intolerance.

In each case, we can take the best alternative only by rising above our personal limitations and centering ourself more solidly in the best within us. This is the basis of detachment.

33. Detachment shifts the attention away from perceptions, feelings, and sensations which limit consciousness, and focuses it on consciousness itself.

The emotions are magnetic by nature and can only become an integral part of a larger whole (the integrated personality) by magnetically orienting them to this larger whole. In the typical person, however, the emotions tend to be magnetized, hypnotically, to the attraction of sensation and form. The emotions therefore thrive on such reactions as grief, anger, pettiness, gossip, fear, misery, and hostility. To put it in popular parlance, they like to be "stroked." But as long as the emotions crave this "stroking," they are unsuitable for the work of integration. Consequently, we must shift the magnetic focus of the emotions. This is the work of detachment.

The activity of shifting the focus of attention is more than just the substitution of one object of attention for another, however. It is really a matter of redefining our sense of identity. If we are ill, but choose to identify with the health of our higher self, we are detached, whereas the person who identifies with his aches and pains is not. If we are under emotional stress, but choose to identify with the calmness, stability, and maturity of our spiritual self, we are detached, whereas the person who gives in to his irritation, reactiveness, and defensiveness is not.

Detachment means that we are in control of ourself—we are focused in a stable, inner perspective, presumably on the mental level. As a result, the whims of external feeling are relatively un-important, even though we may be affected by them from time to time. We are not controlled or substantially influenced by them.

It must be recognized, of course, that the shift in attention to be made is often exceedingly subtle. The higher levels of the astral plane, for example, can appear to be very spiritual—so spiritual, in fact, that many people regularly mistake the higher astral for the soul. But once these energies are examined carefully, it becomes clear that these are just nice feelings about spirit—not the energies of consciousness itself. And so, we must learn to detach from these nice feelings and focus our attention on the genuine substance of the soul—the light within us.

34. The patterns of hostility and anger, dishonesty, lawless-ness, self-indulgence, and greed, whether slight, middling, or great, must be eliminated by the practice of detachment. This is true both in the individual and in mass consciousness, for wher-ever they exist, they obscure the light within us.

These are the distortions of the five ideals of obedience described in instruction 30. As such, they have already been commented on in some detail. But there is a reason why Patanjali brings them up again in the context of detachment. The practice of obedience dealt primarily with the redirection of our active behavior. In addition to transforming our behavior, we must also enlighten our character. Just obeying established guidelines, in other words, is not enough. There must also be complete detach-ment from the lure of old patterns. The problem of selfishness versus generosity is a good example of this point. It is quite possible for a selfish person to "obey" the precept of generosity without actually altering his selfish character. It happens all the time: a wealthy person donates a huge sum of money to a college or a charity, with the stipulation that he be appropriately recognized for his gift—for instance, by naming a building in his honor. The recipient of the gift understandably obliges, lauding him for his generosity. But the gift is really an act of selfishness, not generosity; it is a purchase of fame and adulation, not a true contribution to education or charity. He is obeying the ideal, but falling far short of detachment.

In this context, it is good to remember the statement made by Jesus, that it is not only sinful to harm someone physically, but likewise to harm him in our imagination and our wishes. Such feelings are never excusable, no matter what the provocation; they interfere with integration. We must detach from them and the patterns which led to them, both in ourself and in mass consciousness.

It is important to realize that patterns of anger, greed, dishonesty, self-indulgence, and lawlessness are nothing less than *diseases* of the mind and the emotions. They undermine our health and the processes of integration. It is not acceptable to tolerate even a little measure of these conditions, any more than it is acceptable to allow a small amount of a virus to exist in the physical body. If it is there at all, it will grow.

At the same time, there is a subtle hint in this instruction that we can eliminate these patterns just by withdrawing all interest from them and letting them die. We do not have to beat these vices (and ourself!) to death with guilt, punishment, and self-rejection; we can just stop repeating the undesired habit. If we stop being angry, in other words, our patterns of anger will diminish. But this must be a true cessation. We must stop being angry subconsciously and unconsciously as well as in our outer behavior.

Some of these patterns are very ancient. We may not consciously have a problem with dishonesty, for example, yet as we begin to explore the depths of our subconscious and unconscious patterns of behavior, we may uncover a very old residue of dishonesty that must be dealt with. If we are prepared for such an encounter, however, we will be able to remember that our connection with integrity is also quite ancient—and much, much stronger.

An even greater problem tends to arise as we encounter these patterns in mass consciousness. It is easy to be overwhelmed by the thought of detaching from all of the lawlessness in humanity, but it is not as difficult as it seems at first. To begin with, we must realize that we are not responsible personally for eradicating these conditions globally—the whole of humanity is. Once we understand this, then we must deal primarily with the *pattern* in mass consciousness, not the outer behavior. We must realize that this pattern can be healed by illuminating it with the proper divine quality, just as we have learned to do individually. In other words, hostility is healed with compassion, greed is healed with generosity and altruism.

35. Within the climate of love, all hostility and anger cease.

The word "climate" is chosen to indicate something greater than just the character of the personality. As the aspirant learns to saturate his whole being with compassion, he prepares himself to be able to project this quality into the whole environment in which he is acting. In this way, he creates a climate of self-expression which is automatically healing, comforting, and inspiring.

We have seen how important it is to use the force of compassion to eradicate remaining residues of hostility and anger, through our practice of detachment. But just eliminating these patterns is not enough; we must become an agent of compassion. We must learn to create a positive climate which repels all hostility and anger. Properly built, this climate will lift us above the lower levels of the astral plane where the forces and thought-forms of hostility and anger reside. Thus, a proper climate of love helps us transcend the level where anger functions.

Instruction 35 is a statement of fact which can be relied on. It is not a theory; it is a basic principle of spiritual growth. Love is stronger than hate. In a climate of love, therefore, anger and hate cannot exist. They may hang on for a while, but slowly, inexorably, the transforming power of love will embrace them, overpower them, and redeem them.

In their place, our capacity to be helpful takes root and is nurtured. It becomes one of the strongest characteristics of our life.

36. As integrity is mastered, there is a constant revelation of light.

The person who masters integrity is constantly examining every situation from the perspective of wholeness; he acts in accord with divine purpose and intent. As a result, he constantly reveals the true nature of every situation.

Not everyone encountering such a person would, of course, perceive the light he was revealing. To some, he would just be an ordinary person; to others, he would be a threat, lest he expose them. But a person with any affinity for the light would recognize its constant presence and respect it.

At this level, the aspirant not only sees the truth in all things but also understands how to make the light within visible. His efforts to build, to heal, to redeem, and to create take on a whole new vigor, as he can "sound the word and make it so."

37. As generosity becomes a ruling force, the spiritual person enters into abundance.

Poverty is known only here on earth; it is not an attribute of consciousness. It tends to be created by the selfishness and avarice of mankind, both individually and collectively. Wherever poverty exists (except by renunciation, as in taking a vow of poverty), it generally indicates a serious emptiness at the level of spirit. The nature of spirit is abundance.

The abundance of consciousness, of course, is abstract; it is the capacity of life itself to be fruitful and to multiply. It would be an error to expect the abstract force of abundance to be translated directly into physical wealth. Far more often, it is translated into rich opportunities, the support of friends, or the abilities, enthusiasm, discipline, and courage with which to generate physical wealth. By the time the spiritual aspirant reaches this level of development, however, the abundance he is looking for is seldom money. He is generally far more interested in an abundance of good ideas, love, joy, peace, patience, kindness, goodness, faithfulness, humility, and self-control, which are fruits of the spirit (Galatians 5:22).

The key to unlocking the abundance of life is generosity—generosity with funds, with helpfulness, with support of others, with kind words, and much more. As we learn to give, without strings attached, we also learn to receive, without strings attached. Perhaps more than any of the other ruling forces of detachment, the use of generosity teaches us the basic lessons of managing duality. According to conventional thinking, the duality of wealth consists of the haves and the have nots. But from a spiritual perspective, it is really an issue of those who have mastered generosity and those who have not. For as we learn to give, out of devotion to the light within us, we create the basic structure for the abundance of the soul to pour through us.

38. With self-control comes the ability to direct all energies.

This is another straightforward statement of fact. The lack of self-control at any level of our personality deflects the energies of spirit we seek to contact; we lose control of them. A strong prejudice, for example, will distort new ideas and inspirations we might receive, thereby causing us to misconstrue the guidance of the soul. Only as we achieve a full measure of self-control can we expect to manage the energies of spirit and consciousness wisely, effectively.

Most people, of course, interpret self-control in terms of renunciation of something they crave. But self-denial produces only crude results; it is not the true spirit of self-control. To understand self-control as a ruling force of the soul, we must view it as that practice which maintains the full vigor and force of consciousness:

- Through self-control, we preserve the *intent* of the energies we are seeking to express.
- Through self-control, we preserve the *quality* of the energies we are seeking to express.
- Through self-control, we preserve the *force* of the energies we are seeking to express.

In working with healing energies, for example, we exercise self-control by working impersonally, with a love for both the energies and for the one to be healed, and with a sense of responsibility for the way the energies are applied. By working impersonally, we allow higher intelligence to do the healing in this specific case—we do not impose our own preconceived ideas. By working with love, we magnetically attract the healing energy without changing or corrupting its basic nature. By working with a sense of responsibility, we step down the force of the energy so that we apply the ideal amount needed.

Naturally, there are many levels of proficiency in self-control. Many people assume they are acting with self-control when in fact

166

they are honoring only the intent of their work, not the quality or force. An example would be the tired worker who is still going through the usual motions of his job, "doing his duty," but without any enthusiasm, measure of excellence, creativity, or sense of contribution.

As we become proficient in acting with self-control, the emphasis gradually shifts from controlling the self to controlling the energies the self is expressing. As a result, the art of self-control expands to include such skills as right timing, both of initiative and application. At this point, the personality has learned to act in harmony with the larger forces it seeks to serve.

When we are able to work with this kind of self-control, we have in fact discovered what we need to know in order to safely handle divine energies in our creative, healing, and building work.

39. As lawfulness is mastered, the cycles of life become understood.

We are not talking here about giving up criminal ways and adopting the life of a law abiding citizen. It is assumed that the spiritual aspirant has overcome any tendency toward literal lawlessness eons ago. Instead, the laws in question in this instruction are the laws of life—the laws of the universe. Obviously, these must become the principles of conduct for the aspirant, if he is to grow spiritually in any but superficial ways. Yet many aspirants seem to overlook this obvious need.

One way many aspirants fall guilty to lawlessness is by yearning for miracles to relieve them of their problems. They fall ill due to excessive worry, then pray for a miracle. Or they find themselves in a tight financial bind because they have misjudged their resources, then expect the soul to bail them out. The soul is certainly ready to help in whatever way is possible, and its help often does seem miraculous. But the personality must never expect the soul to suspend the laws of life or even bend them on its behalf. The underlying assumption of such an attitude is that it is all right to demand a suspension of universal law for personal convenience! This is never true. It is an example of serious lawlessness.

The laws of life reveal the pervasive intelligence of God. If we are ever to become proficient in serving as an agent of God and a creative partner of the light within us, we must learn what these laws are, how they operate, and what it means to implement them in our life. We must come to appreciate that everything has an inner, absolute design in consciousness. If we work with this design and seek to fulfill it, we are lawful. If we violate this inner design, we are lawless.

It is not necessary to memorize a lot of laws to fulfill this instruction. Each facet of consciousness carries with it the imprint of law regarding its usage. As the aspirant learns to tune in intuitively to these imprints or designs, and makes it a habit to adhere to them always, he becomes lawful. Indeed, the effort to grow in the soul's wisdom automatically attunes the aspirant to lawfulness.

But this instruction does not just deal with becoming lawful. It states that as lawfulness is mastered, we gain understanding of the cycles of life. This may seem illogical to some, who have assumed that all laws of life apply uniformly, like gravity. Actually, many laws are directly tied into the cycles of growth and transformation. As we learn to act in accordance with our design, we become aware first of the inner law, and then the cycles through which it manifests.

A practical example can be drawn from healing. The average healer believes that he or she ought to be able to heal just about any illness in any condition. The wise healer, however, does not make such naive assumptions. First, he or she intuitively evaluates the inner laws governing this condition—specifically, the law of right action (karma). Is it lawful to attempt a healing or would it be wiser to use this opportunity to help prepare this person to live with this condition—or prepare him or her to die? Only then does the wise healer proceed with the work to be done—acting lawfully.

There are cycles of creating, healing, and building which operate independently of the desires of the personality and the will of the soul. All we can do, as either the personality or the soul, is to cooperate cheerfully with them!

40. The practice of purity leads to independence from form.

In this and the next five instructions, we return to a direct commentary on the five ruling forces of detachment, examining each in terms of how it prepares us to interact with consciousness.

The practice of purity is the ongoing effort to maintain as much of the full potency and quality of the energies of the soul as we can while expressing them through the personality and engaging them in our creative labors. It includes doing nothing to degrade or pollute the energies of spirit in any way, but also embraces the challenge to work always to lift our personal energies to the highest level possible. In practical terms, this means aspiring to work continually from the perspective of the soul, for only the soul can reveal the pure intent, understanding, and love for working with form without being conditioned by the thought-forms of the mental and astral planes, or the forms of the physical plane.

The spiritual principle revealed by purification is "independence from form." It could also be described as the "freedom of consciousness." This does not mean that it is the goal of spiritual growth to withdraw from form and be "freed" of the cycle of rebirth; on the contrary, it is clear that the purpose of consciousness is to be involved in form. But as the work of detachment through purification proceeds, the aspirant learns that consciousness is not a product of form, as so many believe; instead, it is the personality which is the product of consciousness. Consciousness exists independently of form, and the individual who can completely identify with consciousness in this spirit thereby gains the "freedom of consciousness"—the capacity to view any aspect of life without being affected by the distortions of form.

Purity must be the motive for any successful involvement in form. It does not reject form, but keeps us focused in the pure essence of consciousness while we deal with form. It drives mankind toward a greater state of civilization, and the individual toward a more angelic state.

41. The practice of purity also leads to mastery of the physical body, the feeling nature, the mind, and the personality as an integrated unit.

Purity is the ability to handle any divine energy or force without distorting it, while expressing it mentally, emotionally, and physically. It implies that the aspirant is the master of his bodies, not a slave to them. The work of purification is ongoing and constant, but eventually it becomes a habit. At that point, the aspirant thinks first in terms of the archetypes of consciousness and only secondarily in terms of form. Or, to put it more pragmatically, the aspirant has learned to pursue the highest in all that he does. He harnesses a steadfast belief in the higher life with a constant dedication to it, a persistent effort to discover its true nature, and an ongoing effort to embody its nature, quality, and presence in all that he does. Purity, in other words, becomes a heartfelt commitment to expressing the highest level of spirit possible.

The mind is seen as a vehicle for expressing wisdom.

The emotions are seen as a vehicle for expressing compassion and benevolence.

The physical form is seen as a vehicle for achieving productive results in the physical plane.

The personality as a whole is seen as a vehicle for expressing the creative light of the soul.

By mastering the lessons of purity, we are able to act in the midst of imperfect, gross, and corrupted conditions in the levels of form without succumbing to their influence. We may find them repulsive, of course, but we are able to keep our attention focused on the ideal conditions of consciousness, rather than become absorbed in the actual conditions of life. This, then, gives us a basis for calling on the power of the ideal conditions to cleanse and redeem the actual conditions we encounter in our work, in family, and so on.

The ability to act with purity in the push and shove of daily life is an integral part of the practice of detachment. It allows us to preserve our individuality without becoming a slave to the innate life of the mental, emotional, and physical forms—or to the pressures of group minds and mass consciousness. It is therefore important to keep our sights focused on "the highest" and "the best" at all times.

The act of purification—the cleansing of consciousness—should be incorporated as a part of our daily meditative regimen. It is too important to discount or overlook, no matter how far we advance on the spiritual path.

42. The practice of joy leads to supreme fulfillment.

Esoterically, there are three stages of contentment:
- Happiness, which is the contentment of the emotions. If we

are pleased by life, we are happy. If life appears threatening or painful, however, happiness dissolves into unhappiness. By definition, the states of happiness and unhappiness are conditions we cannot control, any more than the weather.

- Joy, which is the contentment and delightenment of the soul. The soul knows that the role it plays in divine life is important, and so it takes delight in it. This joy is constant and permanent; it is unaffected by the trials and travails of the personality.

- Bliss, which is the rapture of identification with the Monad or highest level of spirit. This is the incomparable ecstasy of knowing that we and the Father are one; it transfigures our consciousness. Unfortunately, "bliss" is a word that has been overworked by spaced-out gurus who have seriously cheapened it. As a result, a great many aspirants have come to believe they have touched bliss when all they have touched is a higher octave of happiness—possibly not even their own, but that of their guru.

The challenge of detachment to each of us is to master joy—to leave behind us the duality of happiness and unhappiness and learn to express the joy of the soul in the face of all circumstances—benign, threatening, or uncertain. We must detach from our worries, our sadness, and our grief and leave them behind, as unnecessary burdens that the personality no longer needs to shoulder. In their place, we must cultivate a genuine spirit of joy.

One of the most practical lessons for each aspirant to learn is to pause at the end of each triumph in life, each achievement, and look back upon it, reviewing it. As we weigh the meaning of this success, we must then lay it before the soul. If the soul concurs that it is a genuine accomplishment (and not just self-deception), it will respond with an outpouring of joy. It is not only right and proper to saturate ourself briefly with this joy, but actually encouraged; even though it may seem to some to border on self-indulgence, it is not. It is the proper registration of joy at the end of a creative enterprise.

Another good way of learning to register our inner joy is to make a regular habit of contemplating our internal impulse to learn and serve, as it has guided us into specific experiences and away from others. As we learn to discern the connecting thread which has impelled us to grow and serve throughout life, and begin to identify with it, we touch a measure of the soul's joy.

In these ways, we will discover the secret of fulfillment. Almost everyone craves fulfillment, but they expect life to provide it. This is a serious misconception. We are meant to create whatever fulfillment we taste in life. By adding such rich qualities of consciousness as excellence, joy, beauty, and grace to the work that we do, and by seeking to grow and serve through the experiences which come to us, we fulfill our potential. This, in turn, allows us to know fulfillment.

43. The expression of the will leads eventually to mastery of the reactive process.

For eons, we go through life reacting to external stimuli. As we enter the spiritual path, we are taught that we must master detachment, which shifts our focus from reacting to acting. Obviously, this change cannot occur overnight. It takes many incarnations to perfect. It also requires competence in the use of the will.

• We must use the will to generate a higher sense of purpose and lift us out of our ordinary concerns and habits—the mundane issues of life which keep us stuck in reactiveness.

• We must use the will to provide the power to break away from the thrall of personal whim.

• We must use the will to ward off the temptation to yield to cravings, fears, desires, and fascinations.

• We must use the will to sustain our commitment to transforming good intentions and noble plans into permanent change.

The hallmark of the reactive-passive mode of living is that we take our direction from our environment and those in it. The active-creative mode puts us in control of our behavior. We take charge of the personality and act instead of reacting; we become an effective force of creative change in our environment.

Part of detachment, of course, is learning the difference between our personal will and the spiritual will. In the early stages of detachment, the personal will can be used almost as effectively as the spiritual will. But as we mature and become more aligned with the soul, we must detach from our personal will as well, and cede authority to the soul, where it belongs.

The will is not an imaginary force, however. As we learn to draw in the spiritual will and use it to master our personal will and our reactiveness, we are definitely stimulating the subtle bodies in our system, leading to a series of changes in the subtle bodies. The various force centers corresponding to our physical organs and the endocrine system become animated and may even produce some discomfort. Energies begin to flow from one center to another; there may even be a sweeping ascent of energy part way up the spine. This is a normal reaction of the energy systems of the subtle bodies to the awakening of consciousness within us. It can be controlled by thinking of the energy flowing through the centers in a steady, judicious rate, under the control of the soul.

It must be clearly understood, in this context, that the arousal of the centers and subtle energies is entirely a result of the changes in consciousness occurring through identification with the spiritual will. Any attempt to activate these centers or energies on their own, without the corresponding changes in consciousness, puts the aspirant in serious jeopardy. It overemphasizes the importance of form at the expense of consciousness, thereby sabotaging the real work of spiritual growth.

44. The development of spiritual skills enables the aspirant to become an active partner of the soul.

It is only as we acquire and refine skills that we are able to begin acting, instead of reacting. The stupid and untutored are helpless and therefore at the mercy of those around them and their environment. But as we develop useful skills, we gain a measure of liberation from "welfare dependency."

At first, the acquisition of skills is determined largely by the needs of the moment—we develop skills that will produce some kind of benefit or payoff. It is only fairly late in the growth process that the aspirant learns to cultivate skills based on their ability to help him live a spiritual life. As a result, he ends up with an assortment of different kinds of skills:

• Mundane skills, which enable the personality to operate effectively in the world of forms.

• Skills in the art of living, which enable the personality to perfect his or her expression in the world of forms.

• Spiritual skills, which enable the personality to cooperate intelligently with the plans and goals of the soul.

In order for the personality to become an active partner with the soul, it must outgrow its mundane skills and focus primarily on cultivating the skills of the art of living and spirit. Yet even this can pose a problem of great dimensions. The skills of the personality can become so powerful and effective that the aspirant falls into the bad habit of relying exclusively on them, instead of turning to the even greater power of the soul and invoking its help and guidance. At this stage, he needs to detach from his faith in his personal skills, and redirect this faith toward the skills of the soul. These are not meant to replace his personal skills, but they are meant to assume prominent importance in the conduct and acts of the aspirant.

45. The expression of compassion leads to active participation in the life of the Christ.

Prior to detachment, it is very difficult for the aspirant to express compassion. The emotions keep personalizing his efforts to be loving. But as he begins to bring the emotions under the control of the soul, he develops more of a sense of rapport with the light within other people—indeed, within all of life. This becomes, in time, a mystical rapport, producing a continuous state of compassion and benevolence which cares about, nurtures, and supports all of life. This is the practical expression of the Christ consciousness.

As the expression of compassion is mastered, it reveals to the aspirant the nature of the inner life of the Christ, too, and stirs within him a greater dedication to participating wisely and responsibly in the activity of that Life.

Ultimately, this means that we have detached from our personal life and selfish needs and now are focused in the Christ life, the body of humanity which is the one disciple.

46. Attunement consists of three elements: a well-trained mind, a proper self-image, and a stable and unstrained awareness of the soul.

We now begin our consideration of the third practice of integration. It is interesting to note that after fourteen instructions dealing with the adjustment of physical habits and the detachment of the emotions, only three are given to attuning the mind—and in the traditional Oriental commentaries, these three instructions are usually interpreted in terms of the posture of the physical body! This is because the approach to spiritual growth has, until now, been almost entirely oriented toward passiveness—getting oneself "out of the way" by surrendering to the soul, and then letting the soul work through the personality. Almost no attention has been given to training the mind or creativity, because few people have had the capacity to do so. In the West at this time, however, there are sufficient numbers of people with minds which can be used as noble spiritual instruments. It is important, therefore, not to be distracted by the brief treatment given the mind here. These three instructions are, for the modern aspirant, far more significant than the preceding fourteen. They deserve careful study and thoughtful reflection.

The mind is of paramount importance to the work of integration. The emotions are not capable of fully integrating the personality—nor integrating the personality with the soul. Only the properly prepared mind is able to do this work. If left to the emotions, integration becomes a process of adoring the soul and submitting to higher guidance. The personality never really develops skills of its own, and is therefore unable to master the archetypal skills, will, and compassion of the soul. The capacity of the soul to use the personality is restricted.

The first of the three elements of attunement is therefore a well-trained mind. This means a mind which has been educated, both formally and informally, is exercised daily, and is continually challenged to expand its horizons and understanding. A stupid mind cannot do the work of attunement. But intelligence involves more than the ability to manipulate facts—it also involves the capacity to use all skills of thinking: discrimination, discernment, analysis, logic, induction, intuition, abstraction, and so on. In addition, unless the mind is exercised and used every day, it quickly becomes lazy and careless. It compromises on quality. It develops bad habits. Such a mind is also incapable of attunement. Of course, the same can be said for the closed mind as well, the mind which is unwilling to grow beyond its limitations.

Consequently, the spiritual aspirant approaches this third practice of integration by training the mind and making the use of the mind an integral, important part of his daily life. He feeds the mind good ideas, enriches it with meditations, and uses it to work creatively and intuitively.

The second ingredient of attunement, a proper self-image, is also of great importance. A belief in inadequacy is a tremendous barrier to integration. Before the personality can properly respect and love the soul, it must be able to respect and love itself. After all, the soul's intent is to create a personality that can act as its agent in the worlds of form. The soul would not attempt to create something unworthy of love and respect. There is therefore no good reason not to cultivate a similar perspective, loving and respecting our noble potential to embrace and express the light within us mentally, emotionally, and physically.

It is an important step in attunement to take the time to contemplate what a proper self-image would be and construct, nurture, and maintain a suitable one. Such a self-image should not be an ego trip, of course; it should be based on a mature understanding of the nature of the soul and its intentions in incarnating through a personality. A good model for the self-image is that of the proper child of God—not a child in the sense of being an inexperienced infant, but a child in the sense that we have a rich inheritance of support, guidance, and abundance from a loving Father that we can claim as we demonstrate our adult responsibility and maturity.

The third element of attunement is a stable and unstrained awareness of the soul. This only becomes possible when the first two elements have been cultivated. A stupid mind cannot have a proper awareness of the soul, and a person who habitually doubts his worthiness as a child of God would not be able to sustain true poise. Indeed, this kind of inconsistency is one of the great hindrances to a stable awareness of the soul.

178

In no way does the use of the word "unstrained" endorse passiveness, however. Rather, it implies that a natural, comfortable rapport is developed between the personality and the soul. If the personality felt ill at ease in the light of the soul, it would indicate a strained relationship. Or, if the personality wanted contact with the soul only to gratify its lust for power, this would also constitute a strained condition.

The ideal, by contrast, is a state of attunement based on the personality's deep conviction that contact with the soul is the most important element of its life, and it will permit no distraction, internal or external, to interfere with this contact. For this to occur, the light within us must become the issue of greatest interest to us, so that whenever it calls to us, we respond instantly.

47. The purpose of attunement is to acclimate the finite mind to the infinite nature of life.

An excellent way to accomplish this acclimation is to adopt the daily habit of contemplating the soul as a point of light within the universe of life. The soul is sustained by this universe, and through it, the personality is also sustained. We can therefore trust in the benevolent power of this universe—not because we ought to, but because it makes sense.

Indeed, we can take time to expand our awareness outward into this universe of love, wisdom, and power and consider how this unlimited reservoir of strength serves to strengthen us, as we in turn serve it. We can realize that this love, wisdom, and power interpenetrate our mind and heart and body at every moment, wherever we may be; we are never really alone. We are never really limited. We are in tune with the infinite resources of life.

Another way to approach this same process is to dwell on the everlasting nature of the divine ideals and qualities of life. Our personality is temporal; it will live a number of years and then disintegrate. But the joy and grace and beauty of life that we touch and express never die; they are immortal, just as the soul is immortal. Whatever we create with these qualities gains an element of immortality, too—and so do we, the more we identify with these qualities and regard ourself as an agent of some divine, immortal force.

This is not just an interesting philosophical exercise, however; it is an important step toward enlightenment. The nature of the concrete mind is to establish limits and boundaries. The soul and divine life have no limits or boundaries. The lower mind, accustomed as it is to the problems of daily living, must therefore be taught to overcome its temporal nature and begin to register the abstract, fifth-dimensional perspectives of the higher mind, through which we become aware of the soul.

48. Through attunement, the aspirant conquers the glamours which distract him and establishes a connection with the light within.

It must be understood that not all light emanates from spiritual sources. The aspirant must therefore learn to distinguish between the light of the soul on the one hand and the light of the mind and astral light on the other. Many spiritual seekers who fervently believe they are in touch with the light of the soul are in touch only with the astral light. Because this is psychically perceived, they believe they have contacted the one great reality. But they may have contacted only the glow of the glamours and illusions of humanity.

How do we tell the difference? It is not all that difficult, if we let common sense prevail. The astral light has no real substance; when contacted by the aspirant, it does not produce growth, transformation, understanding, or inspiration. The higher levels can produce some healing and enrichment of negative feelings, but its primary appeal is that it entertains, soothes, and fills us with warm, pleasant feelings.

The light of the mind, by contrast, is distinctly cool—devoid of the feeling and the rich colors of the astral light. It will produce a sense of detachment—perhaps even loneliness when first encountered. But this quickly passes as we begin to use it to explore the level of the mind. The light of the mind can reflect either mass consciousness or the wisdom of spirit, depending upon which level we contact.

The light of the soul will seem, to the average personality, to be almost empty of feeling, color, or stimulation. At first, it may even be rejected or ignored, because it does not fulfill our somewhat trite expectations. In fact, it has a tendency to expose our favorite prejudices, glamours, and comfortable feelings; as a result, there may be a short period of discomfort and even guilt when we first encounter this light, until we learn to cooperate with this process. Once solid contact is made, though, the light of the soul will inspire, inform, and enrich our awareness at all levels. It will nurture our growth and heal our inadequacies. It will transform our sense of identity.

As the mind develops, and learns to attune to the light of the soul, it is able to direct and focus this light into the full scope of the aspirant's character. Where glamour and susceptibility to mass consciousness exist, they will be exposed. Indeed, if the mind continues to direct the light of the soul at the glamours that have been uncovered, it can actually break up and dissolve these illusions. In this way, attunement enables the aspirant to conquer the false light of glamours and establish real contact with the light within.

Attunement is the practice which establishes "the path"—the connection which actually permits the work of integration to proceed. Along this path, health flows to the physical body, love flows to the emotions, and wisdom flows to the mind. Along this path, the impulse of creativity and the divine will flows into the personality.

The following practices of attunement, sensibly pursued, will all assist in building this connection:

• The effort to examine our life and make sense of what has happened to us—and our reactions to it.

• The attempt to discern the ideal in any condition, as defined by the soul—whether the condition be an opportunity, a problem, or an inner crisis.

• The effort to reconcile significant pairs of opposites, finding the middle point or apex which harmonizes them.

• The interpretation of dreams or symbols which seem to indicate some element of the plan or light of the soul. The study of symbolic systems such as the Tarot, the I Ching, astrology, or the Kabala can be especially helpful in building an attuned mental structure.

• Extensive reading of enlightened writings, for the purpose of meditating and reflecting on their significance.

• The invocation of guidance from the soul to help the personality meet the situations of daily life with as much love, wisdom, and maturity as possible.

• The attempt to work creatively in life.

• The effort to serve humanity and God.

49. When attunement has been established, the aspirant is ready to learn to use the energies of consciousness for transformation.

Transformation is the fourth practice of integration; in the Oriental texts, it is generally referred to as *pranayama*—the regulation of breath or the right control of prana. Esoterically, however, pranayama is considered to be more than just physical practices of breathing; it is the inspiration and expiration of "breath" by each of the subtle bodies—and by the spiritual person. While the symbol of breathing is very thought-provoking, it is usually a mistake to link this practice too literally with actual breathing techniques. For one thing, "prana" is not the same as the air we breathe; it is actually the sum of the energies used to sustain our subtle bodies. For another, the absorption of prana is not dependent upon breathing.

On the other hand, if we place the symbol of breathing in the context of transformation, we can understand why Patanjali used it. As we inhale oxygen into our lungs, we absorb it so that it passes into our blood system, circulates through our system, and nourishes our cells. There the vitality of the oxygen is taken and transformed into physical energy. By the time the cycle is complete, and exhalation occurs, we are discharging carbon dioxide, not oxygen—a symbol of the transformation that has occurred.

We are designed to draw energy from each level of our existence—physical, astral, mental, and spiritual. But it is not a simple matter of just breathing this in. The energies must be transformed to be useful to us. To some degree, this process is automatic in the world of forms, as is breathing—but only to a degree. Knowing what we know of the astral and mental levels, we do not really want to inhale their energies indiscriminately—any more than we want to inhale someone else's cigarette smoke when we are breathing air. We must therefore learn to filter and transform any energies we draw in from the levels of form for the use of our subtle bodies.

In general, as we learn effective meditative techniques for the transformation of our thoughts, emotions, desires, and habits, we also acquire the basic knowledge we need for cleansing and transforming the energies we draw in on a daily basis. This is because these energies are magnetic. The presence of patterns of hostility and anger in our subconscious will draw in energies of hostility and anger from the astral environment around us. As we eliminate these patterns in our character and replace them with patterns of forgiveness, tolerance, and goodwill, we are likewise transforming the nature of subtle energies we will draw in for our emotional sustenance.

The major step forward the aspirant must take, however, is to begin drawing the majority of his energy for self-expression from the light within him—not from the circumstances and conditions surrounding him. In this way, he begins working more and more with the pure, undiluted force of spirit, not the tired, dissipated energies of the lower levels. It is therefore important to take time each day to nurture the health and vitality of each of our subtle bodies—the mind, the emotions, and the etheric body—with the pure light of consciousness. Over time, this activity will literally transform the quality of energy that we use for our self-expression.

Each of the three bodies of the personality is well-equipped for this interaction, thanks to an elaborate system of force distribution. This system is built around numerous force centers—what the Hindus call "chakras." As energy is brought into the system, it can be circulated throughout the major and minor centers, to create specific results.

There is a complex science of the best way to distribute energies throughout these centers. At a certain stage of development, knowledge of this science can be quite valuable. But the aspirant must take care not to become overly absorbed in a fascination with the form. *The centers and the subtle bodies are all manifestations in form!* Paying excessive attention to them can result in a major setback for the work of integration.

The emphasis, therefore, should not be placed on seeing how

much energy we can suck up the spine, but on how effectively we can transform the energies available to us into meaningful service, creativity, and assistance to others. If we can treat others compassionately, we do not need to know that the energy is flowing through the heart center. And if we try to stimulate the heart center *without* expressing compassion, all we are likely to produce is a bad case of heartburn. We are designed to transform the energies of spirit into spiritual self-expression. It is important for us therefore to strive to live up to our design.

We are transformers of consciousness. We can draw on universal qualities of healing and transform them into focused help for others. We can draw on universal energies of intelligence and transform them into ideas, plans, and insights. We are able to contemplate divine joy and transform it into a personal expression of cheerfulness, good humor, and contentment with life. We are able to take energies which are abstract and infinite and reproduce them in our life as forms which are concrete and finite. As a result, we are able to consciously promote growth in form, function, and character—in ourself, in others and in all of the many forms of life expression found on earth. No other life form is able to do this, at least in the same way.

Transformation actually sets the stage for the integration of the energies of consciousness with our personal system.

50. The aspirant must first learn to deal with energies coming to him, leaving him, and in their pure state. He must learn to account for astrological conditionings of these energies, and whether or not they are waxing or waning in strength.

This instruction may seem unnecessarily complex, but once it is understood, it is not all that much more difficult than walking and

185

chewing gum at the same time. But it does advise the aspirant that working with subtle energies is potentially dangerous, unless we approach it with humility and common sense. As the aspirant learns to master and express more and more spiritual energy, the impression he can make on others becomes greater and greater. If this impression is harshly critical or just abrupt, it easily can do great harm. So the subject of transformation must be embraced with respect and reverence.

"Energies coming to him and leaving him" deal with the processes of transformation. As we have already seen, energies coming to us from the worlds of form may be polluted or dissipated; they need to be transformed into a higher quality before they can be used. Energies coming to us from archetypal sources will not be contaminated, but they may need to be "stepped down" by us before we can use them for creative work, healing, or other forms of service. This involves translating the power, quality, and design of the divine force into some kind of expression which adequately embodies its nature.

Once the energy has been shaped into a form of self-expression, then it becomes energy leaving us. But this does not mean that we have nothing more to do with it. The aspirant discovers that he is responsible for all of the energy leaving him—whether this is the energy of speech, helpfulness, money, creativity, or thought and emotion. We learn, as we grow in spiritual maturity, that what we do *will have* an impact on humanity, for better or worse. We may or may not live to see this impact; indeed, it may never be visible. But if we are truly working with divine forces, the impact is certain. So we must exercise great care in making sure that we are acting in accord with the divine plan. Many aspirants take a good inspiration and then personalize it, making such a big enterprise of it that it loses all its original impact. As a result, they end up working against the divine plan, instead of serving it. It is therefore of great importance to make sure that the "energy leaving us" remains true to its original creative purpose. If it begins to get out of control, it must be brought back into control—or brought to a halt.

"Energies in their pure state" are, of course, the archetypal energies untransformed by the aspirant. We can dip into the universal pool, draw forth what we need, but the pool remains in its pure state. These energies are there for our exploration and interaction.

The phrase in this instruction admonishing us to account for the astrological conditions of these energies reinforces once again the need for intelligence and a well-trained mind in pursuing spiritual growth. Many aspirants are prone to dismiss astrology, numerology, and other ancient systems as mere fortune telling—something the sincere seeker should avoid. It is true that many of these studies have been corrupted by stupid and silly people, but this does not gainsay their value to the aspirant. Every archetypal energy we must learn to deal with is itself influenced by astrological factors. As we pursue the activity of transformation, it is important to learn to predict the behavior of these energies as precisely as we can. Otherwise, we will never be able to control the process. An intelligent understanding of astrology and its relation to spiritual growth is indispensable. For more insight into this subject, the book to read is *Forces of the Zodiac: Companions of the Soul.*

The final phrase in the instruction deals with the duality of all energies in manifestation. They are either waxing or waning. It is often a waste of time and energy for the aspirant to try to build with an energy which is waning in influence; he will probably be out of step, both with human style and divine plan. He would be better advised, in most cases, to work with a waxing energy. Conversely, if the intent of the aspirant is to clean out a certain type of habit pattern, he will find it easier to do when the energy that fed the pattern is waning, rather than waxing.

51. Second, he must learn to control the same energies by sounding the keynote of the soul.

In instruction 50, we examined the skills the enlightened personality learns in the process of transformation. These skills are of great importance, for it is necessary for the aspirant to consciously participate in the work of transformation. But the true power of transformation ultimately lies with the soul. This is the capacity of the soul to sound an appropriate keynote and thereby cause all energy within its scope to conform to the intended design.

It is important not to overdramatize this capacity. Only the advanced aspirant will have need to learn to act in this way, and even then, he must proceed carefully. The substance of the subtle bodies must gradually be raised to a high enough quality that they can respond to and absorb the rapid changes induced by this method. If this work is attempted prematurely, certain protective veils may be sundered, producing the exact opposite of integration.

For the typical aspirant, the relevance of this instruction is that it underscores the importance of *cooperation* in the relationship between the personality and the soul. It is by cooperating as completely as possible with the plans and intent of the soul that the personality learns the lessons of transformation. There is no question that he will make mistakes, but because his commitment is firmly set on cooperation, he will profit from his mistakes and become wiser.

One of the great problems, however, is that few aspirants have learned to cooperate in this fashion. They still believe that the proper way to deal with higher levels of energy is to worship them and perhaps fear them. Worship certainly has its value, but it is never designed to stifle activity.

Here are some simple ways of cooperating with these higher forces of life and thereby integrating with them:

- Before beginning any project at work, take a few minutes to establish a proper focus of concentration and to invoke the ideal level of poise and power from the soul.
- Examine areas of responsibility, to see how they can be expanded to better fulfill the intent of the soul.
- Strive to work always at the highest level of quality possible—and periodically redefine what this level is.
- Determine what archetypes ought to be expressed through specific activities, then strive to embody them as fully as possible as appropriate opportunities arise.

52. As transformation proceeds, the veils of separation are burned away.

What are the veils of separation? At the most obvious level, they are our own limitations, ignorance, flaws, and separativeness. As transformation proceeds, we eliminate these obstructions. The veils are lifted, and the light within us shines through all that we do. Our aura brightens considerably, and we become, progressively, a source of radiance on the earth.

At a deeper level, the term "veil" also refers to those divisions between the subtle bodies which serve to protect us during the long eons of our growth. There comes a time in the process of transformation when these veils are no longer necessary; we have developed enough self-control. At that time, the soul exercises its option to burn away the protective veils and seize more direct control of the personality.

53. More and more, the aspirant is focused in the light within him.

One of the major veils to be burned away is the separation between the concrete and abstract minds. As the aspirant learns to interact with the higher elements of the mind—the home of the soul and the archetypes—he gradually changes his perspective toward life. He starts to think of himself as consciousness, not form; impersonally, not personally. This is not an abrupt change, but a progressive one. And it prepares him for true meditation, which is always an activity of the abstract levels of consciousness.

54. Transcendence leads the aspirant to a state of identification with the light within him.

In the Oriental texts, the practice of transcendence is called "abstraction" and is described as total withdrawal from form and its senses. Yet a moment's reflection should be enough to indicate that *withdrawal* cannot be a legitimate part of any practice of integration or union. These terms clearly imply movement toward wholeness—not abandonment of the personality.

Simply put, transcendence is the act of stepping up to a higher level. If a person happens to be lying in a gutter, it would be a transcendental experience for him to get up and walk on the sidewalk. For the aspirant who is already practicing the first four steps of integration to one degree or another, however, transcendence has a special meaning. It is the practice of outgrowing the conventions and habits of the personality and the form world and identifying with the life of the soul and the archetypes. It does not necessarily involve withdrawal from these conventions or habits, although this may at times be appropriate, but it most certainly does mean putting them in a higher context.

Perhaps the best way to describe transcendence is to think of it as "growing toward the light." A plant does not just let the sun come to it; it actively seeks out and grows toward the sun. In this context, then, transcendence is something more than detachment, something greater than attunement—it is the emergence in the personality of a refined and highly focused impulse to grow toward the light. This impulse is always present as part of our potential, of course, but now it becomes a conscious motivation.

By the time this stage is reached, it is not really applied in a personal way. If there is great need for personal transcendence, the aspirant would be better served to devote his attention to the work of detachment. Usually, the activity of transcendence is applied more to the need to achieve a higher perspective regarding the accepted ideas and beliefs of mass consciousness, the natural limitations of form, and past teachings. At this time, for example, there is occurring an integration of the Eastern and Western traditions of spiritual growth. This process began about one hundred years ago with the large-scale importation of Oriental beliefs and teachings to the West. So far, little time has been spent separating the usable ideas from the worn-out ones. Yet genuine spiritual growth is not served just by accepting one tradition and adding it onto another like icing on a cake. First, there must be a healthy interaction between the best of both traditions, leading to transformation in both systems. Then, *the best of both systems must be transcended!* Something new and appropriate to the ongoing growth of spirit in form must be developed. This is an example of transcendence all aspirants should pursue.

55. The personality therefore becomes a perfect expression of divine will, compassion, and skill.

The echo of the first instruction in this book is deliberate, for the goal of integration is implied in the methods of attaining it. At this level of growth, however, the aspirant is no longer trying to master these expressions; they have become automatic elements of his behavior, attitudes, and thoughts. The seeds of his character have been so thoroughly purified, reoriented, and enlightened that it is the very nature of the personality to act with divine will, compassion, and skill.

There is nothing accidental about transcendence; it is built on a carefully prepared foundation of devotion to God, intelligent action, creativity, wisdom, compassion, and service. As our dedication to and skill in using each of these qualities and activities become natural, we take another step toward transcendence.

At this stage, the capacity to work with abstract ideas comes into its own. We are as involved as ever in serving on the physical plane, but we are guided always by the appropriate abstract ideals or archetypes. We work not for our own glory, but for the glory of our Father.

The work of integration is not complete with transcendence, however; there yet remains the need for the soul to respond to the efforts of the personality. This it does through the practices of initiation, meditation, and enlightenment. These will be taken up at the beginning of Book Three.

CREATIVE MASTERY

1. Initiation accelerates the expansion of consciousness.

In Book Three, we start with the last three practices of integration described in instruction 29 of Book Two: initiation, meditation, and enlightenment. These are the three practices which bring the soul closer to the personality and harmonize the two, so that light embraces form and form reveals light. These three practices set light in motion; in a very real sense, the work of the spiritual aspirant can now begin. All that has preceded has been a preparation.

The theme of Book Three is creative mastery, and all of the practices set forth in it will be defined in this context. This is an admitted bias, but one which is appropriate for and best suited to the Western aspirant. There are other ways of approaching this stage of spiritual life. Nonetheless, it must be remembered that the soul did not engage in the long saga of incarnation just to teach the personality how to escape it. It has a definite creative purpose which should be understood and honored.

Initiation is a word which has been glamorized by drooling aspirants who like to dream of the sudden acquisition of magical powers, without the need to work too hard to gain them. Yet, if we put it in the context of common sense, it is possible to approach this subject with a certain amount of understanding.

An initiation is an infusion of a new measure of spirit into consciousness, thereby accelerating its expansion. The actual initiation occurs within the soul, at the level of causal consciousness, although awareness of it eventually does filter down to the level of the personality. From the perspective of the personality, initiation imbues the aspirant with new powers and abilities, and some of these will be outlined later in this book. But the soul does not place nearly so much emphasis on the acquisition of new power. There, the focus is much more on expanding its spiritual environment and

195

the scope of its creative potential and responsibility, as expressed through the personality.

There are major and minor initiations which occur along the spiritual path. In many cases, the aspirant only becomes aware of the process near the end of it—when he has finally mastered the skills which reveal to him the larger scope of service and activity that he has entered. It is not necessary here to enumerate specific initiations—they are spelled out quite well in the essay "The Trials of Initiation" in *The Life of Spirit Volume II*. It is sufficient to note that each initiation substantially expands our capacity to express wisdom, compassion, and creativity. The personality no longer works alone. It is consciously aware of its partnership with the soul and its ability to tap the resources of spirit.

At its simplest level, initiation refers to the ability to take responsibility for a new line of work, service, or growth. Even at this level, it is a more complex science than the ordinary person realizes, involving the correct perception of the best time and climate for beginning a project, a proper evaluation of the needs which have called forth this effort, and a correct gathering of the forces needed to carry the work through to success. Many spiritual aspirants, schooled in the nonsense that all they need to do is "believe" in God and His capacity to materialize everything they desire, find it difficult to understand the significance of initiation.

At a higher level, initiation is the process of bringing a new measure of a spiritual quality into manifestation on earth. This may result in a new form or just a revised expression of an existing one, but the success of the initiatory work is not measured in terms of form. It is measured in terms of the emergence of this new life. It could be a new expression of compassion, goodwill, generosity, courage, or some other ideal of human living; it could be a new revelation of spiritual will or intention; or it could be the discovery of a new scientific or engineering principle.

The founding of America is a good metaphor for the kinds of changes which occur in outer life as a result of initiation. The founding fathers created a "new" form of government, but this was *not* their most important achievement. Their true contribution was the far more brilliant definition of freedom which emerged at that time. It is this abstract pattern of freedom which has continued to inspire us for 200 years—and which provides a large measure of the vitality and health of the country. This legacy of freedom has expanded our awareness of citizenship in much the same way that a spiritual initiation expands our awareness of the role we are to play in the divine drama.

2. Through meditation, the soul gains control of the personality.

It is important to understand that there are many levels and applications of meditation. Every spiritual aspirant, from the person who is just stepping on the path to the highest initiate, practices some kind of meditation. He reflects upon the nature of spirit and what lies before him on the spiritual path. He uses it to transform his character and add the light of the soul to his self-expression. There are many techniques of meditation, each appropriate to a different level of development. Indeed, almost every spiritual practice covered in Book One and Book Two is best performed as a meditative technique.

This instruction does not refer to the meditations of the personality; it deals with the meditation performed by the soul. The soul is in constant meditation during the life of the personality, but it must be clearly understood that this is an active, intelligent meditation, not at all like the cheapened forms of meditation so common today, which emphasize relaxation, mental numbness, and hyperventilation. The meditation of the soul is quite the opposite of passive relaxation—it is a state of active mindfulness and sharp awareness, in which the soul sounds the keynotes of its creative plans and destiny. In addition, it is constantly bathing the personality in the spiritual resources it needs to fulfill these plans. In a sense, the personality *is* the meditation of the soul—the expression of the soul's activity to add the quality of its consciousness to form. It seeks constantly to create a vehicle in form which is able to embody progressively more of the qualities and riches of heaven.

As the work of integration proceeds, the meditative work of the soul is to gain the complete cooperation of the personality, so that it becomes a vehicle for the expression of spirit. This begins with the work of purifying the personality so that it can operate on spiritual wavelengths, and then continues with the work of imbuing the personality with an ever stronger sense of responsibility, altruism, and duty. As the personality demonstrates its reliability and trust worthiness, then the soul expands its activities further, revealing to the personality the nature of its group ties on the inner planes, specific details of its plan, and its perspectives on a myriad of issues of living.

The more we identify with the soul, and strive to think as it thinks, the more this kind of meditation influences our life and activity. Our very acts slowly begin to be permeated by the living presence of the soul.

3. Through enlightenment, the light of the soul fulfills its potential to be the light within us.

This is a very straightforward conclusion to the commentary on integration. Enlightenment or illumination occurs as the personality becomes responsive to the light of the soul and begins to radiate it through its thoughts, emotions, and deeds. The light of the soul becomes the light that illumines the personality as well. This fulfills the promise of the phrase, "the light within us."

It must be remembered, in this context, that not all flashes of light that the aspirant might perceive, in or out of meditation, will necessarily be the light of the soul. The subconscious is quite willing to put on elaborate stage shows for the entertainment (and delusion) of the personality, and this includes mimicking what it believes to be the light of the soul. As always, we must look for the signs of maturity and wisdom which are the true indices of enlightenment, not occasional surges of white light. The stage of enlightenment means that we are identifying with spirit, not matter. As the Christ put it, "It is the spirit that gives life, the flesh has nothing to offer. The words I have spoken to you are spirit and they are life." (John 6:63.)

At this stage, we are no longer an agent of light. We have become one with light. The light of the soul is not something we turn on and off; it is a constant feature of our consciousness.

4. As the soul uses the three practices of initiation, meditation, and enlightenment, the work of integration is completed and creative mastery is attained.

Integration is a term we use to describe the unification of the personality and, as this is achieved, the unification of the personality with the soul. As this work is completed, the primary focus of the aspirant shifts from growing to making a useful contribution to life. He sets his sights on creative mastery.

The average person thinks of creativity as something done by artists, writers, musicians, and inventors. In its fullest sense, however, creativity is the process of bringing the light of the soul into form, to transform the form. The true creative essence of the human being is the soul. Integration prepares the personality to participate consciously in the creative work of the soul. Creativity therefore includes:

- Enlightened teaching.
- Inspired parenting.
- The redemption of the personality.
- The wise use of leadership and authority.
- True scientific discovery.
- Genuine religious devotion.
- Inspired service.

Creative mastery is a state of achievement in which the personality has become a full, cooperative partner with the soul in its creative endeavors. He has also become the master of the physical and psychological forces of life—he has learned to control reactiveness, harness duality, dominate the influences of mass consciousness and social tradition, and neutralize the impact of failure and opposition. As a result, the personality becomes less and less preoccupied with his personal growth and more and more interested in the creative work he can do—the contributions he can make to humanity. This is the true sign that a person is beginning to think and act as the soul would have him think and act.

5. It is through creativity and service that the light of the soul shines forth.

The ability to perceive the light of the soul is of little significance, whether it is a clairvoyant glimpse of the actual light or a more figurative insight into the wisdom of the soul. It may be a sign of progress, but *using* the light of the soul is of far greater importance than just seeing it. Staring at the light will do nothing to

200

increase it, except in our imagination, but putting it to work serving humanity and the creative plan of the soul will.

In this regard, it can be useful to recognize that all that we think and feel and do *can* become light itself, shining in the darkness. We are not trying to perceive the light, but in fact become the light, so that it may shine forth into our world, through our involvement in living.

The light of joy shines through our ability to express joy in the face of jealousy, hardship, and grief.

The light of wisdom shines through the insights and inspirations we put to work in practical ways in our life.

The light of compassion shines through the help and support we give to others as they struggle with the difficult challenges of life.

This is the creative challenge to each human being, and the reason for the admonition by Jesus not to hide our light under a bushel but to put it on a stand, so it can give light to all in the house. (Matthew 5:15).

6. The illumination of form is gradual; mastery occurs step by step.

A number of observations can be drawn from this instruction.

1. Our personal growth occurs best when it is careful and thorough. Excessively rapid growth is more of an illusion than a blessing. Learning anything valuable always involves a certain amount of repetition and practice, and this applies every bit as much to learning the lessons of the soul as it does to addition tables. We are trying to become creative, and this is not a haphazard venture. The soul is much more interested in a personality which is willing to devote its whole life to diligently pursuing mastery of its lessons than in a personality which strains and

struggles to eliminate all problems by next Tuesday at the latest.

A good example of this point would be the effort to learn charm and etiquette in polite society. We can read books on the subject and become a clone of Miss Manners, but real mastery of politeness does not occur until we become so motivated by charm and good-will that we express politeness and gracious behavior *automatically*, without being in any way forced or artificial. At this point, our behavior demonstrates a state of consciousness in which all lesser alternatives have been eliminated, and we are guided solely by the inner motives of graciousness and goodwill.

2. The goal of mastery is illumination, not the elimination of problems, deficiencies, and frustrations. It must be recognized that a large majority of aspirants strive not for illumination but for a release from their problems and frustrations. It is for this reason that passive systems of growth, which emphasize the achievement of serenity and peace, are so popular. Nonetheless, reality is reality, and sooner or later the true goal of mastery—illumination—must replace all other goals.

3. The steps involved in achieving illumination are to be taken in the right order, not out of sequence. Careful attention to the soul's guidance is enough to guarantee this.

4. We are dealing here with *order*—a universal archetype. There is a pattern for the illumination of form, known to the soul. The personality may not always be aware of this order, but by seeking to express greater order and organization in its life and affairs, the personality prepares itself to work and act with greater mastery.

5. In working creatively to improve conditions in the world or to help others, we must keep in mind that illumination is gradual for them, too. There is much to be done, but we are not working against the clock; the archetypal patterns of life are not about to go away. Neither is form. So, while working diligently and without

losing opportunity, we can still work patiently and without undue frustration.

6. Light must descend tier upon tier in order to reach the physical plane. Proper forms for receiving the light must be built first on the mental plane, before it can be received astrally and physically. This is one of the keys to effective creative work.

7. The key to accelerating the gradual process of illumination is *service*. There is great danger in trying to force the phenomenal results of illumination by a premature awakening of the psychic nature. However, the effort to serve as the soul would have us serve is a noble one. Service is a radiant expression of illumination—the radiance of love, nobility, goodwill, dignity, wisdom, and grace into the world about us, for the benefit of all life. We are meant to be helpers of our fellow man, stewards of the garden Earth, and agents of the plan of evolution. Ways to serve can be found in all three of these activities. Service is the best way to ground the life of spirit on earth; moreover, grounding the life of spirit forces the personality to accommodate the design and the life of the soul. Once we embark on genuine service, inspired by the soul, the pace of our growth increases exponentially. A life of service also insures that our growth will be safe and protected, because the effort to serve forces us to blend practical work in the physical plane with guidance from the higher self. This prevents us from becoming too unbalanced, one way or the other.

7. Through initiation, meditation, and enlightenment, the polarity of the aspirant is shifted from the personality to the soul.

During most of the long process of spiritual growth, the focus of effort is the personality. Recognizing a flaw in our character, we are motivated by our desire to correct it. Perceiving an opportunity, we are motivated by the need to demonstrate competence to seize it. Our motives are primarily the motives of the personality. At this stage in the relationship, the personality is the dominant pole; the soul must be content with a supporting role. This helps us complete the integration of the personality.

During the latter stages of growth, however, the effort shifts from making improvements in the personality to enabling the soul to take effective control of its instrument of self-expression. Initiation, meditation, and enlightenment are the means by which the soul claims control of its creation. The soul slowly becomes the dominant pole, with the personality assuming a more secondary position. It is still important—it is the focus of our self-expression, after all—but the soul now controls and directs our self-expression directly.

Naturally, this results in major changes in motivation, priorities, and even our world view. Our creative work and service become more and more important, but not for the standard reasons which motivate others and once inspired us. Having become well acquainted with beauty, we serve beauty. Having become familiar with benevolence, we act with goodwill. Having discovered justice, we serve justice.

Slowly, the world of the soul and divine qualities becomes more real to us than the world of form. This is not to suggest that the physical world is an illusion—nothing which is a creation of God can be an illusion. But our polarity has shifted from form to consciousness, and so we are motivated to serve the soul, not the personality.

The soul-centered consciousness uses the personality to serve its agenda, purpose, and needs, not the other way around. The appetites, cravings, and habits which once were so important to the personality now have little impact on the daily life of the aspirant, simply because they are largely irrelevant to the soul. It is important to stress this point, because far too many aspirants envision enlightenment in terms of the personality achieving the pinnacle of success, popularity, and influence. The genuine state of enlightenment, by contrast, is far more humble, boring, and inconspicuous than most people would like to believe. Indeed, the shift of polarity which occurs in enlightenment is so great that the average aspirant would probably fail to recognize a truly enlightened person if he chanced to meet him, and rush off to embrace the first convincing imposter.

8. There is an even higher level of development than these, however: full identification with spirit. At this level, there is no differentiation or distortion.

Even though we have no intention of exploring the nature of the Monad in this text, this instruction is inserted to remind us that consciousness is not the highest level of being. Consciousness is the second aspect of God; life is the first. The divine archetypes and forces we deal with as we acquire creative mastery are themselves the emanations of a single, divine creative impulse—undifferentiated, undistorted.

It is useful to keep in perspective the fact that consciousness is the emanation of an even higher source of life. Growth is not an end unto itself; it serves life. For the same reason, neither meditation nor creativity is an end in itself; it serves life. We will continue to encounter the challenges of spiritual growth even after we achieve illumination. First, we will learn to interact with the spiritual triad; this, in time, will lead us to direct identification with the Monad.

It is helpful to know this, but equally important to keep our focus directed toward the lessons of growth at hand. Some aspirants want to go directly to the Father, bypassing all preliminary steps. This simply is not possible. Even if it were, it would not be desirable. We must master the finite before we can work with the infinite. This is the practical value of differentiation.

When differentiation occurs, it limits life or consciousness to some degree. This is a natural phenomenon, not a sin. In order for the divine will to be done, it must emanate to and eventually control all levels of manifestation—including the physical plane. This limits spirit, but the limitation is endured for a specific creative purpose. As our creative mastery is perfected, however, the limitation is overcome. Each step in spiritual growth teaches us something important about the nature of divine life and its purposes on earth.

The next several instructions explore this idea in greater fullness.

9. To achieve creative mastery, we must learn to focus divine forces and archetypes without significant distortion or reaction. The moment an abstract idea is precipitated into form, a reaction is created. This reaction must be controlled. When it is, then the intelligence of form is able to respond to the idea. In this way, consciousness is able to direct and supervise the creative activity to follow.

The work of creativity always involves bringing something new from the higher worlds down into the earth planes. Inevitably, this results in a certain amount of distortion or reaction. It is helpful to understand both processes.

Distortion is usually a result of our own habits and biases. The mind will tend to interpret inspiration in terms of what it has previously known or accepted; the emotions will tend to color insights to fit what they want to believe. Even the physical body may distort incoming guidance through the momentum of its ingrained memory patterns and traditional behavior.

Reaction is generally far more severe. The mind may react to new ideas defensively and critically, discrediting them before they can take root. The emotions can become angry and resentful, rejecting the new ideas sarcastically. The physical body generally follows suit, shouting, screaming, and stomping its feet in a show of disapproval.

This instruction teaches us the simple truth that these distortions and reactions must be controlled, if we are to achieve creative mastery. Otherwise, there will be no guarantee that the creative process will be connected and supervised by the soul. It could be run by the basest instincts within our psyche. This principle can be illuminated by many simple examples.

When we attempt to establish a new habit of behavior, there is immediately a strong resistance to this endeavor. The subconscious rises to protect what is comfortable and familiar. If we give in to this resistance, we do not succeed in our effort to grow. But if we control it, then the intelligence of the subconscious itself responds in a relatively short period of time, and we can establish the new habit.

When new policies are issued in a business, there is an immediate reaction of resistance and grumbling from the office troops. If management is effective, it will be able to control this resistance—perhaps even by taking care how the new policies are presented. But if it is not careful, the resistance may all but sabotage the new policies.

When a parent attempts to teach a child something new, there is often a similar strong resistance or rebellion. If the parent could understand, anticipate, and control this reaction, he or she would be able to teach with genuine authority.

When new ideas are introduced into mass consciousness, there immediately ensues a strong reaction toward them. If not protected, they will be rejected and buried. But if the agent responsible for introducing the ideas is able to act to control the reaction, the ideas will eventually become established and accepted.

Duality is one of the great principles of life. As new life descends, tier upon tier, it divides into a positive and a negative expression. If the difference can be harnessed and harmonized, it can be used creatively. If not, the creative work may get out of hand. It is therefore important for the spiritual aspirant, in learning about the nature of creative mastery, to respect and become familiar with the Holy Spirit—the third aspect of God. Simply loving God is not enough; we must learn the practical science of controlling the natural phenomena in God's life that would distort our creative work—or protect it, if we work properly.

One of the keys to understanding this instruction is the immediately preceding one. If we recognize that there is a part of us which remains constant and unchanged even while we are engaged in this creative activity, then the distortions and modifications can be controlled. Nor do we have to be in contact with the Monad to activate this capacity. *Whenever* we can focus the mind to become aware of the intent of the soul in some creative endeavor, we are harnessing the power and strength within us to achieve mastery. We align the concrete mind with the will to control. This is the ideal use of the mind, and the recommended way of gaining control of the creative process. Control has nothing to do with repression, masochism, or self-denial. It is a healthy expression of the active, well-trained mind blended with an understanding of the intent of spiritual will.

Suffice it to say that consciousness is *meant* to control form—and is meant to control the creative process. The aspirant must learn what constitutes this measure of control.

10. When this dynamic process of control is mastered, the perceptions of the spiritual man become objective and his creative endeavors become true.

We are exploring here the proposition of establishing a *habit* of creative control, so that the binding of distortion becomes automatic as it occurs. This habit is constructed just as any other habit would be: by repeatedly grooving the subconscious in the proper way.

The key to this work is a simple one. The spiritual aspirant must cultivate a higher quality of habits than the ordinary person. It is not enough just to be as good as others, or even one step beyond them; the spiritual person must make it a habit to embody and express spiritual qualities. He must therefore establish a wide range of appropriate traits:

- A sense of humility toward the divine.
- A sense of commitment to honoring the spiritual will with intelligence.
- Dedication to playing one's role effectively.
- Periodic self-examination.
- The love of truth and accuracy.
- The custom of viewing circumstances from the perspective of the soul, rather than the personality.
- A capacity for sacrifice.

The process of establishing objectivity involves every level of our self-expression physical, emotional, and mental. For many aspirants, the most difficult level to master is the emotions. This is because we habitually tend to identify with our moods and feelings. If an unpleasant mood suddenly sweeps over us, for example, we will probably accept it as a mood of our own creation, even though it may well be a mood we would normally not indulge. In many cases, it is nothing but a free-floating mood that has become attached to us. Nevertheless, misidentification with such moods and concepts can create havoc in the effort to achieve objectivity. If we would but make the effort to detach from the mood, we could discover that we can send these moods away and not be troubled by them—or even dispel them entirely. This is a simple level of control and the binding of distortions. The ability to act in this way is crucial to the development of objectivity. We must be able to discern among the thinker, the thought, and our emotional reactions to it!

Later, we must learn to work in this way with the currents of mass consciousness. This is more difficult, because the force of mass consciousness can easily overwhelm a single individual. Moreover, it is not possible to dispel entirely a thought-form or distortion which has existed for thousands of years. But it is possible to control these currents, by working impersonally and in harmony with the appropriate archetypes.

Some philosophers would argue that complete objectivity is impossible to achieve. It is perhaps true that the average man or woman exercises so little control of the thinking and emoting process that objectivity seems beyond human capacity. But it is well within the reach of the sincere spiritual aspirant, if the effort is made to establish the proper habits of striving toward perfection.

11. The spiritual man is thereby able to bring the light of heaven into earthly expression without interruption.

This instruction gives us a big clue into the meaning of the last two. The light of heaven is continual. It does not go away or diminish. It is a constant factor. We can always call on it and always use it, no matter where we are, what we have done, or how sinful or inadequate we may feel. We never fall out of favor with heaven, and heaven never ceases to operate.

210

Once upon a time, the spiritual aspirant was motivated to work creatively to solve a specific problem or correct a certain error. His imagination was filled with this problem; step by step, he learned to overcome it through the use of spiritual techniques and divine guidance. At this stage on the path, however, he no longer operates in this fashion. He still works creatively, but with a much higher perspective. He is motivated not so much by the need to fix what is wrong as by the need to establish what is right. His imagination is filled with the inspiration of the divine plan. He is aware of the problems of earthly life, but not enslaved by them. Indeed, he does not distinguish between his life in heaven and his life on earth. They are just two elements of the same life.

Divine life expresses itself without interruption, and so does the spiritual person. This does not mean that he does not stop to eat or sleep; it means he has discovered how to harness the creative power of the soul. He knows how to control the distortions and resistance which inevitably will arise. So he does not regard them as interruptions, but as parts of a dynamic process. He uses the light of heaven to redeem them, and presses on toward his goal.

It is not enough just to meditate once a day and then go forth into the workaday world and behave as everyone else does. Meditation, or any spiritual practice, is meant to transform our character and our self-expression, infusing it with spirit, so that we begin to express the light within us in all that we do. We replace our crabbiness with kindness. We replace our confusion with lucid thinking. We replace our irritability with patience. We replace our self-centeredness with generosity. Most importantly, we refine these changes and improvements in our character until they become continual—until we can express them without interruption.

12. The aspirant becomes completely focused in the light of the soul, although still active in the world of form.

The aspirant now understands that he is not just a human being, but a creation of light. He has been born in light, not in sin, and now rediscovers his birthright. He serves the light and finds the fulfillment of his personality and individuality in expressing light.

To help understand better what this may mean, a useful exercise is to reflect on what a proper expression of light would be:

Mentally.

Emotionally.

Physically.

At work.

Religiously.

As a citizen.

As a parent.

In dealing with friends.

In the use of money or other resources.

Many people, upon reading the phrase "focused in the light of the soul," immediately draw a blank, as though the soul is vague and probably nothing more than sugary niceness and cuddly warmth. But this is not the case at all. Abstractness in no way reduces the richness and complexity of the soul—or the need for precise definition and understanding. The soul is the heart of our individuality; there is an immense amount to be learned about it. Being focused in the light of the soul means we have some understanding of the perspectives, plans, and goals of the soul—and are able to harness the motivation and power to act upon them. The sciences of the soul must be studied and practiced; through this study and practice, creative mastery is gradually attained.

13. The aspirant has full access to the archetypal resources of heaven, and thereby knows forms in their fullness: their intended manifestation, their potential for growth, and their proper function—as well as their actual appearance.

Instructions 13, 14, and 15 will set the stage for the remaining forty instructions in Book Three, which will deal specifically with the archetypal resources of heaven, how to contact them, and what to do with them creatively. These three instructions teach the aspirant how to focus the mind and the intuition to contact the archetypes. It can be interesting to compare the three instructions to the three processes of initiation, meditation, and enlightenment.

In this first instruction, the aspirant is encouraged to recognize that forms are made of intelligent substance, his mind is made of intelligent substance, and the archetypes are patterns of divine intelligence. Therefore, by training the mind to be properly responsive to intelligence, he can become attuned to the archetypes and at the same time know forms in their fullness. It is important for the aspirant, as he seeks knowledge of the soul and of archetypes, to explore the nature of intelligence and learn its potential. Some basic statements can be set forth here:

Intelligence is living substance.

It draws its life from the patterns of intelligence of the archetypes.

Intelligence is the medium for growth in this system.

Thinking is the process through which the mind eventually becomes saturated with wisdom and governed by the will.

The human becomes proficient in thinking by training the mind, both in its ability to work skillfully with forms and its ability to work skillfully with archetypes. Four basic ways of training the mind can be mentioned:

1. By becoming aware of the actual appearances of form. This

213

is the purpose of conventional education: to teach us the history, science, philosophy, and language of the appearance of form. Without a decent understanding of these subjects, it will be difficult to proceed to the other three methods.

2. By becoming aware of the intended manifestation of forms. Conventional education *ought* to teach this, but usually falls short. So the aspirant must learn it on his own. Basically, it involves comparing the appearance of form with the divine patterns from which it developed, and examining what the ideal expression in form would be. The study of cosmic law is one of the great branches of this line of learning.

3. By determining what can be done with what exists. This is the process of teaching the basic principles of reform, based on the intended design. By learning the lessons of reform, the mind acquires the pragmatic skills it needs to harness the genuine power of growth and apply it in meaningful ways. In many cases, reform includes creativity—the process of going beyond what is known and discovering that which is needed to enrich and expand present knowledge.

4. By becoming aware of the proper function of forms. The mind can be trained to recognize this proper function by contemplating the spiritual purpose of any given form. This purpose is not the same as the goals to be achieved, but rather the originating intent which stimulated any given facet of divine life to seek manifestation in form. The purpose may not be fulfilled for millennia to come, but if we understand it, we can then discern the proper function of the form at this point in time much more easily.

It should be kept in mind that forms can only be known in their fullness in the context of the intelligence, potential for reform, and purpose of divine life.

14. The aspirant can discern the character of forms, their stage in evolution, and what will best help them unfold at any point in time.

The second great key to learning about the spiritual resources of heaven is that they *individualize* themselves through form. As a result, their infiniteness becomes finite, their universality becomes individual, and they can be known—not by the appearance of the individual forms, but by their character, evolution, and approach to growth.

Much insight can be acquired by examining the nature of individuality, not just in the human kingdom but in all facets of life, from the tiniest cell to the solar system itself. Inevitably, this study will lead the aspirant into the realm of the archetypes, because individuality is always measured in terms of the true expression of these forces and patterns. It is not the differences between two kinds of rock which give them their individuality; rather, it is the degree to which each manifests the archetypal forces governing the mineral kingdom. Nor is it the distinct idiosyncrasies of two humans which give them their individuality; instead, it is the degree to which each is attuned to the soul and capable of expressing it in life.

Understanding this, the aspirant learns to evaluate individuality in terms of spirit first, personality second. There are three keys to this evaluation:

Character is the sum of the various patterns of individual expression which have been developed over the eons of personal experience. In the later stages of growth, these patterns may reflect or embody archetypal resources, but the character is part of the personality, not the soul. It is a collection of subconscious and instinctual patterns. It may be strong or weak, well-rounded or very narrow. By knowledge of the character of any form, the aspirant can evaluate how this person or form will probably respond in differing circumstances and how well it manifests the plan of the soul. Can the form be self-determining? What is the degree of stability? What is the basic type of temperament? Is there an inner development of ethics and principles, or is it generally reactive only to external pressures? These and many other questions need to be asked in the pursuit of a true understanding of character.

The stage in evolution needs to be examined in order to relate actual behavior with the archetypal principles of individuality. Adolescent emotional behavior is not inappropriate to the development of individuality in a teenager, but it would be in a forty-year-old. The same idea can be extended to the evolution of any entity or form through the course of many incarnations. Not all species, or members of any species, are at the same level of development. Indeed, the spectrum of evolution is vast; the outpouring of archetypal life tends to be continual. We therefore need to ponder: is this entity primarily emotional or mental in orientation? How much has the principle of individuality been developed—is he a slave to mass consciousness or his own person? How much is he influenced by glamours and illusions? Is he on the path—and if so, is it the right-hand path or the left-hand path?

The nuances of this study are exceedingly subtle. At times it is necessary for a certain species or human racial type to become extinct or modified. The purpose of divine life is best served in this way. The attempt to preserve such a species or racial type would therefore be an obstruction to the evolution of form. At the same time, however, it must be understood that this statement is not an endorsement of callous, irresponsible attitudes toward our environment and the life forms we share it with. Above all, mankind is meant to be a loving steward of all life on earth. It is merely an illustration of the fact that the extinction of a life form can only be understood fully in the context of the ruling archetypal forces, and the stage of evolution of the form as dictated by the divine plan.

What will best help a form unfold can be partly determined by an understanding of character and the stage of unfoldment, but it also requires an ability to envision what changes, modifications, and assistance will best enrich the experimental life of the archetype. Luther Burbank had an uncanny ability to pick the three or four plants out of several thousand of a single species that would best serve his purpose of developing new varieties of plants. This was an intuitive ability that linked him with the appropriate archetypes and allowed him to assess the unfoldment of the species. This is a very practical skill which should be developed by anyone seeking to work creatively.

This instruction is *not* to be interpreted as an endorsement of the silly practice of guessing what stage of enlightenment or spirituality others have reached. When found in most occult circles, this activity is nothing but a sophisticated form of gossip and oneupmanship.

15. The imperfections of form are the result of the stage of development, not the nature of the archetypal patterns.

The creative work of the aspirant continually exposes him to the imperfections and distortions of form, to the point where it is easy to be tempted into believing that imperfection is a natural state for form. It is this temptation, for example, that has led to the formulation of the idea that humanity was born in sin—an idea that has been seized with delight and sustained by lovers of evil, for it allows them to dominate and manipulate good people.

Humanity and all of life is born of consciousness, not form. All of life is therefore born of perfection, harmony, order, and love, not sin or error or imperfection. It is also born with a very strong impulse to grow, to serve the plan of God, and to involve itself in form. As this occurs, imperfection appears, but only as a transition stage to perfection.

It is not the power of divine life which generates imperfection. Imperfection is the incomplete response in form to the creative work of the archetypes. It falls into two classes:

1. Imperfection due to a lack of growth.

2. Imperfection due to deliberate distortion. There are people who are so in love with materialism that they openly oppose and try to sabotage anything which seeks to serve God and spirit. Materialism comes in many clever disguises. The obvious one is the lusting for material possessions. But many beliefs and practices which seem acceptable—perhaps even spiritual—are actually highly materialistic:

• The practice of hatha yoga, with its emphasis on the body, not consciousness. The practice of martial arts falls into the same category.

• The kundalini lust of some spiritual aspirants, as well as the growing preoccupation of many aspirants with their force centers or chakras.

• The Christian emphasis on the literal resurrection of the physical body.

• The recent craze of one "pop meditation" group for the practice of "levitation" as a means of growing spiritually.

• Excessive worry about physical health.

• The degree of pessimism and fear present in the world today, often in the guise of religious fervor.

Whatever the symptom, imperfection is always the result of a lack of maturity. It is not in any way inherent in the divine resources or plan.

It is of great importance for the aspirant to understand this principle, else it will not be possible for him to effectively tap the spiritual resources of heaven. He will not turn to them, but rather seek to find solutions in the world of form. Or, if he does turn to them, he will not have proper faith or confidence in their ability to help him.

In this light, it can be helpful to realize that the vast majority of people respond to imperfection in purely materialistic ways. They become disgusted and revolted by it. They condemn it and seek to destroy it. These typical responses indicate how widespread materialism actually is, because the genuine spiritual response is very much different. The true spiritual person never fights imperfection; instead, he stands up to it, embraces it, and then transforms it. In other words, hate is never matched with hate; it is mastered with forgiveness. Grief is never matched with sadness; it is mastered with optimism. The limits of physical living are never corrected by despair or destruction; they are mastered by marshalling the divine possibilities and applying them!

Jesus warned us against resisting evil. This does not mean that it is permissible to let evil flourish; it simply means that resisting it is a misapplication of energy. If we meet evil on its own terms, we lose the battle. We must respond with the love, joy, benevolence, and compassion of God. When we do, then we have won the battle within ourself.

Indeed, the more we recognize that our primary opportunity for discovering and learning about imperfection will be within ourself, and that we should be more concerned with removing the mote from our own eye than the speck in the eyes of others, the more rapidly we will discover the real presence of divine resources in our own life.

16. Study of the spiritual roots of any form, how the form has responded to its roots, and how it will continue to respond

in the future will reveal to the aspirant the constructive use of time.

We now begin the specific examination of the archetypal resources of consciousness, how the aspirant becomes familiar with them, and how best he can honor them productively. This study will occupy us for the rest of Book Three. To put this activity in religious terms, we are learning what heaven is like.

The study of time can be approached in a variety of ways:

1. Chronologically, by the literal mapping out of the calendar and clock.

2. Historically, by what happened when and how it relates to other events of the same period.

3. Cyclically, as in the study of astrology.

4. The synchronicity of time, in which we study the intersection of various kinds of cycles.

5. By its productivity—how much can be produced in a certain interval of time.

6. By our "sense" of time—the subjective sense of the astral body. Five minutes of waiting can seem longer than an hour of watching an enjoyable movie.

7. By evolution, where we gauge the proper amount of time in terms of the growth expected to occur.

This instruction implies that while the aspirant will find all of these approaches to time helpful, he will gradually come to understand it primarily in terms of evolution. The soul does not respond to the ticking of a clock; it sets in motion a plan for a lifetime and then determines how many years this plan will require. The aspirant must learn to work in a similar way.

Time is a tool of archetypal expression, not a limitation. God has set aside billions of years for the evolution of the solar system, knowing this length of time is required for the full maturation of divine patterns, qualities, and forces as they seek to permeate all levels of substance.

Still, time can be a major source of frustration to the aspirant, until he sees it in harmonious relation to his work. He prays for healing, but little happens. Is it because his faith is not great enough? Is it because the archetypes are disinterested in responding? Is it because the universe is not really benevolent after all? These are the kinds of concerns which creep into the mind and threaten to undermine stability. In reality, it is probably none of the above. It is just a question of time. It takes time for the adjustments which lead to healing to be made.

The spiritual perspective on time can perhaps best be understood by realizing that time is one of the major "intersections" between the infinite and the finite. The timeless, eternal nature of the soul is difficult to understand from the perspective of time as we know it. So we need a new perspective. Many religions have developed the concept of "The Eternal Now" to fill this need, but the phrase itself is a paradox and leads to a great deal of confusion. A better label would be "timefulness"—the awareness, as we go through the days and years of our physical activity, of being guided by a timeless, immortal purpose of spirit. As we become mindful of these inner dimensions of time in this way, then we will gradually master the skills of time. Otherwise, we will remain mired in confusion.

It is skill and understanding which best harness time. The highly-skilled person can do the same task in far less time than the unskilled person. Indeed, the more we understand the nature of the spiritual resources influencing the growth of form, and build skills and wisdom in expressing them, the more we can effectively gain control of time.

17. Study of the way in which any form expresses its archetypal roots will reveal the creative use of sound.

It must be remembered that we are dealing throughout this text with energy, rather than concrete substance. All spiritual forces, divine ideals, and archetypal patterns are living streams of energy, each with it own vibratory rate or "sound." In a very real way, we learn to identify and relate to these energies by their sound. In the same way, the measure of how successfully the personality has integrated with the soul is the degree to which the personality has learned to express or sound forth the qualities of the soul. The soul uses sound in evoking a response from the personality, just as the personality uses it to invoke the support and guidance of the soul. There are also many other important uses of sound, such as the ability to discern the call sounded by any form as it strives to achieve perfection.

As sound is used creatively and constructively, it becomes language. The soul communicates to the personality, and the personality expresses itself to the world. If we approached the use of the many languages of mankind as vehicles for the communication of abstract ideas and spiritual guidance, and only secondarily as means of communicating from one person to the next, the purpose of language might become clearer. Certainly the value of right speech would be more fully recognized, and the spiritual purpose of literature and the arts would be easier to understand.

Each archetypal pattern can be thought of as having its own "language." This language is to be learned by the aspirant, as appropriate for the work he is doing. It is learned intuitively, but it is every bit as much a language as English or German. It can be misunderstood, mispronounced, and misapplied—but it can also be learned with great fluency.

Once one of these archetypal languages is learned, it is much easier to learn others, but there is still a learning process involved. At first, we just translate these languages, gradually learning something about them. Later, we are able to sound them ourself, and this is when we become creative in their use. We understand the way the many forms which are responsive to the archetype sound forth the language of its radiance, growth, and intelligence. We also learn to use sound esoterically to build forms on the mental and astral levels, to sustain forms, to control them, to energize them, and to destroy them.

In this context, it can be observed that Nikola Tesla spoke the language of electricity, Albert Schweitzer spoke the language of loving service, and Rembrandt spoke the language of art.

18. Study of earlier incarnations will teach the aspirant about the plan of the soul.

There is much foolishness in the public mind about the recall of past lives. The vast majority of people who want to know about past lives want only to know about details and specific events—preferably favorable ones. But a moment's thought on this instruction will indicate how worthless this pursuit is. The details of specific events represent just the *form* of past lives; they tell us nothing about the growth, the service, and the creativity which occurred or failed to occur.

This instruction makes it clear that if we are going to study previous lives, it is best to do so from the perspective of the soul. The value of this study is to teach us:

• About the cyclic manifestation of archetypal patterns.

• About the themes of karma and dharma (growth and duty) which characterize this particular cycle in the expression of the form. We learn the principles of resolving karmic patterns and how

223

pronounced, perhaps even abnormal, traits may be introduced into the personality in order to promote karmic growth. We likewise learn to respect more fully the dharmic patterns of unfolding talent and opportunity, through which the soul seeks to expand its self-expression in form.

• About the remarkable consistency of the soul as it pursues its creative goals. One of the realizations gained from the study of previous lives, for example, is the thematic precision with which the soul plans its lives, especially at the more advanced stages. Life-times are often cumulative, with a sequence of seemingly difficult lives leading to a lifetime of dramatic triumph or resolution. There is true mastery involved.

• About the skill with which the soul is able to respond to those divine patterns which guide it.

• Why conflict exists and how it can best be managed.

If we are going to be truly responsive to the soul, it behooves us to learn as much as possible about the methods the soul uses to influence us. This is often much easier when put in the context of several lives. The study of earlier lives, therefore, when properly approached, can truly enrich the understanding and skill of the aspirant. He must first take care to outgrow his glamours about re-incarnation, however. The current fascination with "reincarnation therapy" through some sort of hypnosis is just one example of how easily people are seduced by popular glamours. Hypnosis is a grossly inadequate tool for examining past lives; it merely leads people on a fanciful trip through their own vivid imaginations.

19. Study of the ways in which others respond to archetypal impulses—to grow, to serve, and to obey cosmic principles—will teach the aspirant about the role humanity plays in the divine plan.

It is not difficult to pick up random images concerning others; with practice and discipline, this ability can be built into a productive skill. Caution and discretion must be exercised, of course, lest this ability be used for snooping or psychic mischief, thereby sabotaging contact with the soul. But as long as the ethics of the spiritual life are carefully observed, much can be learned by studying others intuitively. This study can be divided into two categories: learning from role models and learning from object lessons.

The key in learning from role models is to study how they are inspired by and work with archetypal forces. To what degree have they mastered an archetypal language and learned to speak it? How are joy and peace expressed through their daily activities? By using this intuitive capacity in this way, we become acquainted with a much broader range of archetypal expression than we would normally encounter through our own experiences. We gain tremendous insight into the patterns of human nature. And we begin to perceive the role humanity is meant to play in the divine plan.

Obviously, this means choosing the role models we study with some care. While we can learn a great deal by intuitively studying the way the Christ responds to archetypal impulses, we probably will learn little if anything at all studying our next door neighbor. For this reason, we should pick models known for their saintliness, genius, and leadership skills. And we should keep our study focused on the ways they harnessed divine life to grow, to serve, and to obey cosmic principles. These are the lessons which will reveal to us a working knowledge of the divine plan for humanity.

When it comes to learning from object lessons, the field of study is understandably larger. Here, we *can* learn from our neighbor—as well as our colleagues at work, our parents, our children, and our friends. In particular, we can learn from the mistakes they make. A friend who is hypercritical may teach us the real value of compassion—by never expressing it—far more poignantly than someone with great empathy. A colleague who continually mis-judges the character of people he relies on may teach us a powerful lesson about the need to intuitively examine the roots of character of those we trust. These lessons are an important source of learning for us all—provided that we have cultivated the eyes to see them and the mind to comprehend them.

As Alexander Pope put it, "The proper study of Mankind is man." We are involved, individually and as a group, in the work of humanity. For long eons, we are focused primarily in our selfish needs and wants. But as our interest in the life of spirit expands, we gradually replace our selfishness with a more altruistic perspective. This is accelerated by the study of how others respond to arche-typal patterns.

20. This study of others is the study of force, not form.

Psychic perception is the use of astral or mental senses to per-ceive conditions and forms not apparent to the physical senses. No matter how refined it may be, it is still the perception of form.

Intuition is the use of consciousness to become aware of spiritual forces. Strictly speaking, the intuition does not deal with forms, except indirectly: by knowing the trends and forces already set in motion in any given circumstance, the aspirant can predict what forms will be generated as a result. But the interest lies in the force, not the forms.

In using our inner skills of perception to study great examples of responsiveness to divine life, we must focus on force, not form. We must study their ability to express joy, compassion, wisdom, beauty, or peace—not specific events from their lives or works. After all, we are instructed to study how they respond to the inner life—not how they react to day-to-day pressures of living.

This is an instruction that modern psychology needs to study. It needs to see the pointlessness of gathering tons of statistics about the form of human life, from which it generates misleading hypothesis after misleading hypothesis. In lieu of statistics, it needs to focus its study on the divine laws, principles, qualities, and forces which govern human behavior—and construct an effective model of psychological health and well-being. This would be a radical departure from the present state of things.

21. Study of the principles of appearance and non-appearance gives the aspirant insight into the laws of manifestation.

We are now entering upon a portion of the text which requires major paraphrasing. In the original text of this instruction, for instance, Patanjali describes a way meditation can be used to render the aspirant invisible. While this particular feat, and others like it, can be done, the performance of seeming miracles is no longer a high priority of the spiritual aspirant. Many of the thirty instructions which follow have therefore been translated *as appropriate to the modern spiritual person*, not as originally worded. In each case, however, great care has been taken to preserve the archetypal integrity and purpose of the original instruction.

We are dealing here with the third aspect of God—appearance—and its use by the one who would appear, the soul. The significance of the idea presented here goes far, far beyond the possibility of becoming invisible to the physical perception of others. A few statements can be set forth here as starting points for investigation:

1. There are three levels of appearance: mental, emotional, and

physical. The principles and laws of manifestation are the same at all three levels, but the appearance is more subtle at the inner levels.

2. Not all forms are to be found in physical appearance. Many have only astral or mental appearances. The aspirant must learn to deal with these, and realize that what he does not know *can* affect him. What he does not take into account may also thwart his creative efforts.

3. Habits are forms animated by force. They can therefore be altered by deciding to render the unwanted habit invisible and, if desirable, by replacing it in the world of appearance with a new habit. The same principle can be applied to the manifestation of any form, within us or outside us.

4. The entire subconscious may seem invisible to the average aspirant, but it is an appearance in the world of form. It can therefore be investigated, charted, and then reorganized so that it is more disciplined and effective. We can restructure the subconscious so that only noble elements and skills appear through our self-expression, and the ignoble elements of our character fade away, until they disappear altogether.

5. There are times when the spiritual person finds it more desirable to operate invisibly, humbly and silently, rather than acting directly, openly. This can be especially useful in creative and healing work, where the greatest results might come by creating a proper psychological climate for growth or productivity. The actual work may be performed through prayer, meditation, or invocation. The intent to operate invisibly can also serve to protect creative work until the time comes to unveil it, and to reduce the threat of psychic interference.

As the aspirant learns these simple and very necessary techniques, he learns about appearance and nonappearance. As appropriate, he finds he can apply them in other ways, as well. He also comes to discover that the soul is, at this point, in complete control of its appearance in form, and can shape and structure it to fit its own needs.

22. Study of the Law of Cause and Effect, both in the present and in the future, gives the aspirant insight into the principles governing the term of any expression of form.

By learning the meaning and purpose of the genuine causes of life, the aspirant can learn the likely impact of those causes in form, both now and in the future. These genuine causes, of course, are the motivating forces of the divine plan. The events, predicaments, and circumstances of the form world are *not* causes—they are effects. One effect may be traceable back to an earlier effect, and from it on back to hundreds of other effects—but it must be seen that the only true causes in life are those set in motion by the divine plan. All that happens in form is the result, directly, indirectly, or in opposition to, the purposes, goals, and action of God, the soul, and the divine archetypes. A good knowledge of cause and effect is therefore indispensable for creative mastery of archetypal forces.

The lessons of cause and effect are generally very practical ones. By looking intuitively to the future to evaluate what the long-and short-term outcome of decisions we are making in the present will be, we are learning the lessons of cause and effect. We are seeking to deal intelligently with the resources and opportunities of life. And we gain insight into the "term of expression" of our decisions and projects.

The "term of expression" is not hard to discern. When the strength of any initiating cause dissipates, the term of expression of the form it created comes to an end. The enlightened aspirant can recognize this consummation of effort and detach himself quickly, turning his attention to other creative projects. Indeed, by withdrawing his attention from the effects or manifestation at the proper time, he hastens the "end of the term." Usually, there are clear signs indicating the consummation of any effort and the need for new beginnings. These signs are examined in some detail in the essay, "Seeking Intelligent Guidance" in *The Art of Living Volume II.*

This study, fully worked out, also indicates the enlightened approach to making adjustments for errors—for setting "wrong causes" in motion. The term of expression of these "wrong causes"—and their effects—can be reduced by the aspirant, if he is willing to act immediately to correct the injury caused. If he tries to hide his mistake, or pretend he did not make it, the term of expression may be quite long—until he finally makes the adjustment. But if he acts swiftly, the term will be short, and he will be able to get back to creative activity.

Ultimately, the aspirant realizes that while forms are cyclic and appear for a specific term and then disappear for another term, life continues uninterrupted. The paintings of a master artist may survive for centuries, for example, whereas the work of a lesser talent may draw attention for a few years and then disappear. Yet the divine force of beauty which inspired both of them, to the limits of their abilities, is eternal.

These principles of Cause and Effect can also be applied to groups, businesses, and nations, producing much insight.

23. Study of the creative expression of compassion, cooperation, and communion gives the aspirant insight into the Law of Attraction and the principles of right human relationships.

In considering this sequence of instructions, it is important to keep in mind that "study" is not just a passive contemplation or an intellectual inquiry into abstract principles. The study being enjoined is the advanced study of creative mastery. It is assumed that the work of integration is already well underway, if not completed, and now the aspirant is using the tools of initiation, meditation, and enlightenment to refine his skills in serving the divine plan. The heart of this study is therefore the use of meditative and intuitive skills to investigate the spiritual patterns and principles which govern the outer appearance of life.

Study also involves practicing methods and techniques until proficiency and skill are achieved. Nowhere is the need for this practice more evident than in this instruction. Understanding the nature of right human relationships amounts to nothing unless it leads to *building* right human relationships, based on archetypal principles. It is shameful that more psychologists and psychiatrists do not appreciate this fact.

What is the value of competence in human relationships to working with divine life? At first, there might not seem to be any direct relevance. But it should be remembered that it is through individuality that we bring the life of consciousness and the light within us into expression in the world of form. And we are not the only one seeking to do this. We are one of a very large group (humanity), and this group in turn is part of an even larger group of life forms busy serving the divine plan. If we do not establish good relationships with the other members of our own group, we will be constantly distorting the archetypal life we seek to serve—and distracted from the work we propose to do.

Beyond this, it should be understood that the key to working with energies of all types is establishing a proper and cooperative relationship with them. Our work in learning to build good relationships with friends, family, and colleagues is therefore excellent preparation for working at spiritual levels. It is for this reason that the Christ enjoined us: "As you do unto the least of these My brethren, so you do it unto Me." This is a statement of fact. The way we treat other people reveals the way we will treat the riches of heaven, the spiritual treasures of life, and opportunities.

It must be understood that this instruction is dealing with a set of principles and ethics which do indeed constitute a discipline or study of life. It is not enough, as some modern psychologists advocate, to give our friends and colleagues their "space" and permission to do whatever they want with it, in return for a similar indulgence in our own selfishness. Nor does right human relationships have much to do with unconditional love, which is usually a buzzword for a nice, warm feeling that has no sense of maturity, responsibility, or obligation. A lot of nonsense has been propagated about human relationships in recent years; in part, the study enjoined in this instruction includes piercing through such nonsense and understanding how it fails to explain either the Law of Attraction or the basis of right human relationships.

Under the Law of Attraction, we attract to us people, forces, and events similar in quality to ourself. If we are wise and generous, we will attract friends who are likewise wise and generous. If we are cruel and self-serving, we will attract colleagues who delight in sabotaging our efforts. Indeed, one of the best ways of discerning what lessons we most need to master is to examine the primary lessons our friends and associates are facing.

The Law of Attraction governs much of the life of an aspirant—his participation in groups on the inner planes, his ability to gather and focus creative energy, and his skill in focusing himself on differing levels of consciousness. But the basic principles are learned by interacting with others, wisely, humanely, tolerantly, and lovingly.

The three great expressions of this law are compassion, cooperation, and communion.

Compassion is the practical expression of love and understanding toward those we share our life with. It is the fruit of our in-

232

dividual experiences blended with empathy, goodwill, wisdom, and helpfulness. There is a temptation among many aspirants to condemn or criticize those who have not accomplished as much as they; compassion negates this separative instinct. It enables us to remember that we once struggled with the same lessons our companions and colleagues are coping with, so we offer support instead of criticism. At times we must stand firm in the face of the self-deception or mischief of others, but we know that discipline is one of the strongest threads of compassion. It enables us to focus tolerance, benevolence, and kindness without yielding to the weaknesses or immaturity in others who might try to take advantage of our caring. Ultimately, the wellspring of compassion is the love of the soul; as we grow in compassion, we inevitably transform our relationships into right ones.

Cooperation is a prerequisite to any real spiritual work or activity. To work with divine archetypes, the aspirant must learn to do his share of the work well and without complaint; he must learn to help others serving the same divine forces and purposes without pettiness or selfishness; and he must learn to remain focused in the mutual goals and ideals of the cooperative endeavor. Simply put, he must participate fully in the work of humanity.

Communion is the practice of brotherhood, the culmination of right human relationships. It takes relationships one step further, as we learn to blend with the transcendent spiritual essence of our life. Communion reaffirms our kinship with mankind and with all life, and helps us enter into a conscious awareness of the light and life of the Christ.

Above, all the aspirant must learn that it is not acceptable to love humanity in general while disliking, criticizing, and avoiding everyone in specific.

24. Intuitive investigation of the inherent energy of form will lead the aspirant to the ability to awaken and use this energy creatively.

This instruction is the beginning of a sequence of eleven instructions examining the seven basic types of energy and what to do with them creatively. This study has an obvious correspondence to the seven rays and to the seven chakras or force centers in the human being (or any life system) through which these energies pour. It is interesting to note that Alice Bailey, writing in *Esoteric Astrology*, lists the following creative energies in correspondence to the seven planes:

Parashakti, supreme energy—the Logoic plane (ray 1)
Kriyashakti, materializing ideal—the monadic plane (ray 2)
Jnanashakti, force of mind—the atmic plane (ray 3)
Mantrikashakti, speech—the buddhic plane (ray 4)
Ichchhashakti, will to manifest—the mental plane (ray 5)
Kundalinishakti, energy of matter—the astral plane (ray 6)
None—the physical plane (ray 7)

Esoterically, the physical plane is not considered to be an active principle, and therefore no creative energy is listed. Nonetheless, the elemental lives of the physical plane do have an innate life which can resemble energy to the beginning student. This "innate life" is *not* the same as the inherent energy of form referred to in the instruction, and must not be confused with it. The innate life is what we tap when we "go with the flow" of our feelings and "listen to what our body tells us." It is indulgence in sensation, and has little to do with consciousness.

It is valuable to know about the force centers or "chakras," but it must always be kept in mind what a chakra is: a central point within a form for the distribution of energy. Therefore, the study of chakras should always be conducted from the point of view of

234

learning the effective use of the energies which are to be distributed through these centers. Nor is it necessary to limit this study to the chakras in the human body; wherever energy manifests, one or more chakras can be found, depending on the complexity of the organism. This is because a chakra is simply a center of distribution for energy. Wherever a primary etheric chakra can be found, with its corresponding organs in physical form, an astral or mental chakra can also be located—and these, together, form a system for the expression of some force. The chakra and its physical organ, therefore, can only be properly understood in terms of the force meant to be distributed through it and its spiritual purpose.

If medical researchers understood this principle, much could be learned about human health. If scientists delving into alternate energy sources understood this principle, the energy shortage could be resolved. If dilettante spiritual aspirants, who become so entranced with running kudalini up and down their spines, understood this principle, they would go on to more serious endeavors. Like all energies, kundalini is a creative energy; it is therefore of no value to us unless we have a creative purpose for its use.

What is the creative purpose of this inherent energy? An analogy may help explain it. In building a fire, to produce light and heat, we need three elements: a combustible substance, such as wood; oxygen; and an igniting spark. Just so, in creating light in manifestation, we need three elements. The igniting spark is the light of consciousness. The oxygen is the atmosphere of manifestation—the world with its opportunities and resources. The combustible substance is the inherent energy (or kundalini) in form itself. Like wood, it remains solid and apparently useless until ignited, but once ignited, it reveals the full measure of energy which it had stored up within itself.

The light of consciousness cannot appear on earth without interacting in this way with the inherent energy of form. Thus, as the aspirant pursues the work of integration and creative mastery, this inherent energy is awakened and he learns to use it creatively. The more he studies this subject and its practical relevance to him, the more rapidly and safely he will progress.

The applications of this understanding are tremendous, and have very little to do with hot flashes up the spine. For a creative person to work in any medium, he must first understand the inherent energy within the substance of that medium—and learn to release it. This is true for the sculptor, the writer, the parent, the scientist, the leader, and the business person. It is especially true for the occultist and esotericist.

25. Practice in blending this awakened light with the light of consciousness will lead the aspirant into a greater awareness of the relationship between the occult and the mundane.

Once you have kindled your fire, it does no good to gather more wood unless you add that wood to the fire. Just neatly stacking it by the fireplace does not produce warmth or light. Just so, once the inherent energy of form has been awakened, it must be blended with the light of consciousness—*and used creatively!*

This is a point many aspirants neglect. They become aware of the light of consciousness and the light of form, but do nothing to intermingle them. Heaven stays heaven and earth stays earth. It is this passive approach to spiritual development which has led to the distorted belief that the goal of growth is to escape the earth. If earth is not being improved, and we gain access to heaven, who would not leave earth and move to heaven? But there is a better alternative: bring heaven to earth.

This blending is not difficult, and can be accomplished in meditative reflection.

The knowledge of the soul, focused in the abstract mental plane, is directed into the inherent energy of the etheric form, awakening it and moving it to intelligent action.

The love of the soul, focused in the buddhic plane, is directed into the inherent energy of the astral form, awakening it and moving it to compassionate self-expression.

The will of the soul to make life sacred, focused in the atmic plane, is directed into the inherent energy of the mental form, awakening it and moving it to service of the divine plan.

The light of the soul, focused in consciousness, is directed into the inherent energy of the personality—consciously, subconsciously, and unconsciously—awakening it and moving it to creative mastery.

If this basic relationship between the occult and the mundane is kept in perspective, the countless details and facts concerning this science will begin to make sense.

As a practical exercise, it can be useful to reflect on how well we blend the awakened light of form with the light of consciousness in our primary activities:

- Our work.
- Parenting.
- Spiritual growth.
- Our recreation.
- Art.
- Music.

In parenting, for instance, what would be the awakened light or potential light of the form? What would be the light of consciousness? What does it mean in practical terms to blend these? Answering questions such as these can stretch our mind and our understanding, and put the issue of kundalini and energy into a much more wholesome context.

26. **Intuitive investigation of the multidimensional radiance of the sun's emanation will lead the aspirant to an understanding of the seven worlds of creation.**

The philosophical implications of this instruction are immense and well worth considering. It is said, for example, that the seven planes of creation in our solar system are but the seven subplanes of the cosmic physical plane. In this sense, the creative emanation with which we deal comes from a source greater than our consciousness can comprehend. But as valuable as such philosophical ponderings may be, it should also be realized that there is a very practical reason why this instruction is inserted in the text at this point.

The creative individual must recognize the true source of his creative inspiration, power, and purpose (symbolized here by the sun), and strive always to work consistently with this source. If he does not, he will become sidetracked into irrelevancies.

Moreover, as he tries to manifest this creative inspiration, power, and purpose, he must respect the seven steps it must be brought through in order to make a full appearance on the physical plane. He cannot instantaneously precipitate a creative idea from the highest level to the lowest. God does not operate in this way, and neither can we. Instead, we must see the relevance of nurturing a creative project through each of the seven planes, from highest to lowest.

The Logoic. Obviously, we have no creative interaction at this level; it is God Who brings through the creative emanation and gathers it logoically. This provides the creative spark for the entire solar system.

The Monadic. Only the highest initiates work consciously at this level, but the Monad of each human is the true creative master, responsive to the creative impulse of God and Father to the Son.

The highest, most powerful level of human creativity is that which involves the Monad.

The Atmic. At this level, the creative impulse stirs the will to act and draws to it appropriate archetypal forces.

The Buddhic. The creative impulse is defined in terms of the divine ideals to be expressed and the growth that will occur. Inspiration is released.

The Mental. Definite patterns and plans for manifestation are generated, first at the abstract, archetypal level and then at the concrete, intellectual level. Details take shape, proper timing is determined, and specific ideas unfold.

The Astral. The receptivity of the world to this new creative impulse is prepared. Anticipation, eagerness to cooperate, and adoration of the ideal are focused so that the climate will be as receptive as possible.

The Physical. Etheric substance is gathered and a network or framework for manifestation is assembled. The form emerges.

To work in this way, we must gradually learn to focus ourselves on each of these planes, especially the lower five, and to do so simultaneously, so that we can embrace the spectrum of creativity in a single thought. This is not difficult, but it does require patient practice. In working with the higher planes, however, it is always important to keep in mind that the soul must be used as a "clearing house" for translating ideas, forces, and patterns contacted at these levels. There is a temptation for some to try to bypass the soul and work directly at atmic or Monadic levels. This cannot be done. The soul is the central spiritual reality of our life, and must be the focal point of all of our meditative and intuitive work.

27. Correct investigation of the mother aspect of God will lead the aspirant to the ability to create and sustain forms intelligently.

Having studied and come to some understanding of the nature of divine creativity, and the role we can play in the divine drama, we now turn our attention to the nature of human creativity, which occurs primarily in the three worlds of form.

It should be understood that human creativity is but a pale reflection of divine creativity. We deal with forms. We do not create new substance or even new life forms; our challenge lies primarily in taking the resources of earth and discovering new and more important uses or applications for them. As a result, our creative efforts involve the Mother aspect of God far more than the Father. They involve the form aspect more than the life aspect, while embodying the aspect of quality (consciousness).

The division of divine life into Father, Mother, and Son is *not* sexist; it reveals something very important about divine expression—and human expression as well. Whether we happen to occupy a masculine or a feminine body, we are meant to express both masculine and feminine characteristics. Esoterically, the masculine characteristics are active, creative, and penetrating; feminine characteristics are responsive, intuitive, and absorbing. The aspirant learns to be equally comfortable with both kinds of expression. The person who espouses "maleness" or "feminism" at the expense of the other is generally not far advanced on the spiritual path.

It must also be understood here that the Mother aspect of God is not matter or form itself—it is the part of divine life which specializes in manifesting through form. As we study the archetypal patterns of manifesting through form, therefore, we become acquainted with the Mother. We also learn some of the most important lessons of creative mastery. The primary archetypal patterns to be investigated in this regard include:

Order. We are familiar with ordinary expressions of organization, efficiency, and planning, of course, but we still need to learn that in order to become creative at the divine level, we must learn to work with the structure and order inherent in archetypal patterns.

Harmony. Life depends upon the maintenance of balance between cause and effect and other polar opposites, ultimately producing harmony rather than discord.

Reproduction. The aim of human creativity is to reproduce the life and light of consciousness as fully as possible in the world of form. To accomplish this, it is necessary that forms have means for reproduction—for example, the skilled, creative mind. The creative master must have a full and rational understanding of this principle.

Productivity. Forms must serve their function, or they are not worth sustaining.

Abundance. The Mother is responsible not just for sustaining life in forms, but also for creating abundance. This is not personal abundance for the gratification of selfish greed, but abundance in light. It is produced through creativity, genius, and inspired service. There can be no genuine creativity without a full understanding of the principle of abundance. This is a point worth contemplating.

As should be obvious, this instruction opens up a huge realm for intuitive investigation. It is the study of the receptivity of divine life and how to harness it for the work of redemption.

28. The esoteric investigation of the "five-pointed star" will lead the aspirant to a complete knowledge of the distribution of energy.

It is important to keep in mind that this current sequence of instructions is profoundly symbolic, dealing not only with the network of force centers in the human system but also with the major centers within the solar system—and every organized system in between. The choice of the term "five-pointed star" is therefore intentionally figurative, not literal. It pertains far more to function than to appearance or description—to the fifth principle and the activities of the fifth ray, the work of the son of mind. In some translations, it is referred to as "the Pole star"; in others, "the fixed star." The basic idea is that in any system, one center serves as "headquarters" for the distribution of energy throughout the entire system. In the human network, it is the center located just in front of the forehead.

This instruction tells us that investigation of this key center will give us complete knowledge of the proper distribution of energy throughout any given system. This is invaluable to anyone seeking creative mastery.

• It permits the aspirant to gain control of the energies flowing through his own personal system, and to bring all of the centers to full activity and balance. This is a key not only to health but also to the development of many of the extraordinary skills that advanced disciples tend to manifest.

• It permits the enlightened leader to harness the energies flowing through the group he leads, be it a business, a movement, or a nation. The type of leadership demonstrated by a Winston Churchill is not just an example of outstanding charisma (which all too often is the only quality some leaders possess); it is a dynamic example of what a true leader can do with the proper esoteric skills and knowledge.

• It enables the conventional scientist to grasp the principles of occult science, when he or she reaches the point where the answers of conventional science have been exhausted. The most obvious application of this instruction is to the study of astrology, where direct intuitive examination of the flow of zodiacal energies throughout the system can lead to tremendous insight, as detailed in *Forces of the Zodiac*. But it has similar applications to every branch of science.

29. Intuitive investigation of the center of self-expression will lead the aspirant to knowledge of motivation and the quality of life.

Self-expression is the object of every form. To achieve self-expression, some type of energy must be directed through the form, colored by personality or character, and then expressed in harmony with the dominant quality of life. In the aspirant, the energy which animates the form is primarily of divine origin, even though it still may be highly colored by ancient patterns which are not divine. In the average person, however, the energy which animates the form may be nothing more than selfish desire, colored by the dominant characteristics of mass consciousness.

All of the force centers contribute to self-expression, but the one which is most directly involved, especially for the average person, is the solar plexus. It is the energy pouring through this particular center which activates our patterns of habit, instinct, and character. It is also through this center that access to the subconscious and mass consciousness is primarily gained. In some people, the examination of the solar plexus will reveal the dominant influence of another center—for example, the sacral center in a highly materialistic individual, or the heart center in a very devout person—but it is still the solar plexus which manages and coordinates these energies.

As a result, the right investigation of the solar plexus (of an individual, a nation, or a solar system) can reveal a great deal about the motivation of that entity, as well as the quality of life. It can give a quick picture of the nature of its self-expression.

Nevertheless, it is important to investigate this center with care. The careless investigator is likely to tune into patterns which are best left untouched—the fantasies of mass consciousness, images of fear, and so on. The first step in studying this center, therefore, should be to put it in the context of the other major force centers. These are, from the lowest to the highest:

1. The base of the spine.
2. The sacral center.
3. The solar plexus.
4. The heart.
5. The throat.
6. The front of the forehead.
7. The crown (at the top of the head).

The lower three centers are so closely aligned with the sensory nature of man that it is only possible to study the divine life which ought to pour through them if we examine them in the perspective of the other four centers. The function of the solar plexus, for instance, can best be understood in the context of lifting its energies up into the heart, transmuting them with love. This would be the transmutation of desire and feeling into love—one of the goals of true self-expression. It is best accomplished by contemplating the ideal expression of each of the three bodies of form:

- The ideal expression of the mind is wisdom.
- The ideal expression of the emotions is compassion.
- The ideal expression of the physical body is productivity.

To achieve this ideal expression, the daily conscious and subconscious activity of self-expression—of each of the three bodies—must be carefully monitored. Improper expressions should be patiently revised and the ideal reinforced. New skills in each of the three expressions should be learned. Proper archetypal forces should be invoked and focused. The resistance of past habits and tendencies should be dissolved, so they no longer control.

None of this work requires the ability to focus consciousness in the solar plexus; as mentioned earlier, it is actually more desirable to lift our energies from the solar plexus to the heart. The work just outlined will do not only this, but will also enable the aspirant to lift the energies of the sacral center into the throat, thereby enhancing creativity, and the energies at the base of the spine to the head. But once the basic lessons of mental housecleaning and self-expression have been mastered, then the aspirant can gain much knowledge of the larger implications of this work by carefully examining the functioning of the solar plexus and the quality of energies which flow through it.

It should be added that as the aspirant advances along the path, the solar plexus will no longer be the dominant center of self-expression. It will become one of the higher centers—the heart, in most cases, but possibly the throat, the brow, or the crown. By ascertaining which center is now the focus of self-expression, and knowing the kinds of energies which characterize each center, it is possible to learn a great deal about the motivation, dedication, advancement, and quality of the aspirant. This will only be the case for aspirants of advanced degree, however.

30. Investigation of the throat center will lead the aspirant to a new level of creative inspiration.

The standard commentaries discuss this instruction in terms of enabling the aspirant to conquer all hunger and thirst. To Hindus of ten thousand years ago, this was probably a dramatic goal. But the modern aspirant who has reached the stage of creative mastery ought to have his or her desires, hunger, and thirst well under control.

As the energies of the solar plexus are lifted into the heart, those of the sacral center are lifted into the throat, and those of the base of the spine are lifted into the head, a powerful transformation occurs. The head, throat, and heart become the three major centers of the body. The throat center assumes special importance because of its location at the top of the spine. Being the intermediary between the upper and the lower, it therefore becomes the major center for coordinating creative inspiration and its application.

Activity in the throat center indicates that the mental body is being organized, and the aspirant is becoming responsive to the inspiration of the soul. The throat is often one of the first of the higher centers to become activated. The stirring of activity in this center indicates there will be a renewed need for discipline and restraint. Indeed, the advanced aspirant, working creatively, frequently encounters problems which parallel the earlier problems of hunger and thirst. As creative inspiration and mental energy pour into his or her awareness, they will stimulate all aspects of the system. This can reactivate desires and lusts which the aspirant had thought to be conquered long ago—as well as counterparts on the mental level. Even more discouragingly, these "born again" longings are stronger than ever before. This is not a bad case of backsliding, however. It is the predictable result of subjecting the system to much greater energy than ever before.

As the throat center becomes organized and fully activated, it is able to regulate and coordinate these energies and forces, thereby reestablishing control of the creative process.

31. Self-control in the use of creative energies will lead to steadfastness.

The person who is focused in the lower force centers is reactive

246

and at the mercy of whim. As we lift our focus into the higher centers, our reactiveness is cleansed and replaced by steadfastness, courage, and dedication—an immovable measure of goodwill and benevolence.

This is an instruction of great hope, for nothing plagues humanity more than fear and superstition—the reactiveness of an astral focus. Yet as Franklin Delano Roosevelt put it, "There is nothing to fear but fear itself." As we discover the quality of spiritual force which flows into the upper centers, we see fear for what it is—an illusion. We know that as long as we are working with the forces of divine creativity, we will be filled with strength and devotion, and we need not fear. Indeed, we will have the strength to cast out fear.

Steadfastness is one of the prime characteristics of creative mastery. Taking on the responsibility to introduce new ideas, qualities, or possibilities to humanity exposes us immediately to rejection, criticism, and perhaps even prosecution. Steadfastness is the inner quality which protects us from such reactiveness and enables us to continue pursuing our goal. It continually reminds us of and helps us stay identified with our creative purpose. In this way, it helps us stand in the light and remain steadfast in our vision, our priorities, and our goals.

Esoterically, this quality of steadfastness is symbolized by the capacity of the human to stand upright, with the spine erect. The throat being the center at the top of the spine, it is the chakra most closely associated with this capacity.

As with the other instructions in this sequence, however, this one also applies to groups, nations, and solar systems. Meditation on the higher purposes of any system reveals that which will hold it together.

32. The person who has achieved creative mastery can be known and contacted by the light within his or her head.

There are any number of people on the planet today who claim to be spiritual leaders. Some of them undoubtedly are; there are always enough real leaders to meet the needs of real aspirants. But many of the self-professed leaders are nothing more than charlatans in robes.

How does one tell who is a spiritual leader—a creative master—and who is not? By intuitively examining the quality and presence of light in his or her head. Under this criterion, many of the best-known and most widely adulated leaders would fail miserably. Upon direct intuitive observation, it becomes obvious that in many of these people, the only "light" they radiate emanates from the sacral center—not the head! Indeed, it is not even necessary to meet these people personally to discover this—often, just picking up a book they have written or a tape they have recorded will be enough to reveal their orientation.

In others, there is a genuine dedication to the life of spirit, but the light is focused still in the solar plexus and the heart—it has not yet been lifted into the head. Such a person will often be saintly in attitude and impact, yet still fall short of creative mastery.

It should be noted that as the light within the head develops, it encompasses not just the two major centers, but also a set of subsidiary centers which come to represent the higher correspondence of all the lower force centers. These are the last centers to develop. When these centers are illuminated, therefore, it is a sign of spiritual dominance of the lower centers and their functions.

This instruction also indicates that as we awaken the light within the head, and make gains toward creative mastery, we gradually enter into the company of others who have achieved the same measure of illumination. In fact, there is a network of light which links aspirants of similar levels of development, and knowledge of this network becomes a part of the awareness of the individual as creative mastery unfolds.

Finally, this instruction gives us the key to making genuine contact with the Christ and others who have achieved mastery. But it must be understood that it must be the light within them that we contact, not just preconceived impressions about them (our own or someone else's). There are millions of thought-forms that have been created about any master or true spiritual leader; none of them has any substance. We must distinguish between these glamorized thought-forms and the genuine being.

33. Through the light within us, all things can be known.

This is a straightforward statement. As we become a full citizen in the kingdom of heaven, and are willingly governed at every level of our being by divine patterns and ideals, we gain full access to the range of divine thought. In this range—the divine plan—lies the ideal patterns for all manifestation, all things. Therefore, "all things can be known." And they can be known:

Fifth-dimensionally, as the patterns of all manifestation.

Six-dimensionally, as the motivating force behind manifestation.

Synthetically, in the context of the spiritual will which impels the archetypal forces of life to seek expression to the fullest extent of God's intent.

In other words, the light within us is the "missing link" between the microcosm and the macrocosm—between the finite and the infinite, the mundane and the spiritual, the individual and the universal. As we stretch our awareness into the higher dimensions of life, we discover light and learn that the light is within us. This is unity, the oneness of all life.

34. Right investigation of the heart will lead the aspirant to an awareness of his creative destiny and identity.

This is the final instruction in the sequence on the seven major centers and their use by the soul. It is interesting that it follows one which states that all things can be known through the light of consciousness. What can be greater than such knowledge?

This is an important question for the aspirant to consider, for it reveals much about the nature of archetypal life. It could be answered: *knowing what to do with it.* Investigation, even in the intuitive realms, must be followed by the digestion and application of the knowledge gained. Knowledge must be converted into wisdom. It must become *heartfelt understanding.* This has nothing to do with the emotions and the feelings. It means that we have taken the knowledge we have gained and blended it with the very fabric of our being. It has become a functional part of our identity and creative destiny.

To understand these issues—our identity and our creative destiny—we must consider the soul and the personality as a single unit. It is true that knowledge of one's soul ray or ashramic contacts can shed a great deal of light on these subjects, but these clues point more to potential than to actuality. It is only after substantial progress has been made in becoming a productive citizen of heaven, familiar with the creative divine forces, that a conscious intuitive awareness of the creative destiny begins to emerge. At this stage, two events occur:

• The aspirant begins to see the structure and beauty of all the earlier training he has undergone, in this life and earlier ones, leading toward this creative destiny.

• Without jeopardizing his own sense of identity, he is able to identify with groups, forms, and beings who can help him fulfill his creative destiny, and gain their cooperation.

It is through the heart that true knowledge of our connections with humanity and divine life is learned.

For those who automatically assume that the function of the heart center must be to express love, this commentary may seem odd, even foreign. But it must be understood that all of our life expression is meant to be dominated by love and compassion. The heart center will indeed be activated by a mature expression of spiritual love, but the primary quality associated with it is actually *purpose*. It is the center where the life cord is anchored. It is likewise the center through which group contact and group purpose is known, and is therefore our link with the Hierarchy and other spiritual groups. The proper keynotes for this center are therefore responsibility, sacrifice, and cooperation—not the standard sentiments of our feelings and emotions.

35. Meditation on the pairs of opposites instructs the aspirant in the value of the principle of duality in creativity. Gradually, he learns to spiritualize his creative assignments, not personalize them.

A simple example may lead to understanding. When a creative work is put on exhibition, there is generally a dual response: some like it and are inspired by it, while others dislike it and criticize it. If the creative person listens only to his fans, he may stagnate in his creative skills, because he hears nothing but praise. Conversely, if he listens only to his critics, he may well prostitute his inspiration, by endlessly modifying his work to please those who will not be pleased. What he needs is a proper balance of these opposites, drawing on the praise and support of those who appreciate his work to continue on, and heeding the relevant comments of the critics, so that he can truly improve the quality of his work.

The creative master will gradually become less affected by both praise and criticism, as far as his personal esteem is concerned; he will be able to evaluate these opposites objectively, because his creative work is motivated by the spiritual will, not personal ambition. But he continues to need and use the duality of life for his creative work.

The principle of reactiveness tells us that we cannot initiate any activity in the worlds of form without producing an opposite reaction to it. This is neither a moral principle nor a moral prohibition; it is just a statement of fact—and one we must learn to account for. The "opposition" is not really an obstacle, but more precisely a polar motivation. The creative person learns to harness this polar motivation and put it to work. Often, this is very simple to do. The force of opposing arguments, for example, can be undercut and redirected by addressing them at the same time the initial point is being made. The disapproval of others concerning the way we conduct our life or business can be neutralized by affirming our commitment to the ideals which guide us, and by giving this commitment a higher priority than the comments of others.

To master creativity, we must learn to anticipate and prepare for the distortions of our work, not just in the reactions by others but also in the unbalanced understanding and acceptance of the spiritual force being expressed.

It is interesting that this instruction follows immediately after the one recommending intuitive investigation of the heart. The effort to harness duality always leads, eventually, to the discovery of that which links the two poles. In the human system, it is ultimately the heart that links the higher and the lower, spirit and form. It could therefore be said that the link between the two opposites is the heart of the integrated whole.

Indeed, there are times when we feel alone, alienated from the soul and God, unable to make effective contact. This experience comes to us all, sooner or later. If, at these times, we will simply face the light within us and fill our heart with the love and life of God, being thankful for His gifts of life—His beauty, wisdom, and all of the treasures of heaven—then we can bridge this gap. We can heal the schism in our consciousness with the life essence and unity of God.

This is always the challenge to the creative master.

36. As a result of these investigations, the aspirant is able to perceive, sense, and interact with the life of heaven as readily as he can perceive, sense, and interact with the life of earth.

These perceptions, senses, and interactions, are of course, more subtle than what we experience physically (or what a psychic experiences astrally), but at the same time more powerful. They are a direct contact with the spiritual world. This transcends psychic perception and allows us to work intuitively without the need to translate abstract thoughts into concrete images and symbols. The major problem is one of familiarizing ourself with the "landscape" of the more abstract archetypal regions. Instead of being presented to us as forms, the life of heaven is presented as ideals, principles, qualities, and purposes. We must therefore develop skills in working with these abstractions and build a proper framework for making points of reference. This is one of the great values of pursuing a careful study of any mantic device based on fifth-dimensional thought, such as the I Ching, the Tarot, the Sabian symbols, or the Runes, or an occult science such as astrology or numerology. If used to pursue an understanding of the archetypal forces and their qualities, these systems can be a great tool for training the mind to think in the language of the archetypal and spiritual forces.

This is the easy part. The more difficult assignment is realizing that all of our standards, beliefs, values, and thoughts have been defined in terms of the earth, and must now be redefined in terms of heaven. We think of "purity," for example, in terms of forms, and what can and cannot be done with them. Yet the real issue of purity is always how cleanly and perfectly we can express any given spiritual force through form. As a result, it may actually vary from form to form—or from user to user.

We must leave behind the standards of earth and adopt those of heaven. This is the meaning behind the parable of the rich young man, who was told to give his possessions to charity and follow the Christ. We must give up our possessions of earth and claim our possessions of heaven. This has little to do with actual wealth or possessions—the strict interpretation, as usual, tends to trivialize the esoteric meaning. Instead, it deals with our standards and ways of approaching life. We must give our "ways of the world" to charity—transform them so they are based in generosity—and follow the soul as the sole authority in our life.

When we have learned this lesson, then our contact with the life of spirit will not only be direct, but also *balanced*.

37. The aspirant must take care, however, not to become captivated by these powers of perception and expression, which will seem magical to anyone not familiar with spiritual realities.

The person of genius, brilliance, and inspiration is to be respected, and it is important for those who have not yet achieved such levels of ability to honor the works of true genius and spiritual insight. But the aspirant must not allow such honor to unbalance him. What he has done is worthwhile, but nothing more than anyone with access to the realms of heaven would be expected to do. It is not he that is magical, but life itself.

To become engrossed in the power and impact that creativity can have in the worlds of form is to court disaster. Intoxication is, after all, intoxication, whether the intoxicant be liquor, drugs, or one's own creative or spiritual powers. It is useful to set before the public our perceptions of heaven, but if we expect our followers to believe in these perceptions as a show of faith in us, or because we are a "chosen one," we are abusing the responsibility which comes with our achievement. It is valuable to share our creative accomplishments with others, but if we pursue creativity because of the impression we can make, we are a spiritual fraud.

The instructions in Book Three are directed at helping us build the skills of creative mastery. These skills must be used responsibly and not given any unusual importance. This is just a matter of common sense. The skills of the astral plane are sometimes more significant than the skills of the physical plane, although not always. The skills of the mental plane are definitely more significant than the skills of the astral plane. But it is only at the level of divine archetypes that the skills we develop are spiritual skills. And even these are to be transcended when they become outmoded. If we view them as magical, however, we will be unable to leave them behind.

Indeed, if we become too distracted by the magical ways the life of consciousness can affect form, we will soon become "earthbound" and lose touch with heaven.

This instruction is a warning from Patanjali not to become unbalanced in our use of the skills of consciousness. It is one of the most clear and lucid statements in the entire text. Yet this has not stopped one of the more popular "transcendental" figures of our age from doing exactly what Patanjali has warned against—trying to teach the phenomenal skills of consciousness for magical purposes, without a proper grounding in the true workings of spirit. As a result, much damage has been done to unsuspecting followers.

38. **Mastery of the patterns of form results in the capacity to pass readily from body to body.**

People are sometimes amazed by the ability of chess masters to play fifty or more games simultaneously with aspiring chess players, winning them all. Often, they must make moves after glancing at the chess board for only a few seconds. Yet this capacity is not so stunning; these masters understand the patterns and fundamentals of the game so thoroughly that they can make quick judgments and take rapid action. In much the same way, the creative mastery of any discipline or study allows us to pass readily from project to project, from form to form.

With this instruction, we begin consideration of the "siddhis" or creative powers of the advanced aspirant. There has been much publicity given these siddhis in recent years, and certain meditative groups offer classes which purport to help the student develop these powers. But as we have seen in the last instruction, such emphasis on the value of these powers is actually contrary to the spirit of Patanjali's advice. The effort to cultivate these powers for their own sake will distract us from the real work to be done: perfecting the expression of spirit.

For this reason, we should shun the temptation to make wild interpretations of this instruction—for instance, seeing it as a justification for the theory of "walk ins." It is much more reasonable to interpret these instructions in terms of advanced creative work. Once the aspirant understands a true archetypal pattern, for instance, there is no limit to the number of forms he can express it through—or even the number of people in a field that he might be able to inspire.

There are other meanings to this instruction, of course. Each individual has five bodies: the dense physical form, the etheric body, the astral body, the mental body, and the causal body. As mastery of these bodies is attained, it becomes possible to shift the focus of attention quite rapidly from one form to the next. It even becomes possible to enter into "other bodies"—the body of the Christ, the body of an ashram, the body of planetary awareness, the body of a specific organization, and so on.

As long as we are acting at archetypal levels, we are in tune with all the forms which are legitimate manifestations of any particular archetype. We can therefore move rapidly from one body to another. At no time is it actually necessary to leave the physical body to do this; we act fifth-dimensionally.

39. Mastery of the impulse to grow results in freedom from the dangers of the water, the mire, and the thorny path, as well as the capacity to rise to greater heights.

This is an instruction which has probably generated more glamour and mischief among Patanjali's readers than any other. At one level, it can be read as an instruction on how to levitate, which in turn would give the aspirant the ability to walk on water, float over the thorny path, and speed across the mire. As a result, many Hindu aspirants have spent great measures of time trying to manipulate their vital energies and learn to levitate.

There are many well-documented cases of levitation. In the early days of the Quaker church in this country, it was not unheard of for a worshipper of unusual devotion to float up to a height of ten feet or so during a church service, then float gently back down to the pew at the end of the worship. More recently, there were many instances in the life of Padre Pio when he was seen levitating across the courtyard at his monastery. But it must be understood that levitation is no "trick" of the accomplished guru. It is a capacity

257

which unfolds as the result of strong and unbroken devotion to God. As the devotion or aspiration of the aspirant becomes so powerful that it literally lifts the whole of the individual's thoughts, emotions, habit, and character into heaven, it frequently has a corresponding effect on the etheric substance as well. This is the basis for the physical body levitating.

Levitation, therefore, should never be seen as an end in itself, or even as a skill to be worked at and perfected. This trivializes and mechanizes something much more powerful. Instead, it should be viewed as a symbol for the power of aspiration and the impulse to grow—a recognition that our love for God can be so strong that it can literally lift us to greater heights.

It is in this context that this instruction should be interpreted. The impulse to grow is to be used creatively, just like other spiritual forces. Unfortunately, most of us do not use the impulse to grow in a creative way. We let the processes of growth drag us along, perhaps, but we seldom become a master of it. We still get stuck in the mire or tripped up by the thorns on our path. We develop a "problem consciousness" and define our progress and growth in terms of the lessening of our woes, rather than an increase of divine life.

When we reverse this process, and start defining growth in terms of added measures of compassion, joy, wisdom, courage, and peace, then we begin to harness the power to grow. We become absorbed in the perfection of these divine forces and qualities, and they lift us above ourself, to greater heights.

40. Mastery of talent and skill results in the direct manifestation of the light within us.

The light of the soul does not shine directly through the personality but through the talents, skills, and achievements produced by the personality. The highest priority, therefore, should be given to the development of those talents and skills which will be useful to the soul and help it fulfill its creative destiny. Being pledged to the soul counts for little until we can translate this pledge into light.

Nonetheless, mastery implies that the soul is in control of the use of these talents and skills—that we are trying to glorify our Father through our achievements, not ourself. The person who becomes self-important, arrogant, and vain because of his many accomplishments is no master. He is more interested in putting himself on exhibit than in making legitimate creative contributions.

It should be the goal of every aspirant to try to acquire such talent and skill that whatever he or she does in the world glows with the light of divine life. This is not as far-fetched as it might seem at first. The works of a William Shakespeare or a Rembrandt glow with the light of divine inspiration, and the power of their flame has not diminished over the centuries. The contributions of an Albert Schweitzer are much more intangible, living now only as an example, yet they burn with the vigor of divine compassion and goodwill.

Once established, these skills and talents become a continual source of radiation, whether or not they are actively in use. A person with strong healing talents does not have to be deliberately engaged in a healing effort, in other words, for the light to shine forth from him. The light is there and radiating regardless of the focus of his outer consciousness.

The process of bringing heaven to earth and translating spiritual forces into inspired forms produces light on earth. This is a literal occurrence in etheric substance, and can be observed by all with eyes to see.

41. Mastery of resonance results in the capacity to hear spiritually and to create through the use of the Word.

The word resonance means "resounding"; it describes the way sound travels through any medium. Our physical ears are attuned to sounds created only by a limited band of cycles; they are normally unable to hear any sounds from outside that band, let alone from different planes of consciousness. As we become acquainted with the various levels of awareness, however, we can see how a given creative thought sounded at a spiritual level can be transferred into movement and action at the three levels of form. We also learn to expect that a sound encountered, for example, at the mental level, will probably have a creative counterpart at the buddhic level. By anticipating these resonances or echos, we gradually develop the ability to listen spiritually and to speak creatively.

The true skill of resonance is to create a form which is *responsive* to the archetype or divine pattern from which it evolved, and will remain responsive after the creative process is completed. By the same token, the key to spiritual listening is to learn to respond to divine guidance as the soul hears it—as opposed to responding to what we want to hear. To reach this level of creative mastery, we must not only purify and cleanse our own consciousness, so that it is devoid of all prejudice, personal preferences, and private preconceptions; we must also achieve mastery over mass consciousness, so that it no longer can influence our thinking without our registration of the fact. In addition, we must coordinate the subtle energies of our system so that they are attuned to or in harmony with the voice of our creative inspiration.

It might be added that this capacity for spiritual resonance has absolutely nothing to do with the modern fad of "channeling," in which the claim is made that the channel is in tune with a voice of great wisdom, usually a discarnate who lived several thousand years ago. Without even going into trance, the channel permits the discarnate to speak through him or her. This fad has led to the appearance of an incredible number of hoaxes—frauds who try to imitate a spiritual reality in order to impress gullible people.

In this context, it should be understood that the resonance described in this instruction does not even refer to clairaudience, let alone channeling. Clairaudience—the ability to hear astrally or mentally—is a legitimate psychic capacity, but we are not dealing with psychic skills in this text. We are dealing with their higher counterparts—the skills of the spiritual person.

42. Mastery of the pervasive nature of energy results in the capacity to create without the ordinary restrictions of time, space, and circumstance.

One of the most difficult steps for the aspirant is to overcome the limitations of finite thinking. Some people limit themselves by using the mind too literally, others by superstitiously giving their fears and worries too much importance. These are problems of being earthbound. Once we recognize that we have full access to heaven, we begin to learn to use the pervasiveness of energy as a tool of our creative work. We begin our creative work at the formless levels of spirit, which automatically means we are acting without the limits of time, space, and circumstance. As we bring our creative work into manifestation on earth, however, we will have to account for the usual restrictions. Yet we will tend to see their creative potential, not their limitations. This, in turn, gives us a whole new perspective on "restrictions."

• We come to realize that we do not actually have to travel through space to work with spiritual forces or use our intuition.

Any element of the universe can be brought into our perception by concentration. Astral travel or the so-called "soul travel" is a limitation of the fourth dimension—the only "distance" we need travel is compassed by stretching our awareness to embrace the wisdom of the soul. Because our consciousness pervades life, too, this distance is but a single step on the spiritual path.

• We do not have to do all the creative work by ourself, although it is necessary to be the prime initiator of the creative responsibilities we take on. There are many ways the automatic processes of the universe can be set to work for us, just as the physical body performs many vital functions automatically. It is up to us to discover these automatic processes and put them to work. A simple example would be the process of letting the universe correct certain injustices, rather than exhaust ourself in seeking revenge.

• The future can be known, thereby enabling us to guide our creative activity through possible obstacles and capitalize on new developments on the horizon. If we rise to a point where we are working at formless levels, then we are able to understand ongoing trends and anticipate future developments, including these factors in our plans.

It is useful to train the mind to think in these more universal terms and not be limited by the little we know from our life in form. The greatest barriers to soul consciousness are the restrictions we place on ourself.

43. The limitations of the unenlightened state become the creative matrices of the master of light.

Limits do have their usefulness. We would not attend to our business on the physical plane if we continuously had access to the higher planes—at least the average person would not. And so blinders are built into the mechanism by the soul, so that the intended focus will be sustained. As growth occurs, the blinders are gradually removed, but not entirely. The true creative master recognizes that limits are still useful, in order to ground the abstract forces of his inspiration. But now the blinders do not blind; they help him sustain his vision and focus.

Paul talked about "a thorn in the flesh," to keep him from getting too proud. "About this thing," he writes in II Corinthians 8-10, "I have pleaded with the Lord three times for it to leave me, but he has said, 'My grace is enough for you: my power is at its best in weakness.' So I shall be very happy to make my weaknesses my special boast so that the power of Christ may stay over me, and that is why I am quite content with my weaknesses, and with insults, hardships, persecutions, and the agonies I go through for Christ's sake. For it is when I am weak that I am strong."

Like Paul, we should be wise, and learn to regard our weaknesses as emerging strengths—and in our strengths, see the residue of conquered weaknesses. Both our weaknesses and our strengths emerge from our impulse to grow, yet only the strength connects us with the life of spirit. As a result, we do not need to be defensive or apologetic about our weaknesses—or retreat from the weaknesses and foolishness of others. Of course, it is never desirable to merely redefine our weaknesses as strengths, and then dismiss the need to grow, as so many modern psychologists advocate. On the contrary, the creative master learns to use every variable of his life to serve his ultimate spiritual purposes. He can use defeat as well as triumph, weakness as well as strength, because he acts not on his own behalf, but for the glory of God. Only the weak wear their weaknesses as medallions; competence is always the best defense against fools.

Simply put, we should expect the "master of light" to appear as an ordinary person—highly talented, to be sure, but very much a human being. The true magician seldom uses overt magic; the soul is not interested in staging a show. It has gone to great trouble to create the conventional channels of creativity, and it is through these conventional channels that most of the real magic is performed. If this idea is kept in mind, it will be possible to keep the notions of mastery and supernatural powers in balance with the practical work an aspirant must perform. Creating a spectacular shower of rose petals out of thin air is not nearly as impressive to the soul as is growing better roses.

In spite of this deliberate involvement with form, the aspirant has a great advantage over the ordinary person: he is able to observe the drama of the world with detachment and a spiritual perspective. The circumstances of life are nothing more than creative matrices through which to work; the aspirant's true home and interest is in heaven. He recognizes himself to be spirit in form—a discarnate clothed in incarnation—and while he is in meditation, it would be almost impossible for someone meeting him on the inner planes to know if he were incarnate or discarnate. His creative work serves his larger purpose; it does not bind or restrict him in any way.

44. There are five primary matrices through which each archetype or divine force is expressed in form: the plan, the intelligence, the character, the borrowed substance, and the appearance. These must all be mastered.

Not only must each of these matrices be mastered, but each must be patiently developed. The following can be stated:

The plan is the pattern or blueprint which is shaped in the mind, based on archetypal inspiration. It will either be sketchy or precise, depending on the level of the aspirant's mastery.

The intelligence refers to the skills and talents through which this expression can be made—including many aspects of intelligence which have "dropped below the threshold." Indeed, one measure of this intelligence would be the degree to which we can perform a creative activity on "automatic pilot." A great pianist, for instance, does not have to think about what his fingers are doing—his practice and skill guarantee they will function properly. Instead, he can focus his attention on communing with the spiritual dimensions of the music. The same idea can be applied to non-human forms, too. The intelligence of a rose—its capacity to express archetypal beauty—would be quite advanced, while the intelligence of gravel would be less so.

The character is the individual's ability to translate the qualities of the soul into expression in form. It includes the accumulated wisdom of our experience, our temperament, our basic line of sustained interest, and our habitual focus of concern. The character of one variety of rose would differ somewhat from others, for example, even though the basic intelligence of all roses would be identical, it being an achievement of the species, not of individuals.

The borrowed substance is the material of the mental, astral, or etheric levels which must be gathered to make a creative manifestation in form. This substance is borrowed from the angelic kingdom and is made of elemental lives. Even our own physical, emotional, and mental bodies are borrowed substance.

The appearance is the actual manifestation of the form, at whatever level or levels that occurs.

It can be most informative to take any aspect of life or a project and plug it into this formula. For example, what would be the five matrices of the creative effort to express more joy or gracefulness in life? What would be the five creative matrices of teaching a child arithmetic? What would be the five creative matrices of pursuing a career? What would be the five creative matrices of leadership?

In answering these questions, it will quickly be seen that true growth, inspired by divine life, will create new expressions at all five levels. But much "growth" is not inspired; in these cases, the growth of one matrix is often at the expense of another. This is a clear sign that the ballyhooed progress is really counterproductive.

45. As this mastery is perfected, the aspirant attains the full power of archetypal skills.

These skills, being skills of creativity, are developed through the interplay of the pairs of opposites. Therefore, they can be best defined in terms of five sets of seeming opposites. The skills, of course, when properly developed, actually balance the opposites. They are:

1. The power to work abstractly or concretely. This is the ability to work comfortably either in the abstract mode of universal concerns and energies or in the concrete mode of the individual.

2. The power to renounce and to redeem. Renunciation is the active demonstration that we are not controlled by form. Redemption is the transformation of the character of any form so that it becomes more responsive to the light.

3. The power to nurture and to harvest. This is the ability to feed, inspire, and teach—or, as appropriate, to consummate, judge, and reap.

4. The power to create and destroy. This is the ability to build new forms or destroy old ones which obstruct the new.

5. The power to invoke and to respond. This is the ability to call on the life and patterns of the divine archetypes as needed, while being able to respond fully, free of convention and preconception, to the evocation of the soul.

46. Glory, beauty, nobility, and joy constitute the power to respond.

In the creative master, the acts of the physical body bring glory to the Father of all creation. The expression of the emotions fills life with beauty. The wisdom of the mind is a constant tribute to the nobility of the human disciple. And the integrated, enlightened personality acts always with the joy of the soul. These qualities do not emerge out of the nature of form, but rather through year after year of training to respond to the true nature of divine life.

47. Liberation from the senses occurs as we master their reliability, their function, their sense of personality, their universality, and their purpose, both at outer and inner levels.

This instruction is something of a conclusion to the sequence which began with instruction 36. A parallel was established there between sensing and acting at the level of heaven and sensing and acting on earth. This was followed by five instructions which depicted, in essence, the five "senses" employed in working at the level of spirit. These, in turn, led to the development of the ten skills. We now are presented with an instruction which indicates how to use our archetypal senses and enlightened skills to gain liberation from the conventional restrictions of the senses.

There are two elements to consider in dealing with our senses: first, the physical sense itself, such as taste or hearing; and second, the subconscious mechanism which interprets the sensation and relays on to our conscious mind its meaning and significance. Of the two, the second is the more important. We can have perfect vision, after all, and still distort the meaning of what we see. Or we can be deaf, and still "hear" the inner voice of spiritual guidance better than someone else who enjoys perfect hearing.

It is the subconscious mechanism of sensation that we need to connect with the archetypal patterns, and thereby gain liberation. In essence, we need to teach each sense to discern and respond to glory, beauty, nobility, and joy—so that not only can we accurately discern these qualities when encountered, but also so we can saturate our whole awareness with them on command. To put this poetically, we need to train our eyes to see divine beauty, our ears to hear harmony, our palate to taste joy, our sense of smell to discern nobility, and our sense of touch to feel the benevolence of life.

Patanjali tells us there are five aspects of each sense which must be mastered in order to gain this level of liberation:

1. Its reliability. Our physical senses tend to deteriorate as the body ages, and many never reach their full potential in any event. An oenologist, for example, will develop his or her sense of taste and smell to far greater levels than the average person. In terms of the inner sense mechanism, the issue of reliability is even more critical. What have we trained ourself to pay attention to? Are we sloppy in our use of our sensory tools, or exceedingly accurate? Do we register fine details at the expense of the overview, or do we excell at observing the general mood and tone but overlook specifics?

2. Its function. Ideally, each of the physical senses and its subconscious mechanism is meant to be the outer tip of a continuous system for perception, beginning at spiritual levels and descending into the concrete physical plane. The function of hearing, therefore, is not just to hear what is said to us physically and background noises which may affect us. It covers a much wider range than that. As we listen to what others say, for example, we should be listening with our clairaudient and intuitive senses as well, examining whether their inner character agrees with what the outer person is saying—and what the spiritual essence within them would say.

3. Its sense of personality. It is amazing how quickly our senses conform to what is perceived to be the convenience of the personality. The eyes simply do not see what would be disturbing to the personality; the ears do not hear. In some instances, this condition leads to denial, suppression, and represssion, all in the name of protecting the stability of the personality.

4. Its universality. Our physical senses to some degree, and our subconscious sense mechanisms to a very large degree, are plugged into mass consciousness. There is a subtle but highly pervasive conditioning of our senses that goes on at the level of mass consciousness. The aspirant must examine these influences in great detail and liberate himself from them in order to achieve mastery.

5. Its purpose. Ultimately, the purpose of any sense is to be able to perceive—and reveal—the presence of light on earth.

It should be added that with liberation, the master begins to view the senses as active organs, not merely means of perception. The sense of touch is used to support, to heal, and to bless. The sense of sight is used to envision and to direct light into the earth plane. Sound is used to invoke, to direct, and to command. Fragrances are used to protect, to preserve, and to uplift. Taste provides a basis for communion.

48. The aspirant who has learned to act with divine forces can think instantaneously, independently of sensory perception, and with mastery of substance.

This instruction again reveals to us something of the nature of consciousness. Through the archetypal force of order, the intelligence of consciousness is able to operate like a huge computer, processing data, options, and calculations instantaneously. The more the aspirant becomes familiar with these levels of thought, the more he consciously acquires the ability to think in this way. Indeed, as this talent develops, there is a corresponding change in the etheric system. It is transformed to the point where it almost begins to "think." It undergoes a complete rewiring and assumes a new function, very much like a sounding board for the mind. In turn, the nervous system of the dense physical body becomes an extension of the brain; the whole system literally becomes illuminated with the light of intelligence. This opens up the possiblity of far greater *conscious* expression of intelligence. In essence, direct awareness of the intelligence of the soul or higher mind is achieved. To some degree, the limitations of the mental and astral bodies are bypassed so that the thoughts of the soul can be registered without distortion or delay. To put this in conventional terms, the practical IQ of such a person would probably be 2,500.

True objectivity is obtained. The feeling aspect and reactiveness of the astral body become dormant; instead, the emotions are used as a vehicle for expressing buddhic qualities and practical helpfulness. Perceptions are made primarily on an intuitive level, rather than through the senses of form.

The mind learns how to interact with substance and impregnate it with the patterns and life of consciousness.

In each of these three respects, the key is the aspirant's increasing capacity to work multidimensionally.

49. When the aspirant can also discriminate between soul and spirit, he attains mastery even of the divine archetypes and enters into omniscience.

The Monad is the true creative master, able to create not just in form but directly in the realm of archetypes itself. It is not our purpose in this text to study this level of creativity, but the following comments can be made.

There are three creative fires we can deal with: fire by friction, solar fire, and electric fire. They are all used for creative tasks; fire by friction is the creative fire of form, solar fire is the creative fire of the soul, and electric fire is the creative fire of the Monad. Each involves a greater degree of skill, control, and power, leading to full creative achievement. These three degrees could be called *competence, mastery,* and *supremacy.* In these three words, the whole range of the human creative experience is summed up. It should be understood that competence, mastery, and supremacy are the only vehicles we have for bringing the light of God into expression on earth. Loving humanity is not enough—it can all too easily degenerate into just feeling good about humanity. We must blend our love with competence and mastery. Then it becomes a tremendous force.

We do not achieve spirituality by being sloppy or careless. We achieve it by caring about the quality of what we do, helping others, and supporting the work of God on earth. We achieve it by celebrating the best there is, whether we find it within ourself, within others, or within God. And when we encounter something less than the best, we seek to redeem it and help it grow into the best, the supreme.

God is the best there is, the supreme. To discriminate even between the soul and spirit, we must embrace the distinction between mastery and supremacy. And this must infuse the whole of our life.

When it does, then we enter into the omniscience which is God, and share fully in His perfect knowledge.

50. The aspirant thereby attains full enlightenment.

He not only is light and able to express light fully, but he is also able to control and focus the expression of light, from the perspective of spirit. This is the highest state of enlightenment.

At this stage, the motives of the aspirant have become the motives of light. His struggles are the struggles of light. His triumphs are the triumphs of light. And yet, he preserves the true characteristics of individuality. He has specific responsibilities and assignments. He is trusted to work out his expression of the plan of God through his own talents, skills, intelligence, and resources. He has full freedom to make decisions and choices. Yet he chooses always to serve the light.

Still, this is not a static plateau. As indicated in the previous instruction, he is aware of an even greater source of life within himself than light. This is the spirit or Monad. "Full enlightenment," therefore, implies that the aspirant becomes aware of the next step before him in spiritual unfoldment. In addition, he not only serves the divine plan, but actually adds to it through his contributions.

Far from reaching the end of spiritual growth, he has reached the beginning of the road of light.

51. But this attainment is genuine only if all temptations are truly mastered, for the principle of duality remains active.

As long as we are involved in creative work—and everyone serving God's plan, at any level of development, is—we are continually involved with duality, with temptation, and with evil. The temptations become more subtle as we advance and become more triumphant over glamour and illusion, but they do not disappear. Indeed, because the scope of our responsiveness and responsibility increases, coping with the imperfection and evil of the world becomes more and more of a problem.

We are not playing games; we are serving the plan of God. Part of this plan is to illumine the shadows of the earth. One does not illumine the shadows of the earth from some luminous "safe spot" high in the upper realms of heaven. To bear light, one must walk in the shadows. Therefore, temptation is ever present.

Of course, the creative master also realizes that God's light is ever present, and a good deal stronger than evil or imperfection. So he continues to walk in the light, even as he passes through the shadows. This is the one sure protection against temptation and evil.

One of the great challenges to all aspirants, in fact, is to learn that the divine forces and archetypes *are* stronger than our problems and temptations. What is weak tends to be our *connection* with light, and our willingness to rely on it. To be an agent of light, we must learn to activate it. This does not happen just by believing. We must practice invoking, focusing, and expressing these qualities, repeatedly—to solve problems, to master temptations, and to eradicate evil. Indeed, regardless of our level of development, we should make it a daily habit to dwell at least briefly in God's benevolence:

The power of divine intelligence to eliminate our confusion.

The strength of divine love and goodwill to neutralize our irritations and fears.

The ability of divine joy to dispel depression.

The capacity of light to overpower darkness.

The more advanced we become, the more important it is to make this a daily habit.

52. True wisdom accepts duality as a basic principle of crea-

tive life and learns to discriminate between the creative impulse and its results. It also learns to view time in this perspective.

There is a strong suggestion in the thought-form surrounding this instruction that one of the primary ways the creative master can still succumb to temptation and evil is through impatience. There is a tendency among aspirants of every degree to want to push humanity through the paces of its growth—and to become disillusioned when humanity fails to respond to their great effort. To guard against this temptation, we must learn to embrace the broad scope of time God has set aside for the completion of His plan (eternity) while simultaneously discerning:

1. The next step forward for humanity as a whole.

2. The next step forward for the spiritual vanguard of humanity.

3. The next step forward for us individually.

Often, the spiritual leader must plant seeds which will not bear fruit for hundreds of years, even thousands. This can be clearly seen in the work of the Christ. But the time frame in which these seeds will grow in the soil of humanity is known in advance; there is no illusion. It is a situation which is entirely different from that of many aspirants, who simply act out of step with the true plan for human unfoldment. A great deal of nonsense is the typical result—nothing creative.

It may be helpful to understand that "discrimination" tends to mean different things for people at differing levels of development.

To the astrally oriented person, discrimination is primarily a choice between right and wrong. As a result, the aspirant is frequently confused, because what seems to be right in one circumstance may appear to be wrong in another. Actually, it is a wholly unsatisfactory way to approach discrimination, because our perceptions of "right" and "wrong" tend to be highly personal. It is this focus which fuels religious wars, fanaticism, competitiveness, and nationalism.

To the mentally oriented person, discrimination is more a choice between what works and what does not work—between what is effective and what is ineffective. This clears up many issues and conflicts, but again can be a source of great confusion, because there are frequently vast differences in effectiveness over the long and the short term.

To the spiritually oriented person, discrimination becomes a choice between what serves the plan of God and what does not. At this level, all confusion disappears and is replaced by clear understanding.

53. Creative mastery is the doorway between the life of heaven and our work on earth.

If we understand the creative design of humanity, we can then find heaven on earth through every new development which helps humanity grow—whether it is a personal achievement or an accomplishment of the whole race. We know what is involved in bringing heaven to earth. We understand the true drama of redemption and transformation. We can see the steadfast presence of divine life on earth, guiding, nurturing, and planting the seeds of ultimate perfection in every situation, no matter how desperate it might seem.

We will also understand that the term "creative mastery" is a broad one, covering many different activities, all of which serve the plan of God:

1. Healing.
2. Redemption.
3. Enlightened teaching.

4. Inspired creativity.
5. Enlightened leadership.
6. Service.
7. The building of right forms.

At this stage, the aspirant is not especially interested in his or her own personal growth or achievements. The stage shifts to the whole of humanity and civilization. Esoterically, the state of civilization at any point in time represents the level of growth humanity has reached in bringing heaven to earth. As we examine civilization, we can see pockets of light and excellence here and there—as well as a great deal that is still shrouded in darkness. By defining these areas of darkness in terms of what can be done to illuminate them, we can gain much insight into what the next step forward for humanity ought to be.

54. The aspirant is now able to work sixth-dimensionally.

Fourth-dimensional perception is the lower psychic state of the astral plane. It is filled with deception, delusion, and error, but if the aspirant proceeds intelligently, the valuable aspects of fourth-dimensional thought can be learned without too many drawbacks. This is done by focusing on the meaning of growth through time, the inner significance of experience, and the constructive uses of the phenomenon of projection.

Fifth-dimensional thinking is the higher psychic state of the mental plane, and the aspirant's first direct contact with archetypal patterns—although not all fifth-dimensional thinking touches the archetypes, by any means. It is learned by trying to conceptualize the full nature of any idea, by grasping the difference between a complete idea and a fragment of an idea, and by synthesizing groups of facts into common meanings.

Sixth-dimensional thinking is the true intuitive state of pure identification with divine ideals and forces. It is at this level that we discover in full our birthright—our potential for full creative mastery—as well as our unity with humanity as a group. It is the level of Christ consciousness. Sixth-dimensional thinking is learned by realizing that our identity is a living spark of light in "the One in whom we live and move and have our being." Communion is a ritual which is meant to be performed at the sixth dimension.

55. The goal of creative mastery is to work with perfect purity and harmony in serving the plan of God.

The instructions in Book Three have all been designed to bring us to this conclusion, where we are able to work with purity and harmony in serving the divine plan.

• The personality has been thoroughly purified, transformed, and trained.

• The soul has confronted ancient patterns within its own experience and that of humanity as a whole and replaced them with the ideal.

• The personality and the soul are fully integrated and able to work as companions.

• The aspirant works exclusively with the divine forces and archetypal ideals of heaven. He has assumed his rightful position in the Hierarchy. His primary motivation and interest lies in serving and supporting the plan of God.

The light within is fully ablaze and serves as a testimony to the intelligence, benevolence, and glory of divine life.

THE LIGHT OF THE WORLD

1. There are five doors to the inner levels of awareness: incarnation, drugs, hypnosis, the mystical love of God, and meditation. The first door is always open; the other four are closed. Of these, two are meant to be opened, two are meant to remain closed.

Book Four will endeavor to describe how the light within us fits within the larger scope of the light of the world. As a result, there is a shift in tone and emphasis which is apparent even in the opening instruction. Patanjali is no longer as concerned with the step by step unfoldment of the individual. He is more concerned that the individual aspirant recognize his or her responsibility to proceed wisely and maturely.

In using the phrase "the inner levels of awareness," Patanjali is not referring just to the consciousness of the soul; he is referring to all dimensions more subtle than the physical. This includes the psychic perceptions and sensations of the astral plane and lower mental plane, as well as the abstract intuitive perceptions of consciousness. It is quite possible to contact portions of the astral plane and the lower mental plane without any dedication to the soul—or any control from the level of the soul. This kind of contact, however, can be exceedingly dangerous, and may alienate the person even further from his or her spiritual heritage. *Any door that opens only to these particular levels, therefore, and not to the higher levels of consciousness, should be kept shut and strictly avoided.*

The first door, **incarnation**, is always open. This is a genuine path to spirit, no matter how much some spiritual elitists scorn it. Having taken on a physical body, we gradually discover that there are inner motives and forces which direct and guide this body. As we learn to recognize and identify with these inner forces, we pass through the door to inner awareness which is open to all of us—the sublimation of experience.

Many people think that incarnation closes the door on the inner realities, but this is just another example of the great illusion at work. Every night when we fall asleep, for instance, our awareness shifts, to one degree or another, to the inner dimensions. Even during our waking hours, the door remains far more open than we realize. Every good inspiration and every accurate hunch comes from some interior dimension—as does every fear and anxiety.

The second door, **drugs,** is meant to remain closed. It has been known for eons that certain drugs artificially establish contact with inner dimensions. But this is never any spiritual dimension—just the astral plane. In the vast majority of cases, in fact, it is the lower astral plane. Every such contact seriously warps our consciousness, distorts our perspective, and undermines our motivation. Some of the most tragic cases of birth defects and retardation can be traced back to serious drug abuse in earlier lives.

It is unfortunate that so many of the popular figures of the so-called "new age" have embraced the use of drugs—and have dredged up worn-out traditions to support their indulgence. Part of ushering in any new age involves purging the worst of the old traditions; these people, by contrast, are trying to enshrine these worn-out customs as a basis for the new age. Shamanism and other tribal practices are not meant to be any part of the new age; neither is the use of drugs.

The third door, **hypnosis,** is also meant to remain closed as a means for contact with the inner dimensions. This is not to imply that there are not valid uses of hypnosis in a clinical setting, any more than the preceding comments should be construed to reject the use of drugs for medicinal purposes. But if the goal is to open awareness to the inner dimensions, hypnosis and self-hypnosis are totally unsatisfactory, because they make contact only with the subconscious. They put the subconscious in control, blocking out any possible contact with the soul. Moreover, they have a tendency to render the person who is hypnotized passive, dependent on the guidance of the hypnotist; and subtly undermine the individuality of the subject. The same problem can also arise in the use of self-hypnosis and even certain forms of "positive thinking," especially if it leads to Godless, arrogant, and hysterical affirmations, rather than spiritual insight. People who have dabbled with hypnosis without a proper focus or control often become highly susceptible to brainwashing and the rape of the mind.

As a corollary, it might be added that the use of magical incantations to alter the focus of awareness is likewise taboo, for the same reasons. Actually, most forms of primitive magic, like voodoo, are dependent either on the use of drugs or a form of mind-numbing, hypnotic repetition of chanting to induce astral awareness. Nothing of spiritual value is ever gained by these practices, and the risk incurred is enormous. These practices are meant to be put behind us; they have no constructive role to play in the new age.

The fourth door, **the mystical love of God,** has long been the accepted method of consciously opening contact with the inner planes. It is pursued by building an ever-stronger devotion to and adoration for the qualities and ideals of divine life—God's love, joy, glory, wisdom, peace, forgiveness, and beauty. The shortcomings of this approach are that there is a tendency for aspirants using this method to become unnecessarily passive, and that most of them end up *only* loving God. They do not make contact with the wisdom and will of either God or the soul. Indeed, they often end up loving God more in the abstract than in the practical, immediate events of life.

The fifth door, **meditation,** is the recommended approach for the modern aspirant. However, it must be understood that there are many different forms of meditation. To be an effective tool of the life of spirit, the practice of meditation must be active; instead of just adoring the beauty of God, for instance, the meditator needs to find a way to put this beauty to work in his own life, through his attitudes, thoughts, feelings, or creative activity. Above all, it should be understood that the purpose of meditation is to make contact with the soul; to the degree that it also opens awareness to the astral and mental planes, these developments should be seen as steps toward ultimate contact with the soul. In addition, all efforts to explore the astral and mental levels should be conducted from the perspective and authority of the soul. In this way, the aspirant can avoid the traps and pitfalls of lower psychic perception.

A complete review of the practice of meditation can be found in *Active Meditation: The Western Tradition.*

2. The transfer of our focus of awareness from our lower bodies to the higher ones is part of the process of spiritual growth.

At first, this instruction seems to be so obvious and clear that one wonders why Patanjali even bothered to include it. But, as usual, he is stating more than the obvious; he is giving us a significant hint for accelerating spiritual growth. As we manage to lift the focus of our awareness to the next higher level and work stably from that perspective, we are able to control and master the energies and forces of the next lower level. In other words, if we are focused on the astral plane, as the majority of people currently are, we need to lift our focus to the mental plane, from which perspective we would be able to direct and control the energies and forces of the emotions. This is true even in the case of those who believe that the loving emotions are superior to the cold, critical mind. The emotions can be trained to love when controlled by the mind, but they are not loving by nature—by nature, they are reactive, instable, possessive, and defensive. Spiritual love—compassion, benevolence, and charity—is an expression of human maturity.

Implied in this instruction is the admonition that it is our responsibility, as a spiritual person, to seek always to work from the next higher level—to deliberately initiate growth, as it were. Indeed, this should be one of the first principles in the philosophy of all spiritual people. The great problems of humanity are the result of immaturity in the human community. There is a desperate need for people who will stand up and advocate responsible growth—who will show humanity how to look inward, to the next higher level, to find the solutions to its problems.

At present, humanity seeks to solve its problems primarily on the physical level. It redraws boundaries, signs treaties, and forms alliances. But it still misses the point. Where there is hatred and animosity, new boundaries cannot solve the problem. That is an attempt to solve problems rooted in the astral level through purely physical changes. It cannot work. Only a new spirit of goodwill and cooperation, rooted in the pragmatism of the mental and spiritual planes, can ultimately triumph.

3. It is not the mastery of the skills and talents of consciousness which causes consciousness to evolve, but the perfection of this mastery does prepare the way for light to shine in the world.

The key word in this instruction is "causes." Mastery of the skills and talents of consciousness is very much instrumental in the unfoldment of consciousness and the fulfillment of its purpose—but it is not the *cause* of this unfoldment and fulfillment. The cause is the divine creative impulse itself. At first, this distinction may seem to be a trifling one, but it is of great importance. The aspirant must learn to distinguish clearly between the actual causes of life on the one hand and the effects of those causes on the other.

On a personal level, we must realize that fulfilling the goals of consciousness is not a matter of personal choice; we are driven by the very force of evolution itself. Sooner or later, we must respond. If this seems unfair, it is an indication that we have a very shaky understanding of the soul and consciousness. We are excessively guided by our sensations, needs, and wants.

We need not activate the soul or the divine creative impulse; it is already awake. Our duty is to become more fully responsive to the life of spirit, and thereby activate our talents and skills in using consciousness. The central skills to be mastered can be classified as follows:

Atmic	Buddhic	Mental	Astral	Physical
Oneness	Communion	Civilization	Cooperation	Community
Expansion	Goodwill	Transformation	Tolerance	Responsibility
Intelligence	Comprehension	Discernment	Association	Coordination
Perfection	Integration	Discrimination	Imagination	Beauty
Realization	Intuition	Insight	Sensitivity	Sensation
Radiance	Idealism	Personality	Projection	Expression
Beatitude	Contemplation	Planning	Discipline	Building

Each of these labels describes a whole classification or set of skills which need to be developed. The person who learns to use these skills and talents prepares himself or herself to be an effective partner with the soul; the person who does not limits himself or herself to a very passive role in the spiritual arena.

4. The individualization of consciousness leads to the development of vehicles, skills, and talents through which light can be focused and expressed.

Just as sensation is often confused for consciousness, the concept of "personality" is often thought to be the same as "individuality." There is a world of difference. Individuality is the sense of selfhood of the soul; the soul's ability to state, "I am." Personality is the sense of selfhood of the lower self. Even when the individuality is focused in form, there is never any loss of awareness of its true nature and purpose. In this regard, it is something like the electricity stored in a battery; originally, part of a vast mass of undifferentiated electricity, this power has now been focused into a single battery, thereby making it useful. Yet its true nature still remains as electricity.

In much the same way, the soul is an individualized expression of consciousness. It creates a personality which can become aware of this individuality, but the true sense of individuality can only be discovered in the context of consciousness.

Indeed, the true basis of individuality in the human kingdom is the One Individual, the Christ. We are individually members of this One Individual. This arrangement in no way robs us of our own potential individuality; only a person still enmeshed in personality would think that. Rather, it greatly enhances our expression of individuality.

The height of individuality is the ability to express a full measure of the power, quality, and intelligence of a particular archetypal force through our well-trained and disciplined personality, without distortion, so that the light casts out the darkness.

A brilliant description of the principle of individuality is found in 1 Corinthians 12, where Paul states: "For just as the body is one and has many members, and all the members of the body, though many, are one body, so it is with the Christ. For by one Spirit we were all baptized into one body and all were made to drink of one Spirit."

We all were made to drink of one Spirit. This is our destiny—to individualize consciousness, produce vehicles and talents through which it can be expressed, and then attend to the labor of serving the light within us.

**5. Consciousness is One, even though the forms conscious-
ness generates are multiple and varied.**

The word "one" is not being used in the sense of counting here,
as though we held one apple in our right hand and three in our left.
Instead, it refers to the fact that consciousness is inclusive or syn-
thetic (synthesis being the process of drawing seemingly dissimilar
elements together and producing a common unity). As consciousness interacts with ideas, for example, it draws them together and
finds their common meaning, origin, and power. This characteristic
is built into consciousness; its very nature is to draw that which is
disparate into wholeness. In its highest level, therefore, consciousness is One, and it acts in this basic way at all levels, to one degree
or another.

To continue the analogy just used for individuality, consciousness is like electricity which can flow through the wires from a central generating station to the thousands of homes in a city. It runs
millions of toasters, television sets, vaccum cleaners, and personal
computers—and yet the electricity itself is one. It comes from a
single source and maintains the characteristics of this source. Consciousness is much the same.

Because consciousness is One, there is no risk in fragmenting itself and sending individual sparks of consciousness into manifestation as the multiple and varied expressions of form; the synthesizing nature of consciousness guarantees that they will be drawn
back together again into the perfect One. This, indeed, is the great
creative process, and the justification for the statement that light *is*
stronger than darkness; joy *is* stronger than sadness and grief;
wisdom *is* stronger than ignorance. These qualities are imbued with
the strength of Oneness, a most dynamic and powerful principle.

To work effectively with any finite expression of consciousness,
therefore, we must understand its higher correspondence to and

288

relationship with Oneness, and use this synthesizing principle to integrate it more fully with its intended destiny. To take any form or entity at face value, without accounting for its roots in Oneness, is tantamount to dealing blindly with it.

We must also see that all mental and emotional processes are but finite expressions or functions of this synthesizing characteristic of consciousness. Analysis and logic, for example, are highly useful concrete mental functions, but to understand them fully and realize their complete potential, they must be seen as branches of the One tree of consciousness. The imagination and sensitivity are useful astral functions, but again need to be seen as branches on the One tree.

Indeed, human psychology and the psychology of all form expressions must be viewed from the top down, from the Oneness of consciousness, or the effort to understand it will create nothing but confusion.

6. Those forms which are generated from a direct realization of Oneness will be perfect and will not be subject to the growth process of duality.

We have already seen that duality is an important facet of the process of creativity. While this instruction may seem to contradict this principle, it does not. More accurately, it completes the thought.

There comes a time in learning and refining any skill that perfection is achieved. At this point, there is a pure realization of how this skill contributes to the Oneness of life. From then on, any use of this skill results in the perfect fulfillment of the divine plan. It is not affected by duality.

As might be expected, there are not an overwhelming number

of examples that can be cited to explain this instruction. One of the best is the way in which Nikola Tesla was reported to have worked. Having been inspired by the divine patterns of electricity, Tesla would conceive a new machine to generate and transform it. He would then proceed to construct the machine, in full detail, in his mind, just as it would be in real life. When the model was finished, he would turn it on in his mind and let it run for three to six months—in his mind. He would then evaluate it for wear, redesign it, and test it again. When he finally built the machine physically, it would work perfectly the first time he turned it on.

It is important to realize that duality is not negated by this principle; rather, it is harnessed so well by our perfected skill that it does not generate difficulty.

Esoterically, it could be stated that this is a level of creativity focused at the atmic level. It usually does not produce results directly on the physical plane, but rather at the abstract levels of consciousness. It produces divine archetypes as well as the power to implement them in the physical plane perfectly.

In general, a person who is fully conscious at the level of the spiritual triad is able to act with this level of skill. They are able to make contributions to humanity without also saddling it with the imperfections and mistakes of misguided experiments.

7. There are three types of reactiveness which plunge awareness into darkness: materialism, selfishness, and ignorance.

The heart or center of all creation is the light of God. The further from the center we may be, the more the light diminishes. At the most distant points, darkness prevails. This is what the Bible refers to as "the outer darkness."

In instructions 6 and 7, we are given a portrait of extremes. The first gives a portrait of the spiritual man who is at one with the light within him. He acts without flaw. The second describes the process by which humans become estranged from God, and drift purposelessly into darkness.

The darkness of the physical plane is materialism. Materialism is the true condition of being earthbound, having such a strong attachment for the earth and the things of the earth that all thought, feeling, and action are determined by this obsession. When the darkness of materialism prevails, there is no understanding of light, except in physical terms. The soul is seen to be a silly concept; consciousness is held to be purely a manifestation of physical awareness.

The darkness of the astral plane is selfishness. In this condition, everything is personalized; the desires, feelings, and wishes of the individual become the focal point of his personal universe. Light may be recognized, but only because it makes the person feel better. All decisions are made based on this selfishness.

The darkness of the mental plane is ignorance. It manifests as bigotry, confusion, dogmatism, arrogance, and sophistry.

There are other problems of human behavior, of course, but they all tend to be produced through a combination of these three types of reactiveness. Envy, fear, malice, pessimism and their many brothers and sisters are all the offspring of these three conditions.

When all three types of darkness are found in the same person, it is a strong indication of a person who is oriented toward evil. He has dedicated himself to the glorification of darkness and reactiveness, and thereby has become anti-creative. He is indulging in deliberate imperfection, which is a denial of everything the soul is trying to accomplish.

Most people, however, do not pursue imperfection deliberately; they simply stumble into it. They fall. The light within them becomes obscured by materialism, selfishness, or ignorance. Bad habits are formed, leading eventually to one kind of addiction or another. But even though obscured, the light remains active, and gradually overpowers the darkness. Eventually, they stand back up, and once again honor the light. The soul understands this and treats the personality accordingly.

Only as the individual becomes quite advanced does the rejection of darkness become so strong that the reactive principle becomes neutralized. Even then, it is still active in mass consciousness and must therefore be accounted for by the individual, if he is to be effective.

The struggle with darkness is such a natural part of the life of the average person that it does not stand out. In the life of the advanced individual, however, it is consciously confronted. Such a person must be firmly focused in his or her heritage of light in order to handle these confrontations properly. It is therefore highly recommended that each aspirant learn as much as possible about light, its purpose, and its proper handling. It is likewise recommended that each aspirant clearly define for himself or herself the difference between light and darkness.

8. The measure of light within the seeds of our character determines the kinds of experiences which come to us. This is a direct result of the measure of light we have expressed in the past.

Once again, Patanjali brings up the issue of right action (karma). In some regards, it is a summary of what has been said before, but in other ways, it breaks new ground. The instruction makes clear that it is not what we have done which generates karmic effects, but how much or how little light we have expressed in doing it. This takes the issue of karma out of the moralistic arena of right or wrong and puts it into the spiritual arena of consciousness. It is consciousness—the measure of light we express—which determines the pattern of future growth and opportunity for us, not appearances.

Many people "do all the right things," but for all the wrong reasons. They are motivated primarily by materialism and selfishness, not light. Even though they may win the approval of friends and neighbors, they have not created the kinds of character seeds that draw in growth opportunities and rewards. The new seeds of character they have planted, to bear fruit in later times, have been colored primarily by their selfishness and materialism.

Another version of this problem is the spiritual devotee who serves and acts out of a sense of duty—but resents every moment of his or her "sacrifice." As a result, he fills himself with so much bitterness and resentment that there is no room left for light to enter in through his acts. His efforts truly are in vain.

As we grow in spiritual maturity, our attitude about karma or accountability changes. At first, it seems a threat to avoid; we refrain from hurting others because we fear the consequences. Later, we view it as a matter of harmony; if we are engaged in manipulating others and pursuing selfish goals, then how can we be on a wavelength of responsiveness to God? Eventually, we realize that the principle of right action is actually an expression of divine benevolence. If we err, we are given a full and complete opportunity to correct the mistake. As we act wisely, we are given the full support such action warrants.

This instruction makes a statement that ought to be seriously considered by all who want to understand the true workings of the human consciousness. Many modern philosophers believe we are largely shaped by the experiences of our life. Patanjali indicates it is just the reverse: our experiences in life are shaped by the seeds of

293

our character, which in turn were shaped by the way we acted upon, or reacted to, experiences in earlier times and lives. The experiences themselves are neutral, for one person may respond to a crisis with nobility and courage, thereby creating a seed of character which is filled with light; whereas another may respond to the same crisis with fear and bitterness, thereby creating a seed of character which sinks into darkness. The experience is the same; the karma is radically different.

Indeed, to fully understand the principle of right action or karma, we must put it in terms of accountability or responsibility. If we steal, we take on an eventual responsibility of helping or protecting those who are victims of theft. If we ridicule a certain class of people, we take on the eventual responsibility of defending their rights and worth as humans. There may be many lifetimes between the time that we err and the time we learn full responsibility, but the time does come eventually. The work of karma is not just to compensate "an eye for an eye." Its purpose is much more benevolent. Karma promotes right action. Until we learn right action, we are tied to the hardships and difficulties induced by our errors and mistakes.

As always, the soul is in control of the process of growth, and is able to use every resource available to it to consummate its goals—even the seeming failures of the personality. Slowly, it replaces the darkness of materialism with the light of the will to build. It fills the darkness of selfishness with the light of the will to heal. And it eradicates the darkness of ignorance with the light of the will to serve.

9. Darkness frequently obscures the patterns which govern growth, but these patterns are clearly seen in consciousness, at every level.

When we have difficulty perceiving a plan or pattern of consciousness—or a type of divine energy—the problem lies not in consciousness, but in us. We are still too submerged in darkness to see clearly. And yet, if we rise above this darkness and explore the archetypal realms of consciousness, the patterns will become visible and will be seen to be benevolent, intelligent, and inspired.

Because consciousness at its highest level is One, the patterns of consciousness are never interrupted. They can be obscured by materialism, selfishness, and ignorance at physical, emotional, and mental levels, but they are never interrupted. Their force and destiny are never broken. They remain continuous, ongoing.

As an example, if the soul has formulated a plan of action for its self-expression through form, this plan of action will carry on from experience to experience, from lifetime to lifetime, regardless of species, time, or place, until it reaches fruition. It may frequently be obscured by darkness in the mind and heart of the personality, but it remains intact, whole, and ongoing. In this regard, the soul is something like a painter who is trying to give perfect expression to a certain theme or ideal. This theme or ideal will appear repeatedly in many of the painter's works, possibly all of them, in different styles, periods, and subjects. Yet the paintings are all marvelously tied together by this common theme or ideal, and each contributes to the further perfection of the painter's skill and depth in expressing the theme. An unknowledgeable observer might criticize the painter for being repetitive, and mistake the growing light for darkness, but ignorant criticism never changes reality. Through the common theme, experimented with on many different canvases, the creative purpose of the painter is fulfilled. The true lover of art will recognize this, "at every level."

For the aspirant seeking to grow spiritually, it is very important to learn to recognize these patterns in his own character—which are, of course, the patterns of right action or karma. These are the patterns which carry and direct our inner impulse to grow; the more we cooperate with them, the more we will understand how and why we are growing. The problem is that few of us consciously co-operate with our karma or our impulse to grow. We spend our time making excuses and being defensive—in other words, doing everything we can to avoid examining these patterns and under-standing them.

The experiences of our life are the creative journal of the soul. As certain kinds of experiences repeat themselves, forming patterns, this is a clear revelation of some facet of our character. If the experiences are beneficial to us—if, for example, others are always eager to help when we experience an inconvenience—it is probably a sign that we are generous and helpful ourself. But if the experiences are limiting, restrictive, or embarrassing—if, for example, we are repeatedly being cheated or misled—it is probably a sign that we are dishonest, manipulative, or unscrupulous. By carefully examining these patterns and speculating on what they tell us about our character, we can learn a great deal about the soul's creative plan and what it means for us. As always, however, we must be careful not to deceive ourself. Some people carefully manage to *avoid* the conflicts and challenges of life, always with-drawing from their real opportunities to grow. If such a person examined the superficial lack of conflict in his life, he might easily conclude that he had mastered conflict. Actually, he has only mastered avoidance. Conflict will still be devastating.

Incidentally, these same kinds of patterns can be observed in groups, professions, nations, and even races. It is not just individuals who are governed by karma or right action; groups are as well. A good example of this in recent times would be the press, which, as it has grown in power, has become arrogant in its abuse of that power. There have been any number of circumstances over the past decade in which the press has been revealed to be not an elite group of professionals, as they like to present themselves, but a bunch of tasteless gossipers who have no capacity to discriminate between rumor and fact. Yet whenever the press shows any tendency to start to pay attention to this repeated pattern, one of the senior, most respected members of the corps will write a column that dismisses the whole problem with a set of stale excuses. The rest of the press issues a collective sigh of relief, and goes right back to its abuses and arrogance.

What the press fails to take into account is that there is an inner, spiritual force governing its activities, just as all of life is directed by an inner, spiritual force. And it intends to reform at least the worst of the abuses of the press. If the press would only cooperate with this campaign, the abuses could be cleaned up without any impairment of the press's ability to report the news. But if the press stubbornly refuses to cooperate, they may precipitate a situation which could endanger its freedoms. In such a case, we would all suffer an enormous loss, because of the pride of those who should care the most.

The need for an examined life is central to all spiritual growth. There is nothing sadder than someone who says, by his or her attitudes or acts, "I don't want to learn; I know enough."

10. The patterns of character have no known beginning.

Most people, of course, believe that the human character begins to take shape at the time of birth. A few farsighted individuals might extend the beginning to the time of conception. But in point of fact, the character of a newborn is well set at both the time of conception and birth. It is this character which, combined with the creative plan of the soul, largely determines the type and quality of experiences that will make up the child's life.

As surprising as it might be to some, it is not especially difficult for a well-trained clairvoyant to examine the patterns of character of a baby still in the womb and accurately predict the kind of lessons and events that he will be facing after birth. In making this examination, the clairvoyant may also become aware of specific events in earlier lives which helped shape these patterns. Nonetheless, it would be a mistake to assume that these patterns had their origin in these particular episodes. They, too, have their antecedents; the effort to find the true and absolute beginning of any pattern of character would either drive us mad—or lead us back to the beginning of divine creation!

The most constructive way the spiritual aspirant can deal with these patterns at any point in time is to seek to cooperate fully with the soul's power to promote growth in his present life experiences.

11. Any mental pattern giving rise to behavior or expression has been created by the interaction of the impulse to grow (the spiritual will), our response to it, our interest in it, and our ongoing support of it. When any of these elements is withdrawn, the mental pattern will become inactive.

This is a profound instruction. It gives us the key to transforming the basic structure or character of our personality, so that it better reflects the creative plans of the soul. In an age when changing hairdressers is thought by some to be a sign of a major transformation of personality, it may be difficult to appreciate the value of this instruction. Suffice it to say that unless change occurs in the structure of character, it will be a temporary change at best.

There are four elements contributing to any mental pattern:

The impulse to grow. This is the soul's intent to express itself through the personality in some ideal way.

Our response to it. This depends on our level of maturity. A highly immature person will reject the soul's intent and perhaps even rebel directly against it. The average person may want to co-operate with the soul's intent, but has his own preconceived ideas what this means. So he colors the intent and distorts it beyond recognition—or he trivializes it. The spiritual aspirant will strive to respond to the intent of the soul as fully as possible.

Our interest in it. The soul may be interested in us learning honesty, but we may still be quite enthralled by the web of deceit that we can spin, trapping others in it. For a while, our practice of deceit may even seem beneficial, thereby strengthening its value to us. As long as we are interested in maintaining a specific pattern of character, we will. It is only when we begin to realize that we have actually been creating problems for ourself through this deceit that our interest shifts from preserving the bad habit to removing it. Even then, it may be a long time before the new direction of our conscious intention is able to control established patterns in the subconscious.

This instruction also implies that sometimes we take the good elements of our character for granted, and lose interest in them. This can weaken them to the point where we can no longer rely on them.

Our ongoing support of it. We "nourish" the mental patterns of our character in thousands of subtle ways every day, through the attitudes we hold, the values we reinforce, the grudges we nurse, the habits we repeat, the words we speak, and in many other ways. We may decide, for example, that we want to improve our self-image, then turn around and discard all evidence of accomplishment and triumph. We are not supporting our intent to improve the quality of our self-image.

The real value of this instruction is the final sentence: "When any of these elements is withdrawn, the mental pattern will become inactive." These few words tell us all we need to know about putting a halt to any harmful pattern of character. Perhaps we have a tendency toward criticizing and condemning others. We want to change it, but have been unable to restrain ourself. According to this instruction, there are three things we should do:

1. As soon as we have gained insight into what this habit is actually doing to us, we should update our values to include our new understanding. In this case, we would need to increase the value we place on the ideas and decisions of others. We should expand our respect for the time and effort they have put into the thinking process. Until these basic values are altered, all other work will be nonproductive.

2. We should then deactivate the elements which created this pattern. The easiest would be our interest or our support. We decide that what others choose to do is none of our business, so we shift our interest from judging their pecadillos to our own self-examination. Or, we realize that we support this bad habit as a means of feeling better ourself by comparison. We therefore establish a new habit of nourishing our self-esteem with the light within us, not by degrading others. As we cease supporting the old patterns of behavior, they atrophy.

3. We should cultivate new patterns to replace the old. If the light within us means anything at all, we must be able to recognize it within others as well—especially people we do not naturally like. So we replace our old habit of criticizing and condemning with a new one which celebrates the presence of light within our friends and colleagues. We learn in this way to respond to the good within

them, instead of magnifying their faults and relating only to their problems.

The first steps in changing these habits are meant to occur at inner levels, preferably through the use of proper meditative techniques. By rehearsing the changes at this level and integrating them with our values and character, we find it much easier to follow through with improved habits of behavior. If we do not lay this groundwork, however, we may produce only superficial results. There are some people, for instance, who believe they can cure their bad habit of criticizing just by shutting their mouth and not voicing their opinions. At inner levels, however, they still entertain critical thoughts and feelings. No change has occurred at all!

The truth of this instruction is testified to, tragically, by the examples of thousands of modern day aspirants who have taken "get spiritual quick" courses led by unscrupulous gurus. These courses typically teach the aspirant a form of "meditation" which blanks the mind and leads the meditator into a state of passive numbness. In theory, this is supposed to let "pure consciousness" take over, but as we have seen throughout this book, pure consciousness needs skills and active love and wisdom to act through. It cannot act through numbness! Nonetheless, many of these people have practiced these techniques for as long as twelve to fifteen years, only to discover, at long last, that the intellectual skills and mental sharpness they had to begin with have been lost. Even their memory is sluggish and confused.

Why is this so? Because they have been repeatedly deactivating certain patterns of mental skill and emotional responsiveness in their character—and they have been successful, as this instruction predicts they will.

As we create new patterns of behavior and expression, therefore, we should strive to make each of these four elements strong and properly balanced with each other. We should also make sure that they do not undermine existing patterns of wisdom or skill. Otherwise, we run the risk of distortion.

12. At the level of form, the experiences of past and present seem to be the only reality; the future is but unrealized potential. At the level of consciousness, however, reality is known to be the radiance of light.

Again, we are being called on to recognize a basic difference in perception and understanding between the light of consciousness and the nature of form. At the level of form, what is real seems to be what has happened and what is happening. But this is an illusion; the sense of time is an impression generated by the duration of forms and the patterns which give rise to those forms. The true origin of reality is the radiance of light, which by its very radiance creates the impression of time.

We worry if there is enough time to do this or to do that. How silly in the light of this instruction! If the soul bothers to create a form, be it a personality, an opportunity, a relationship, or a habit, then this form will obviously endure, in one shape or another, until the creative purpose of the soul is fulfilled—until consciousness ripens and the darkness has been redeemed with light. How can there not be enough time? Our concern would be much more profitably directed at learning to radiate the light.

The restrictions of time we impose on ourself are an illusion, even though time itself is not. Indeed, one of the great skills of consciousness is learning to use time creatively—a skill known as "right timing." This is a complex science involving knowledge of the seasons, astrological cycles, the appearance and disappearance of energies, and many other factors. An important part of exploring the nature of consciousness is learning the lessons of right timing.

302

Equally relevant is the development of the understanding that we are never victims of the past; if we are victims of anything, it is only our interpretation of what the past means.

As we grow spiritually, we need to start thinking of time in terms of the divine plan. The only "real time" is that which is needed to fulfill the plan of God. This obviously includes the future as well as the past and the present. As we begin to be motivated by the creative plan of the soul, we likewise discover that it includes the future as well as the past and the present. We must make sure that our values, attitudes, and personal plans are based on a healthy appreciation of all three of these phases of time.

The analogy which has already been used of the personality being a portrait painted by the soul may help complete the thought in this instruction. An artist will often make many sketches and studies before beginning the actual work on a masterpiece. Once the portrait is completed, the sketches and trial studies no longer matter; they have served their purpose. But they are nonetheless included in the final work. This is the underlying meaning of so much that we experience in our life. An event here and an episode there may be confusing and perhaps even threatening, but only because we are taking them out of the context of the final portrait! The soul knows the creative purpose behind these "sketches," but we do not. As a result, in all too many cases, we put an excessive amount of attention on events and conditions which do not deserve it, thereby warping our self-understanding and coloring our perceptions of life.

If we ever make one assumption in life, it should be this: that the soul knows what it is doing. It has a creative vision, and this creative vision is our reality. It fits into the creative vision of God, and therefore our reality has meaning and purpose. Once this creative vision is achieved, it will be like a radiant burst of light on earth—through us. Until then, there will be many studies and sketches. But these studies and sketches have no meaning in and of themselves, except in terms of the final portrait. Our challenge is to express as much light as possible through each of these episodes.

13. The measure of light within any pattern of character can be known by examining the strength of its creative potential, its animation, and its resistance.

It is important to understand that no pattern of character is inherently spiritual or inherently materialistic. The spiritual value of a seed of character is determined solely by the measure of light it is able to express.

Devotion is a good example. Three devoutly religious people may go through the same religious training, yet end up with three widely divergent expressions of devotion. The first may let his devotion be monopolized by a charismatic cult leader who substitutes himself for direct spiritual contact. The second may direct his devotion at trying to solve the problems of earthly living purely in terms of the earth—not in terms of spirit. As a result, he emphasizes solutions which appeal to him emotionally, but fail to make sense in terms of the larger picture. The third may use his devotion to maintain constant and steady contact with the life of spirit, to promote intelligent thinking and individual responsibility. Obviously, the measure of light expressed by the act of devotion in each case is widely divergent. So is the quality of the seeds of character generated through the expression of this devotion.

Just so, someone might have a fine wit. But instead of animating this wit with the love of God and a deep respect for the individuality of others, he pollutes it with cynicism and pessimism. As a result, not much light is expressed through his wit—although the same skills of humor in another person might indeed be the vehicle for expressing a great measure of the light within.

Many people have strong creative potential, yet let the resistance within their habits of comfort mute it. A good example would be the housewife with a strong spiritual awareness who nevertheless does not respond fully to her opportunities. She has the time, the resources, and the talent to serve spirit, but she is afraid to take any action that would jeopardize her comfort or standing in the community.

Another way in which resistance colors potential and animation is found in the case of the person who is highly interested in the life of spirit so long as everything is going well in his life. But when his marriage begins to fall apart, his career stumbles, or he encounters censure from others, his spiritual habits and outlook begin to fail. Spiritual growth suffers while he takes the time to lick his wounds and burrow in self-pity.

There is no set of skills or character strengths that the spiritual person will or will not possess. But whatever skills and attributes of character he or she does have, they will be expressed with light and love. They will be used to their full creative potential, animated by the benevolence and wisdom of divine life, and they will be strong enough to overpower resistance, not succumb to it.

This instruction also teaches us something important about change. It must occur at inner levels first—not at the outer level. We might perceive, for instance, that there are certain deficiencies in our political system and decide that we need to change the Constitution. But this would be an example of mistaking the form for consciousness, and believing that overt changes in the form—the Constitution—will actually remedy political deficiencies. In point of fact, the actual deficiencies lie in our attitudes toward citizenship, our habits as citizens, our devotion to the ideals of freedom and democratic responsibility, and so on. It is through these elements that the Spirit of America works, more so than the actual form of government. It is in these elements that either the light or the darkness reigns. It is therefore with these elements that we should work, if we are to serve our country creatively.

The attempt to change the form is usually just tinkering. Genuine growth and creativity involves changing the *capacity* of the form to express consciousness and light, and this usually means that the changes required are subtle ones, of attitude, understanding, commitment, and intent. As these changes are made, changes may occur in the outer form as well—but the inner changes must be made first.

14. The appearance of latent seeds as active facets of character, skill, or life's circumstances indicates that the time is right to bring these seeds to a spiritual harvest.

The appearance of any condition in our life, be it physical, emotional, or mental, implies that the time is ripe for us to deal with this condition directly and wisely, and interact with it to the soul's gain and benefit. We can assume that the soul has a reason why we must face or endure this situation or character trait, even though the reason may be utterly obscure at first. If nothing else, recognizing that we do not have the personal strength to endure this situation, and turning to the strength of the soul, will represent a tremendous lesson learned.

Please note that this instruction does not advocate a passive acceptance of fate. Instead, it proposes an active cooperation with destiny. There is an enormous difference. It is one thing to understand that we must deal forthrightly with a problem, accept it without hysteria, and then calmly solve it. It is quite another thing to passively accept a problem and live with it for thirty or forty years without making any effort to correct it! Those who adopt the latter strategy are not participating in the spiritual harvest—they are just waiting for God to do their work for them. God never will.

When problems arise, we are meant to deal with them. If we do not know how, then we should turn to the sources of higher strength within us, and ask for the guidance and strength that we need. Self-pity, guilt, or fear are nonproductive reactions to life's challenges. We must expose our problems to the light within us, and harness this light to heal, improve, and redeem conditions as necessary. This is the work of the spiritual harvest.

15. Although the circumstances of life and substance itself can be impressed and directed by the light within us, matter is not just a projection of consciousness. It is distinct and has a purpose and plan of its own.

It is an enormous breakthrough in understanding to realize that the quality and focus of our thoughts, feelings, and acts invoke a certain type of opportunity or challenge in our life. We are a master of our fate after all! But there is a danger in this breakthrough as well. Some people proceed to leap to the conclusion that they can control *everything*, as though they had suddenly become God. They believe that each person creates his or her own "personal reality"—or even worse, that they can control God's reality. This is a leap in arrogance, not faith, and is actually materialism of the worst kind.

Consciousness is meant to organize and direct matter. The complex forms of our daily life are the fruit of this interaction. Nonetheless, matter does have a separate purpose and plan for evolution that distinguishes it from consciousness. The integration of personality and soul does not mean that matter and consciousness become the same.

Matter is the raw material with which consciousness works. From it, the soul draws the substance it needs to create its physical, astral, and mental bodies. From it as well, the soul draws the conditions and factors it needs to promote growth in its personality. In return, matter is enriched by being organized and vitalized.

It must be understood that the personality is a bifold creation. It is first and foremost the creation of the soul. But in very real ways, it is also a product of its experience on earth. What the personality learns from these experiences strongly influences its spiritual growth. If it learns skill in gathering the resources of the earth, discovering their creative potential, and tapping it in profitable ways, then growth may be rapid. Yet if it identifies too strongly with the inertia, denseness, and darkness of materialism, it can reinforce defensiveness, selfishness, greed, and vanity.

Once again, Patanjali is emphasizing the need for responsibility. The spiritual aspirant has a duty to grow according to the guidance of the soul. He likewise has a role to play as steward of the many forms of life which inhabit the earth. He must take care to understand both of these roles and not confuse them.

16. The capacity of the spiritual aspirant to control or direct matter is directly related to his identification with divine intelligence.

It is not actually the goal of the spiritual aspirant to be able to control matter; the focus of spiritual growth is consciousness, as was stated in the first instruction of Book One. Nonetheless, as the aspirant learns the nature of the true interaction between consciousness and substance, as has been discussed in the last few instructions, he begins to grasp the possibilities. At this stage, it can be a strong temptation to try to control matter directly, through the skills and understanding he has acquired. Succumbing to this temptation, however, would represent a disaster of the first degree. It would subvert the focus and purpose of the aspirant's ongoing growth.

It is expected that the aspirant will learn more and more about directing and illuminating matter, *but always in the context of increased contact with the mind of God!* These are lessons to be learned, as they become necessary, from the divine archetypes which govern and direct growth on the physical plane. They must never become an end in themselves.

17. The inner patterns of life, both of consciousness and matter, can be discerned by the aspirant only if he has trained the mind to register them.

In this instruction lies the key to "mastery." There are no mysteries in life—only ignorance. Every secret of heaven and earth is in plain view, for all to behold. Every miracle of the Christ has been revealed. We fail to comprehend only because we have not trained our mind to register the inner dimensions behind the outer phenomena.

This is not a matter of belief, faith, or charisma—it is a matter of training the mind to register wavelengths of life previously beyond our spectrum. This is what any genius learns to do. A composer such as Beethoven or Bach is a marvelous example of this point at work. They could hear inner sources of inspiration no other composer could hear.

How often we settle for sloppy explanations! Modern psychology is a perfect example. It is riddled with ill-conceived therapies and utterly ludicrous theories which attempt to explain human behavior. Why? Because the vast majority of researchers and theorists have studied only the outer appearances of human behavior—and primarily abnormal behavior at that. There has been almost no study of normal human behavior or exceptional human behavior—the patterns of genius or saintliness. Nor has there been any study of the inner patterns in either consciousness or matter which give rise to human psychology. As a result, the true workings of human psychology remain a mystery to most people.

How does the mind get trained in this way? Through right focus and constant practice. Right focus is the effort to seek out and discern the archetypal pattern which governs a particular line of inquiry. Constant practice is the repeated effort to use the light of the mind to examine a particular facet of life and uncover its secrets. This is not as difficult as it might seem. Energy does follow attention. The more we try to examine our life, for instance, and discover why our friends are constantly leaving us in the lurch, the more we are likely to discover, eventually, the pattern of behavior in our own character which views friends only as a matter of convenience, to be kept as long as they help us, and then dumped immediately.

By examining life, first to discover our own character and then to discover the inner patterns of all phenomena, we acquire the ability to understand what works and what will not. We also deepen our fundamental love for truth, which enables us to wade past the mysteries and the sloppy explanations and embrace reality as it is.

It should be noted, however, that this love of truth emerges from the active, intelligent mind, not the heart.

18. Although our thoughts, attitudes, and experiences are everchanging, the light within us remains constant.

Does it matter whether our thoughts, attitudes, and experiences are ever-changing? Not to the average person. But to the spiritual person, who has refined creative skills and is now seeking to act responsibly in life, it does. A sculptor cannot create a sculpture out of water; it is too fluid to hold a shape on its own. By the same token, we must recognize the limitations of creating new expressions which are doomed to be out of fashion in just a few seasons. The true creative person wants his or her work to endure as long as possible. To ensure this, he or she must be inspired by the light within, not the whims and fancies of society.

This instruction also suggests that while the light within us remains constant, the best way to harness the ever-changing nature of our thoughts, attitudes, and experiences is to enrich them with light. In this way, we bring the light within us into our outer life, for our own benefit and that of others.

This instruction is an echo of Instruction 5 in this book: "Consciousness is One, even though the forms consciousness generates are multiple and varied." Out of the one, come the many. If we can understand this basic principle of life, we can truly become an agent of divine life. Acting with wisdom, all that we do will be wise. Acting with love, all that we do will be compassionate. Acting with a sense of permanence, all that we do will be permanent.

19. Our thoughts, attitudes, and experiences are not the source of illumination.

The mind, emotions, and physical body can become vehicles for the expression of the light within us, but they are not the source of the light within us. Consciousness is not an epiphenomenon of the physical body, or any facet of the personality, no matter what modern psychologists may believe. The source of illumination is consciousness.

We do not generate light. Light is an attribute of divine life. We can know it, identify with it, and express it—but we cannot generate it. Our role is to be an agent of light.

20. Sensation is limited by identification with the vehicles of manifestation.

Sensation is the capacity of any vehicle of manifestation to be aware of the phenomena of its particular plane. With sensation, there is a very strong element of personal identification: "I sense this; therefore, it is real to me." As a result, great importance is placed on personal experience. Judgments are based on what we have experienced, and therefore sensation becomes highly personalized, self-centered. This is understandable, of course, because the whole process of manifesting through form occurs through individualization. The divine is narrowed and focused so that it can be expressed through a single point, to employ a metaphor.

This characteristic of sensation is not undesirable, so long as the aspirant recognizes it and accounts for it. For one thing, it does give him experience in learning the lessons of individuality. For another, it indirectly helps him translate the abstract qualities of goodwill, joy, wisdom, and peace into practical and well-focused humanistic expressions.

When this understanding is lacking, however, and the tendency of sensation to identify with the vehicles of manifestations is left unchecked, great difficulty can arise. The personality becomes highly selfish and materialistic. Sensation becomes glorified, and the quest for pleasant thrills and feelings become addictive. Great attention is given to "listening to the body and the feelings" or some equivalent to that. The greatest danger of all lies in becoming addicted to one's own ideas and intellectual powers, as this is a trap which is difficult to understand and escape. The individual becomes a slave to the elemental life he is meant to master and direct.

This whole problem can be seen in the context of mass consciousness, too.

21. The attempt to comprehend consciousness in terms of the innate limitations of sensation leads to endless confusion. Instead, the aspirant must explore the true source of illumination.

This instruction presents us with a statement almost as sweeping in scope as the first one in this book. In it, we find the reason why intelligent people, seeking greater understanding, are so distraught by identity crises, distractions, moral dilemmas, breaches of faith, and a seemingly endless variety of confusion. We can also find the reason why psychology and religion have come to so little understanding of human nature and mankind's relationship to God.

The aspirant individually, and psychology and religion collectively, must come to distinguish between sensation and consciousness. We must study and catalog sensation, but never rely upon our sensations for understanding and illumination. It is simply not possible to comprehend life in terms of sensations. The limitations are too great. No matter how it is used, sensation produces a self-centered focus that emphasizes problems and ignores solutions. This will blur our perception unless it is wholly under the control of consciousness. This principle applies to society as well as to the individual.

Deep in the thought-form of this instruction, there is a warning that if we attempt too one-pointedly to define consciousness in terms of sensation, we will develop the "inverse skills of conscious-ness," which would literally be talents of perversion. As conscious-ness operates, it imposes order and structure. Excessive identifi-cation with sensation, by contrast, leads to confusion, chaos, and disorder, until eventually the mechanisms of sensation begin to break down. When this happens, the physical body becomes vul-nerable to grave disorders; the emotions become susceptible to self-hypnotism, hallucinations, the wish life, and excessive reactiveness (grief, sadness, frustration, and depression); and the mind becomes fragmented, distracted.

One could spend as much time exhaustively researching the inverse skills of sensation as he might investigating the proper skills of consciousness, and there is value to it, in the right context. But the greater value of a psychology of illumination as compared to a psychology of darkness should be obvious. The aspirant seeks the light; he must learn to cope with the shadows of life, but his primary goal is to learn to carry light.

Therefore, we must make sure that the skills we practice are indeed skills of consciousness. And we must learn to recognize the true source of illumination—consciousness—and turn to it daily.

22. As the soul gains enough control of its creation that it is able to express its light through the personality, then the light within us is formed. Spiritual self-expression becomes possible.

The simplicity of this statement may lead many people to dis-miss it as too vague to be helpful. But it is an idea which needs to be returned to continually in our efforts to understand and act.

In any situation in life—any problem, conflict, challenge, or opportunity—the true source of illumination is the soul. If we can comprehend what the soul is trying to accomplish through this situation and learn to act on its behalf, not just our own, then we set the stage for spiritual self-expression. This enables the soul to use its personality for the radiation of light, thereby illuminating the problem or challenge. This, in turn, reveals the light within us.

The emotions may not always like the direction the soul leads us, or the solution the soul proposes; they may view it as a cup of bitter gall. But if we have genuine control of our emotions, we will know that there are more important goals in life than emotional gratification. We shall honor the will of this divine impulse and not succumb to the temporary hurt feelings we may encounter.

As we try to look at any situation from the perspective of the soul, it becomes relatively easy to comprehend what must be done in order to individualize the light within us, so that it may penetrate the darkness. First, we can survey the world around us and consider what is impeding the spread of this illumination. Are we contributing to this impedance? If so, how must we change? If we are not, how can we serve so as to help others see their impedance and be encouraged to remove it? What are the true hindrances?

This stage of evaluation and planning must then be followed by action, in which the light is honored and embodied in what we do. There is tremendous room for growth in this department. We can all, for example, learn to express more love and joy in our attitudes toward the work we perform, as well as more competence and skill. We can strive for a higher level of quality in our performance. And this is true in all activities, not just work: parenting, friendship, service, citizenship, and many more.

The true aspirant sacrifices all to the light within. This is the meaning of Christ's injunction to the rich young man who wanted to be a disciple, when He said to give away everything and follow Him. He was not necessarily referring to the literal wealth the man possessed, but rather to all of his possessions of sensation—especially skills and qualities which would let him act effectively *without* summoning the soul. It is important to have such qualities and skills, of course, but we must know their limitations. We must never let our skills and talents blind us to our need for the strength, love, and wisdom of the soul.

The aspirant devotes himself completely to the soul by striving always to be an agent of its light. He strives to make everything he does sacred, which is the true meaning of sacrifice. When properly understood, sacrifice does not involve the loss of anything at all—just the gain of enlightenment.

23. As the mind is filled with light and the presence of the soul, it becomes multidimensional in its capacity to know.

Our physical senses operate three-dimensionally. They can measure height, width, and depth, but are limited to observing any object or condition from just one angle at any given point in time.

The emotions are able to operate fourth-dimensionally, in that they add projectability to height, width, and depth. By projecting themselves, they can occupy a limited number of points at the same time. In other words, they could view both the front and back of a solid object at once—and possibly even view through it as if it were transparent. They can also project forward and backward in time, thereby examining the growth potential of the object.

The mind is able to operate fifth-dimensionally, in that it adds simultaneity to projectability and height, width, and depth. In other words, it can view an object, idea, or person from all possible points of view at the same time. It can also study an object, idea, or person relationally—how it relates to any and all other corresponding phenomena.

The spiritual intuition is able to operate sixth-dimensionally, in that it is able to be aware of the complete group in which any object, idea, or person lives and moves and has its being. In terms of people, that group is humanity as a whole.

This is not to imply that the emotions or mind of any given individual are automatically able to act in these ways. To some degree this may be so, but the real power of fifth dimensional thought is something which must be trained for and mastered.

As the mind becomes responsive to the light of the soul, however, it dynamically increases its capacity to serve the soul.

• It discovers that it can focus itself at any of these levels or dimensions, and obtain information accurately.

• It learns that it can transmit energy from higher levels to lower levels—for example, from the level of the soul into the physical body, thereby producing healing.

• It finds that it can focus the light of the soul to penetrate into areas of confusion or darkness that it cannot pierce on its own, both to comprehend more fully and also to break up glamours and illusions.

24. The mind, now capable of dealing with the infinite as well as the finite, becomes the primary instrument of the soul in directing the personality and expressing light on earth.

This instruction is virtually self-explanatory. The mind, having been properly trained, becomes the direct agent for the soul at the personality level. It strengthens the character, bolsters the value system, and manages and coordinates all efforts. It reconciles all duality that comes into the life of the spiritual person—indeed, it is able to embrace both the infinite and the finite simultaneously, and find the creative potential within their duality.

As such, the mind becomes the ideal paraclete. Those aspirants who believe it is enough to love God, and ignore the proper development of the mind (or even worse, seek to destroy it), should tattoo this instruction on their forearms and meditate on it every day, until they begin to comprehend what they are missing.

25. The resulting state of consciousness is focused wholeness.

The state of focused wholeness is not as paradoxical as it may seem. It occurs when the aspirant has reconciled the seeming opposites of universality and personality, thereby achieving true individuality. He is able to act as an agent of universal consciousness, while still maintaining his focus as a single person.

This is not just a state of bliss achieved during peak moments of meditation, although meditation is certainly the venue through which focused wholeness is cultivated. Rather, it is a very active state of involvement in life. The pole of universality brings the awareness of responsibility, which has been growing throughout Book Four, to its highest point. At the same time, the personality has reached the point where it is able to act competently and effectively in service to the soul. Personal needs, while still attended to, give way in importance to the needs of the nation, humanity, and God.

We are meant to share in the life of God and form a relationship with divine life, as well as all life forms. It is not expected that we deny ourself in order to share in this way; by the same token, it is not possible to share if we are continually at odds with others, grim at heart, or constantly expecting others to carry our burdens. Focused wholeness is the state of true sharing. It is a state of mind we can carry with us all day, every day, as we pursue our activities. We share with others the potential achievements of humanity, just as we share in the work of dissolving ancient karma and healing modern problems.

26. **In this state, the agent of light is able to act consciously on behalf of the soul.**

Until now, the aspirant has struggled to understand the direction and guidance of the soul. While doing his best to serve, he has understood only in part. As a result, his efforts sometimes ended up being counterproductive.

Now, however, the aspirant is able to act in full lucidity—with full knowledge of what the soul expects, and why. He is no longer tormented by doubt or indecision; he sees clearly and knows how he fits into the larger perspective. Indeed, the ability to grasp the "big picture" or larger perspective is one of the great hallmarks of this stage of development. He knows what is right at every level, and will not brook the petty ignorance of those who like to make up their own rules for reality.

This does not mean, however, that the process of growth stops at this point. The fundamental characteristic of consciousness is that it promotes and encourages growth. It seeks to reveal that which can be known and leads the aspirant to expand his realm of knowingness. It only stands to reason, therefore, that as the aspirant becomes more attuned to consciousness, he becomes more completely filled with the impulse to grow, to explore, to break down limitations, to serve, and to translate the plan of the Father into a noble reality on earth.

These advanced lessons take the aspirant into new fields of study and mastery. Instead of studying consciousness from the perspective of form, he begins studying form from the perspective of consciousness—and both form and consciousness from a growing awareness of spirit. In addition, he becomes steadily more aware of hierarchical activity, the impact of energies emanating from beyond the planet, and many other new realizations which expand his understanding of the nature of the soul and consciousness. He leaves behind his personal problems and preoccupations, and takes on instead the challenges and tests of civilization. He outgrows the last vestiges of "spiritual selfishness"—the orientation of "what can spirit do for me"—and dedicates himself entirely to spiritual service.

27. However, the agent of light still registers sensations in his subtle bodies.

The soul does not endure countless millenia of preparation in order to throw away its periodic vehicles once they have become attuned to the light of consciousness! It values sensation, knowing it to be its only avenue of contact on the mental, astral, and physical planes. So it uses these vehicles, actively and freely, but is careful to do so with discipline and self-restraint, for it knows that the vehicles of sensation are still just as vulnerable to darkness as ever. In fact, they are even more vulnerable, because they have become more highly sensitized to all impressions. Unless this were true, they would still be too coarse and crude to receive and transmit the light of consciousness.

The advanced individual faces the same problems the average person does, but on a global as well as a personal basis. These problems are registered in the periodic vehicles, and might well have a terrible impact, except for one condition. The advanced individual understands the nature of sensation, takes care not to personalize these impressions, and uses the light at his disposal to neutralize offensive and seductive ones, thereby enlightening the shadows. As this is a daily happening, he also appreciates the value of habitually cleansing the subtle bodies, taking care not to succumb to the temptations of the world and using his talents and skills in a positive manner, not letting them become passive.

There is no "magical protection" for the enlightened individual; he is subject to the same problems as the aspirant, only more intensely. His only protection lies in a carefully worked out sense of individuality, his ability to persevere, and his contact with the soul and divine love and light.

The need for self-discipline does not lie only in handling the problems of creative activity, however; the aspirant also finds that his vehicles of sensation are now able to register far greater measures of joy, beauty, intelligence, goodwill, and fulfillment than before. This greatly enriches his enjoyment of life, but naturally must be kept in balance, lest it become excessively hedonistic—or just over-emphasized. It is all too easy, for example, to become fanatic and obsessed in dealing with brilliant ideas. This is not the fault of the ideas, or even of sensation; it is merely the result of not disciplining the subtle bodies properly.

In many of her books, Alice Bailey mentions at length the diseases and maladies that disciples frequently fall prey to, because they are not handling their periodic vehicles properly. We must always keep in mind that just believing in what is right and wholesome is not enough to guarantee the well-being of the aspirant; we must also learn to focus energy intelligently and apply it productively. These are the keys to maintaining health, balance, and wholeness in the spiritual life.

28. The sensations registered by the agent of light must not be construed for consciousness, but handled with mastery.

Because many of the sensations being referred to in this context emerge only after actual contact has been made with the soul, it is exceedingly easy for the aspirant to become confused and believe them to be the result of soul contact. This is an error in judgment, but it often takes a while to learn this lesson.

A common example would be the aspirant who conceives a certain creative project, based on genuine inspiration. As he endeavors to implement his project, however, he encounters the immaturity of the masses, in the form of criticism, opposition, and rejection. This is a sensation and ought to be handled as such, but because the aspirant has initiated his work as a result of legitimate contact with the soul, he may be tempted to interpret this opposition as a sign that the soul is displeased with what he has done so far. He may even decide that the original idea was not as inspired as he first thought and abandon it, at least temporarily. In this way, he is misconstruing the reactiveness of the masses (sensation) for the guidance of the soul (consciousness).

In other instances, the reaction of mass consciousness may be so strong that it actually does block out the inspiring light of the soul for a period of time. The project must be halted until conditions are more favorable. It is easy for the agent to misinterpret the meaning of this type of situation and believe that he has failed. This problem can be avoided, however, if the agent has learned to act from his understanding of the plan—not in reaction to the reactions of others.

Potentially even more damage can be done by succumbing to the subtle influences of those who support a creative idea, but lack the aspirant's contact with the soul. Their suggestions for modification should be carefully weighed; some will make good sense, but others will all but nullify the original intent of the soul. Nowhere is the truth of this point better illustrated than in the key ideas associated with the so-called "new age movement." In principle, the new age is supposed to be a time of spiritual breakthrough. Few of the leading tenets of new age thinking, however, show any signs of Hierarchical inspiration. Most of them are worn-out ideas from exhausted spiritual traditions.

Even highly advanced individuals can be troubled by some of these issues. It is therefore quite important to discriminate as wisely as possible between consciousness and sensation, and maintain the continual habit of disciplining and regulating our sensory mechanisms.

29. When even the most subtle of sensations can be handled with detachment, the agent of light becomes consciously aware of the source of illumination, the Light of the World.

It is a good idea to remember the distinction between the source of illumination, illumination itself, and sensation. The source of illumination is the Christ, the Light of the World; it leads us back to spirit, the Father. Illumination itself is consciousness, the soul. Sensation is the fragment of consciousness invested in matter which, as it evolves, gives the spiritual person the capacity to perceive and act in the world of form.

This instruction suggests that there is a continuum from one level of awareness to the next, as was first stated in Instruction 45 of Book One. Once the aspirant begins the work of looking for the presence of light behind the shadows of form, he will be led on, step by step, to progressively more subtle manifestations of light, until he reaches the light itself and then the source of illumination. The only thing that can block this ultimate discovery is his own decision to stop looking. Whenever this occurs, it is usually a sign that he has convinced himself that his perception of light is the same as the light itself.

The detachment referred to in this instruction is cultivated by learning to work and act impersonally. Too much of a sense of personality holds us down in the world of form, where personality is king. True creativity and service require us to work *individually*, as an agent of God—but not as personal crusaders, who thirst for the glory of a personal triumph. The moment we personalize God's plan, it stops being God's plan, and becomes our plan. The moment we try to make Christ our personal savior, He stops being the Christ and just becomes our personal demigod.

As we give up our robes of personality for the cloak of true individuality, we discover the source of illumination, the Light of the World, not in theory but in fact. We are able to identify with it and know that we are one with it, a part of it. From this point on, our creative work and involvement in life are marked with a sureness and wholeness which enable us to glorify the Father, even as the Christ has commanded us to do.

30. At this stage, the agent of light has mastered all limitations of form and reactiveness.

The aspirant has learned to use consciousness fully at each level of awareness, and thereby has mastered its use. Life is not static, however; he must continue to use his skills of mastery on a daily basis. Indeed, he must expect to have to master the limitations and reactiveness of the world every single day, as part of the creative work he is pursuing.

Contrary to Eastern thought, the aspirant does not gain exemption from the cycle of incarnation or the principle of karma; these are universal principles and will be with us no matter what level of consciousness we attain. Divine life sustains these laws; why should we want to be free of them? As the Christ stated, "Do not imagine that I have come to abolish the Laws...I have come not to abolish but to complete them. I tell you solemnly, till heaven and earth disappear, not one dot, not one little stroke, shall disappear from the Law until its purpose is achieved." The agent of light masters these laws and uses them in his service to the plan of God. He gains freedom not through exemption but by understanding the purpose of the laws and cooperating freely and fully with them—indeed, using them for his creative plans.

31. In the agent of light, the light shines perfectly through the darkness.

To use a metaphor, the light of the sun travels ninety-three million miles to reach the earth, where it is absorbed into the system of a tiny flower, transformed by photosynthesis into the energy of growth, and expressed once again in the radiant beauty of the unfolding blossom. Indeed, at times the color of a blooming flower is so intense and vital that there can be no doubt that God is present. Just so, the aspirant who has contacted the source of illumination is constantly touching everything in his life, at every level, with the light of this light. He reveals the presence of God.

From this, we can learn a powerful lesson, for the end always indicates the most satisfactory means. To become an agent of light, we must endeavor to shine the light perfectly through whatever darkness we encounter, even though we may not know for sure how to contact the actual source. If we make the effort, constantly invoking the guidance of the soul, the contact will be made unconsciously. We will know the contact has been made from the fruits of our actions. And as we continue, practicing the presence of the light of God at every opportunity, eventually we will achieve a conscious realization.

This instruction also implies that the means by which we express the light will approach perfection. Surrounded by imperfection, we will not whine and complain about it; we will suggest creative ways to heal and redeem it. *Warnings* may be issued, so that the sincere aspirant does not fall into known traps, but little if any time will be given to condemnation, criticism, or fault-finding. This is because criticism and complaining, even when accurate, cannot carry the light. They generate the wrong wavelength. There are times when criticism is unavoidable, of course, but the agent of light takes care to use it gently, humbly—never destructively. The manner of the agent of light always underscores and reveals God's benevolent, forgiving, and understanding nature.

It might be added that at this stage, the skills of consciousness have become automatic, dropping below the threshold of awareness. They are like the skills of coordination or breathing—we do not have to consciously control them. We use them automatically.

32. The agent of light now speaks the pure language of consciousness.

The final three instructions in the text deal with the final level of development, where the master becomes the avatar. An avatar is an individual who is able to reach beyond the known limits of any system, contact a new revelation of divinity, and focus it in his own creative expression so that it makes sense to those within the system. He brings in new light to nourish and spur growth within the system. The Christ and the Buddha both served as avatars, as have many others.

The avatar deals at sixth-dimensional levels, reaching beyond it to the seventh dimension, which is really the first plane on the cosmic scale. He contacts and absorbs pure solar energies and, by focusing them into his own consciousness, steps them down so that they can be revealed to us. Hence, he "speaks the pure language of consciousness." Indeed, he becomes the Word.

33. The state of focused wholeness embraces the major and minor cycles of time.

The major cycles of time are, of course, those set in motion by the divine plan—the time required to complete any one phase of evolution. These cycles require an enormous attention span. As an example, only now, two thousand years after the Christ, are the advanced aspirants of the world beginning to understand what He taught and revealed. The theologians of the world still quibble over minor points and miss the major ones entirely; the average people still fight with one another over their religious beliefs. Yet the teachings and spiritual light of the Christ endure and continue to shine, for those with eyes to see.

The minor cycles of time are those which seem so important to the individual aspirant, until he puts them in their proper context. They trap him in a sense of urgency which has no relevance to divine life.

The state of focused wholeness puts these cycles of time in their proper perspective, so that the avatar is able to reveal that which the people are ready for and need at this point in time—not just what they want. Timing becomes a skill of spiritual self-expression.

To put this idea in practical terms, the need for modern aspirants today is to build for the first few hundred years of the Aquarian Age. It is inappropriate to resuscitate Atlantean teachings or to fight to preserve spiritual practices which were obviously designed for different cultures, different peoples. To be an effective agent of light, we must be in harmony with the divine plan *today*. We must appreciate the kinds of energies which are stimulating the world during these beginning stages of the Aquarian Age—in particular, we must learn to deal with the crystalizing impact of the Seventh Ray, which tends to encourage dictatorships, the bureaucratic mind set, a kind of intellectual fanaticism, as well as other difficulties.

34. The aspirant is fully identified with the Light of the World.

To think of the aspirant in a personal sense at this stage would be an error, for his life and activities have greatly transcended that level. He has become a planetary force, identified with the Christ consciousness. As John wrote:

"The true light that enlightens every man was coming into the world. He was in the world, and the world was made through him, yet the world knew him not. He came to his own home, and his own people received him not. But all who received him, who believed in his name, he gave the power to become children of God; who were born, not of blood nor of the will of the flesh nor of the will of man, but of God."

This true light, the Christ, is fully active in the aspirant, at this final stage. To some, it might seem a sacrilege to suggest that any aspirant could become the Christ, but it is not. The destiny of human consciousness *is* to become fully identified with the Christ and to take our rightful place as loving and creative children of God.

We should therefore seize upon the example of Jesus, who showed us what it meant to be the Light of the World, and strive to live up to this example as best we can. In this, we should remember what He told us: "Truly, truly, I say to you, he who believes in me will also do the works I do; and greater works than these will he do, because I go to the Father."

ABOUT THE AUTHOR

Carl Japikse is one of the leading authorities on meditation and personal growth in the United States today. He has been conducting classes on the instructions of Patanjali for more than ten years now, as a complement to the many other classes in Active Meditation and personal growth that he teaches. With Dr. Robert R. Leichtman, he is one of the founders and principal officers of Light, a non-profit charitable organization dedicated to promoting the right use of the mind and human creativity.

A graduate of Dartmouth College, Mr. Japikse worked for a number of newspapers, including *The Wall Street Journal*, before deciding to devote his full time to teaching and writing. His other books include *The Hour Glass*, a collection of modern fables, and, in collaboration with Dr. Leichtman, *Active Meditation*, *Forces of the Zodiac*, *The Art of Living* (five volumes), and *The Life of Spirit* (two volumes).

Mr. Japikse is also the developer of the *Enlightened Management Seminar*, an intensive introduction to applying the principles of spiritual living to the challenges of managing.

OTHER BOOKS PUBLISHED BY ARIEL PRESS:

Active Meditation: The Western Tradition
by Robert R. Leichtman, M.D. & Carl Japikse, $24.50

Forces of the Zodiac: Companions of the Soul
by Robert R. Leichtman, M.D. & Carl Japikse, $21.50

The Gift of Healing
by Ambrose & Olga Worrall, $6.95

The Art of Living (five volumes)
by Robert R. Leichtman, M.D. & Carl Japikse, $35

Practical Mysticism
by Evelyn Underhill, $5.95

The Life of Spirit (two volumes)
by Robert R. Leichtman, M.D. & Carl Japikse, $7.95 each

The Hour Glass
by Carl Japikse, $14.95

Across the Unknown
by Stewart Edward White, $7.95